Reading WOMEN *Writing*

a series edited by
Shari Benstock
and Celeste Schenck

Autobiographical Voices: Race, Gender, Self-Portraiture
by Françoise Lionnet

Autobiographical

VOICES,

Race, Gender, Self-Portraiture

Françoise Lionnet

Cornell University Press

ITHACA and LONDON

First published 1989 by Cornell University Press.

International Standard Book Number 0-8014-2091-1
Library of Congress Catalog Card Number 88-43236
Printed in the United States of America
*Librarians: Library of Congress cataloging information
appears on the last page of the book.*

*The paper in this book is acid-free and meets the guidelines for
permanence and durability of the Committee on Production Guidelines
for Book Longevity of the Council on Library Resources.*

In memoriam J. L. L.
In posterum J. & D.

Foreword

As the editors of *Reading Women Writing*, we are committed to furthering international feminist debate. To that end, we seek books that rigorously explore how differences of class, race, ethnic background, nationality, religious preference, and sexual choice inform women's writing. Books sensitive to the ways women's writings are classified, evaluated, read, and taught are central to the series. Dedicated primarily although not exclusively to the examination of literature written by women, *Reading Women Writing* highlights differing, even contradictory, theoretical positions on texts read in cultural context. Of particular interest to us are feminist criticism of non-canonical texts (including film, popular culture, and new and as yet unnamed genres); confrontations of first-world theory with beyond-the-first-world texts; and books on colonial and postcolonial writing that generate their own theoretical positions. Among volumes in prospect for the series are a book on women's prison narratives in international context, a study of incest and the writing daughter in Jean Rhys and H.D., and a reading of popular film, sexual difference, and spectatorship in an emphatically social context.

Françoise Lionnet's *Autobiographical Voices: Race, Gender, Self-Portraiture*, the inaugural volume of *Reading Women Writing*, is comparative, theoretical, and political; it is also formally innovative. Lionnet groups Afro-American, Caribbean, and Indian Ocean texts without effacing their differences; by means of comparative analysis, she expands the theoretical boundaries of women's autobiography. In her nonlinear, inter-referential readings of these texts, she avoids hypostasizing either "black women's autobiography" or "Indian Ocean women's autobiography." Then, too, by invoking Augustine and Nietzsche, not as models of masculine autobiography to which she will set contrasting female examples, but *for* the feminine in them, she reads through and against these male texts: both to show women writers' indebtedness to an autobiographical tradition and to imagine that tradition retroactively in the light of women's texts.

The concept of *métissage*, exuberantly elaborated in Lionnet's text, propels *Autobiographical Voices* at every level. The inseparable aesthetic and political functions of *métissage* link the five women authors discussed—Hurston, Angelou, Cardinal, Condé, Humbert—and join the whole comparative reading to the political stance Lionnet takes, appropriating the Darwinian notion of strength in diversity. *Métissage* is also the basis for Lionnet's positioning of herself as a reader/subject; she is herself a *métisse*, born in Mauritius, educated in France, now living and teaching in America. Finally, *métissage* functions as a strategy for approaching her book: a reader may pursue any number of paths through the text, considering out of sequence, for example, the chapters on Augustine, Angelou and Humbert. The reader thereby participates in the book's production by making a commitment—political, as Lionnet would have it—to bricolage, reading, as it were, as a *métisseuse*. The very form of *Autobiographical Voices* is necessarily hybrid. It dares scholarly convention to be adequate to *its* diversity of critical moves. With *Autobiographical Voices* by Françoise Lionnet, *Reading Women Writing* proudly commences publication.

S. B.
C. S.

Contents

Language is no longer linked to the knowing
of things, but to human freedom.
Michel Foucault, *The Order of Things*

Preface

We women are so diverse and live in such varied cultural, racial, and economic circumstances that we cannot possibly pretend to speak in a single voice. It is by listening to a plurality of voices from various corners of the planet and across centuries that we will strengthen our ability to resist demeaning power structures without risk of being recuperated by current or trendy professionalism within our academic disciplines. Women's voices do not and will never constitute *a* "minority discourse." Our voices have existed in a state of greater or lesser tension with other points of view in all historical eras and geographical areas. Always present everywhere but rarely heard, let alone recorded, women's voices have not been a dominant mode of expression or a legitimate and acceptable alternative to such dominant modes. The very inaudibility of these dissenting voices within accepted patterns of traditional and/or oppositional practices is a clear indictment of the processes through which such imperialist patterns have been constituted. Our voices have always been there, but it is only recently that academic and political institutions have begun to take them seriously. This book was written from the deep conviction that it is the foregrounding of our *differences* as women which can ultimately unite us as a powerful force of resistance against all repressive systems of ideology.

By focusing on the autobiographical fictions of some women writers from different—yet similar—cultural contexts (e.g., Afro-American, Caribbean, and Mauritian), I hope to echo some of the most innovative aspects of this global literature, especially its revision of canonical texts such as Augustine's and Nietzsche's and its growing interest in highlighting *alternative* patterns of resistance to cultural and political hegemony. These women writers articulate a vision of the future founded on individual and collective solidarities, respectful of cultural specificities, and opposed to all rigid, essentializing approaches to questions of race, class, or gender. Because of the subtle and nonexclusionary nature of their project, the writers have often been browbeaten by male writers and critics, who have accused them of not being sufficiently "political." I hope my analyses will help to counter such simplistic approaches to their works and will encourage critics to look at that body of writing in a different light. It is indeed deeply disturbing to me, as a woman and as a critic, that writers as intelligent and talented as Zora Neale Hurston, Maryse Condé, and Marie-Thérèse Humbert have been viewed by compatriots—such as Richard Wright, Oruno Lara, and Edouard Maunick—as unenlightened, apolitical, and at best slightly embarrassing sisters because the confessional nature of some of their narratives does not offer ready-made solutions to the problems of racism in their respective countries. Perhaps as a result of such thorough misunderstanding and its disheartening consequences for the creative person, Maryse Condé and Marie-Thérèse Humbert stopped writing about their own islands: Condé's recent successes have been historical novels set in a very distant past, and Humbert's second book was about an imaginary island in the Atlantic. Hurston's fate is well known and need not be rehearsed here: such forms of self-censorship bespeak the coercive nature of narrowly construed "political" interpretations of the works I discuss. By focusing on the language and structure of these works—narrative strategies, rhetorical patterns, and discursive configurations—I hope to elucidate the subtlety of the writers' vision and to stress their unfailing commitment to a process of emancipation that can redefine the nature and boundaries of the political.

Many friends have been there for me from the inception of this project. Ross Chambers believed in it from the start, and my intellectual debt to him is vast and long-standing. His approach to narrative and his seminars at the University of Michigan provided the methodological tools that became indispensable to my analyses. John McCumber, with his philosophical acumen and good linguistic sense, has always been my best interlocutor. Eva Boesenberg, Sarah Kofman, Adlai Murdoch, Jonathan Ngaté, Ronnie Scharfman, and Louise Yelin read and discussed different chapters of the manuscript.

Through their research and teaching, the following people have contributed much to my insights: Michel Beaujour's rhetoric of the self-portrait showed me new ways of dealing with autobiographies; Lemuel Johnson introduced me to the concept of ethnocentrism, and his discussions broadened my approach; Margot Norris's work on mimesis and dissimulation helped me to look at linear narratives in a new light; my reading of Augustine was triggered by Susan Sontag's course at the New School for Social Research. The seminars Gerald Graff, Lynn Hunt, and Barbara Johnson gave at the 1986 International Summer Institute for Semiotics and Structural Studies at Northwestern University provided a very useful context for reflection.

During the 1987–1988 academic year, a postdoctoral fellowship at the Society for the Humanities, Cornell University, enabled me to complete work on the manuscript. The society provided a stimulating intellectual environment in which to refine and sharpen some of my ideas. I especially thank Stephen Clingman, Henry Louis Gates, Jr., and Christopher Waterman for provocative remarks, encouragement, and good times. I also thank Dominick LaCapra, the acting director, and his staff and the other fellows for making this a very fulfilling year. The insight, energy, and interest of the students who discussed the major ideas of this book in my seminar at the society made my teaching there a most gratifying experience. This fellowship year was also made possible by supplements and time off granted by the College of Arts and Sciences, Northwestern University, for which I express my appreciation.

The anonymous readers for Cornell University Press made invaluable comments. Their interest as well as their questions and criticisms encouraged me to better articulate some crucial points. In the final stages of writing, Celeste Schenck's intelligent, thorough, and extremely perceptive advice helped me through some last hurdles. I am also grateful for the careful editing of Judith Bailey and the work of Bernhard Kendler and Kay Scheuer.

Over the years, I have shared ideas and vented discontents with many feminist friends in five different countries: I treasure those exchanges and the discoveries to which they led. Among such friends, my mother has a special place, as do Andrée Fredette and Jocelyne Newberry. Finally, my most profound debt is to those who share my daily life: living, reading, and writing are possible because *you* are always there.

A shorter version of Chapter 6 first appeared as *"Métissage,* Emancipation, and Female Textuality in Two Francophone Writers," in *Life/Lines: Theorizing Women's Autobiography,* ed. Bella Brodzki and Celeste Schenck (Cornell University Press, 1988), copyright © by Cornell University. A somewhat different version of Chapter 7 was first published as "Anamnesis and Utopia: Nietzschean Self-Portraiture in Marie-Thérèse Humbert's *A l'autre bout de moi,"* in the *Canadian Review of Comparative Literature* 15:1 (1988). Both are reprinted here by permission.

I gratefully acknowledge permission to quote the following works:

Maya Angelou, *I Know Why the Caged Bird Sings, Gather Together in My Name, Singin' and Swingin' and Gettin' Merry like Christmas,* and *Heart of a Woman.* Copyright © 1969, 1974, 1976, 1981, respectively, by Random House, Inc., New York.

Marie Cardinal, *The Words to Say It,* English translation by Pat Goodheart. Copyright © 1983 by VanVactor and Goodheart, Cambridge, Mass.

Aimé Césaire: The Collected Poetry. Copyright © 1983 by the University of California Press.

Maryse Condé, *Heremakhonon.* Copyright © 1976 by UGE 10/18, by permission of Editions Laffont/Seghers, Paris; English translation by Richard Philcox. Copyright © 1982 by Three Continents Press, Washington D.C.

Edouard Glissant, *Le Discours antillais.* Copyright © 1981 by Editions du Seuil, Paris; *Caribbean Discourse,* English translation by J. Michael Dash. Copyright © 1989 by the University Press of Virginia.

Marie-Thérèse Humbert, *A l'autre bout de moi.* Copyright © 1979 by Editions Stock, Paris.

FRANÇOISE LIONNET

Evanston, Illinois

Autobiographical Voices

Introduction
The Politics and Aesthetics of *Métissage*

Henry Louis Gates, Jr. recounts an anecdote about the violent fate of a little-known Francophone writer, who refused to continue living in the prison house of a language imposed by historical circumstances beyond his control:

> In 1915, Edmond Laforest, a prominent member of the Haitian literary movement called La Ronde, made his death a symbolic, if ironic, statement of the curious relation of the marginalized writer to the act of writing in a [European] language. Laforest, with an inimitable, if fatal, flair for the grand gesture, stood upon a bridge, calmly tied a Larousse dictionary around his neck, then leapt to his death. While other black writers, before and after Laforest, have been drowned artistically by the weight of various [European] languages, Laforest chose to make his death an emblem of this relation of overwhelming indenture.[1]

The story dramatizes the dilemmas of all those who must survive (and write) in the interval between different cultures and languages. Standard French, as contained within and legitimized by the Larousse dictionary, used to be the only "official" means of literary expression in the Francophone world. Its overpowering and authoritative voice succeeded in suffocating Haitian Creole, the mother tongue of Laforest's childhood, his oral link to a different histor-

---

[1]Henry L. Gates, Jr., "Writing 'Race' and the Difference it Makes," *Critical Inquiry* 12 (Autumn 1985), 13. I have substituted [European] for "modern" in the original text (in the Haitian context, Creole is a "modern" language).

ical past. The fluidity and flexibility of creole dialects are enriched by custom, usage, and tradition but rarely sanctioned by written or syntactical rules. Creole is thus easily devalued and ignored as a creative medium by those who would encourage more "classical" modes of expression. Retrieving and revaluing those social idiolects that contribute to the development of heteroglossia and the dialogic imagination[2] has been the task of contemporary writers in all of the Francophone world, from Quebec to Mauritius, from Brittany to Alsace, from Guadeloupe to Senegal.

But in 1915, Laforest did drown from the weight of the book, the Law of the colonial fathers, which prevented him from floating and surviving in the flowing current of a muddy river, that uncanny symbol of a devalued maternal heritage with its supposedly irrational, unfiltered, and mumbled oral traditions. His predicament concretizes the linguistic conflicts resulting from colonialism and its hierarchical ordering of languages and traditions. This Haitian writer is an extreme case of a Creole who resisted identification with white civilization and managed not to internalize its ideology, although he did not succeed in finding alternative solutions to his condition of indentured subject and reduced himself to silence. He was caught in a social conflict not unlike those described by Clifford Geertz as based on a "confusion of tongues."[3]

In the French colonial environment, the forced integration of the blacks and the *métis* into the dominant conceptual systems of the *métropole* began early. Until fairly recently (some twenty-five years ago or so), in the local schools of the Antilles, Guyana, Réunion, and other French territories, schoolchildren learned to repeat phrases like "nos ancêtres, les Gaulois [our ancestors, the Gauls]," reading official French history from standard French textbooks. With just a few such phrases, a certain weltanschauung, a vision of the world as circumscribed by European modes of discourse, would imprint itself on the consciousness of the young, inevitably leading to the kinds of self-denials that Maryse Condé and Marie-Thérèse Humbert dramatize with such intensity in their autobiographical novels, *Heremakhonon* and *A l'autre bout de moi*. These self-denials, I argue, amount to

---

[2]See Mikhail M. Bakhtin, *The Dialogic Imagination* (Austin: University of Texas Press, 1981), especially pp. 259–422.

[3]See Clifford Geertz, *The Interpretation of Cultures* (New York: Basic Books, 1973), pp. 9 and 28.

forms of suicide, just as surely as Laforest's political gesture did. In the case of marginalized women writers, the situation is compounded by the double stigma of race and gender. This stigma, imposed in a more or less devious way by the social structures of the colony, is then internalized by individuals and groups in their efforts to conform to the idealized images that society upholds as models. Writers who struggled to verbalize these conflicts have in the past often alienated themselves from the community of educated intellectuals, when they did not become the victims of heroic, tragic gestures like Laforest's. Nowadays, others succeed in giving voice to their repressed traditions, initiating a genuine dialogue with the dominant discourses they hope to transform, thus ultimately favoring exchange rather than provoking conflict.

The Cultural Politics of *Métissage*

There is a long Western tradition, from Plato to Maurice Blanchot, including Augustine and Montaigne, which conceives of writing as a system that rigidifies, stultifies, kills because it imprisons meaning in "la rigidité cadavérique de l'écriture [the cadaverous rigidity of the written sign]" instead of allowing a "parole vive [living *logos*]" to adjust fluidly to the constantly changing context of oral communication in which interlocutors influence each other: Derrida has studied how this relation of opposition between *écriture* and *parole* becomes established in Plato, and is thenceforth central to Western discourse.[4] It is worth noting that Montaigne was the first to use the same phrase—"la parole vive et bruyante [a lively and noisy way of speaking]"—in a secular context. He was discussing his efforts to write the way he speaks, instead of using Latin, to use the lively figurative language of his native Gascogne, however hyperbolic, rather than be stifled either by a dead language or by a literal style that follows the "vérité nayfve . . . nue et cruë [the simple truth . . . the naked and unvarnished truth]."[5] These central questions

---

[4]Jacques Derrida, "La Pharmacie de Platon," in *La Dissémination* (Paris: Seuil, 1972), p. 89, *Dissemination*, trans. Barbara Johnson (Chicago: University of Chicago Press, 1981), pp. 114–15.

[5]See Michel de Montaigne, *Essais*, "Des boyteux," p. 1005; also "Sur des vers de Virgile," p. 853, in *Oeuvres complètes* (Paris: Gallimard/La Pléiade, 1962). *The Complete Works of Montaigne*, trans. Donald Frame (Stanford: Stanford University Press, 1948),

of orality and literacy, speech and writing, truth and hyperbole, transparency and obscurity have become the cornerstone of the cultural aesthetics of many postcolonial writers. As Edouard Glissant, the Martinican poet, novelist, and theorist, spells it out:

> For us it is a matter of ultimately reconciling the values of literate civilizations and the long repressed traditions of orality. . . .
> This practice of cultural creolization [pratique de *métissage*] is not part of some vague humanism, which makes it permissible for us to become one with the other. It establishes a cross-cultural relationship, in an egalitarian and unprecedented way, among histories which we know today in the Caribbean are interrelated. . . . We also know that there is an obscure residue of something unexpressed deep within every spoken word, however far we may push our meaning and however hard we may try to weigh our acts [il est au fond de toute parole . . . la matière obscure d'un informulé].[6]

For Glissant, the *métissage* or braiding, of cultural forms through the simultaneous revalorization of oral traditions and reevaluation of Western concepts has led to the recovery of occulted histories. In the effort to recover their unrecorded past, contemporary writers and critics have come to the realization that opacity and obscurity are necessarily the precious ingredients of all authentic communication: "il est au fond de toute parole . . . la matière obscure d'un informulé."[7] Since history and memory have to be reclaimed either in the absence of hard copy or in full acknowledgment of the ideological distortions that have colored whatever written documents and archival materials do exist, contemporary women writers espe-

---

pp. 786 and 667. For a more detailed discussion of this aspect of Montaigne's style, see Claude Blum, "La Peinture du moi et l'écriture inachevée: Sur la pratique de l'addition dans les 'Essais' de Montaigne," *Poétique* 53 (1983), 60–71.

[6] Edouard Glissant, *Le Discours antillais* (Paris: Seuil, 1981), pp. 462–63. All further references are given in the text. The English translation by J. Michael Dash, *Caribbean Discourse*, is forthcoming from the University Press of Virginia (1989). Whenever possible, I have used this translation. But I have frequently had to alter it in order to stress nuances of the French text which are indispensable to my analyses. For example, Dash translates *métissage* by the word "creolization" which is perfectly acceptable when dealing with cultural mixing but not appropriate when referring to the racial context. That is why I shall retain the word *métissage* here. I shall indicate "trans. mod." whenever I alter the English text.

[7] See, for example, Sarah Kofman's stimulating discussion of what can be problematic in "the will to clarity," in "Nietzsche and the Obscurity of Heraclitus," *Diacritics* 17 (Fall 1987).

cially have been interested in reappropriating the past so as to transform our understanding of ourselves. Their voices echo the submerged or repressed values of our cultures. They rewrite the "feminine" by showing the arbitrary nature of the images and values which Western culture constructs, distorts, and encodes as inferior by feminizing them.[8] All the texts I will be discussing in this book interrogate the sociocultural construction of race and gender and challenge the essentializing tendencies that perpetuate exploitation and subjugation on behalf of those fictive differences created by discourses of power.

For those of us who are natives of the so-called Third World, it has become imperative to understand and to participate fully in the process of re-vision begun by our contemporary writers and theorists. The latter are engaged in an enterprise which converges toward other efforts at economic and political survival but which is unique in its focus on memory—the oral trace of the past—as the instrument for giving us access to our histories. These recovered histories have now become the source of creative explosions for many authors, male and female, who are being nurtured and inspired by the phenomenon applauded by Glissant, the egalitarian interrelations in which binary impasses are deconstructed.

Within the conceptual apparatuses that have governed our labeling of ourselves and others, a space is thus opened where multiplicity and diversity are affirmed. This space is not a territory staked out by exclusionary practices. Rather, it functions as a sheltering site, one that can nurture our differences without encouraging us to withdraw into new dead ends, without enclosing us within facile oppositional practices or sterile denunciations and disavowals. For it is only by imagining nonhierarchical modes of relation among cultures that we can address the crucial issues of indeterminacy and solidarity. These are the issues that compel us in this fin de siècle, for our "green dirt-ball" will survive only if we respect the differences among its peoples.[9] We can be united against hegemonic

[8]Sander Gilman has studied the common denominator shared by negative stereotypes in the West and shown how the "other" is always sexualized and racialized: blacks, Jews, women, the mad are described as inferior because they are the reductive antithesis of what is set up as "normal." *Difference and Pathology: Stereotypes of Sexuality, Race, and Madness* (Ithaca: Cornell University Press, 1985).

[9]To use Zora Neale Hurston's humorous phrasing. *Dust Tracks on a Road*, ed. Robert Hemenway, 2d ed. (Urbana: University of Illinois Press, 1984), p. 147.

power only by refusing to engage that power on its own terms, since to do so would mean becoming ourselves a term within that system of power. We have to articulate new visions of ourselves, new concepts that allow us to think *otherwise,* to bypass the ancient symmetries and dichotomies that have governed the ground and the very condition of possibility of thought, of "clarity," in all of Western philosophy. *Métissage* is such a concept and a practice: it is the site of undecidability and indeterminacy, where solidarity becomes the fundamental principle of political action against hegemonic languages.

We who have been oppressed and silenced—especially those of us who suffer from the "traumata of insignificance" (as the Haitian thinker Patrick Bellegarde-Smith recently put it)[10] because we belong to insular "minorities" from some of the smallest countries of our planet—will never be tempted by the illusions of leadership, will never be deluded into thinking that we can represent anyone but ourselves. That is why we have much to contribute to a global understanding of affirmative and egalitarian principles. My country, Mauritius, like a number of small Caribbean nations, has a long history of (neo)colonial encounters. It has the advantage of being farther away from the economic giant that is North America. But its proximity to South Africa and its dependence on multinational conglomerates, which control much of its economy, place it in the problematic zone known as the Third World. Its survival as a small nation is, however, ensured by a political system of checks and balances which allows all the ethnic groups of the island to have a voice in the decision-making process.

As an Indian Ocean island, Mauritius is open to influence from East and West, North and South. It is a true site of *métissage* and creolization, and since its independence in 1968, it has managed to safeguard a measure of freedom for all its citizens without falling prey to authoritarian rulers. It is of course very far from being the "paradise" tourist brochures eulogize, but it is surely a microcosm of the globe. As a Mauritian woman critic who has lived in the antipodes for the last decade—in the United States of America, where

[10]At the Conference on Pan-Africanism Revisited, Pomona College, April 9, 1988. See also the Epilogue in Patrick Bellegarde-Smith, *In the Shadow of Powers: Dantès Bellegarde in Haitian Social Thought* (Atlantic Highlands, N.J.: Humanities Press, 1985), p. 176.

this book was written—I have become increasingly convinced of the urgent necessity of looking at this New World from the perspective of that small island (and others like it). This book articulates that perspective. My purpose is to demonstrate connections and to share some of the views that have guided my cultural production in this hemisphere.

The interdisciplinary nature of my inquiry will become obvious to my reader; however, my choice of texts may at first seem quite incompatible with the perspective I have just outlined: why Augustine and Nietzsche together with twentieth century women writers? To some, this may either seem an artificial combination of autobiographical texts or, much worse, reveal a colonized mind focused on some patriarchal and canonical figures whose presence is meant to give scholarly legitimacy to my enterprise. My answer to such queries is simply that this particular collection of writers happens to exemplify, for me, all the various facets of my own background as a Mauritian critic, born and raised as a cultural Catholic in the second half of this century, the period of gradual decolonization around the world. The works of Augustine and Nietzsche are examined here primarily for their cultural importance and for the hidden dimensions of their scholarly reception. My analysis foregrounds aspects of their texts which confirm the possibility of a different interpretation. By its very breadth, this book may fly in the face of the scholarly conventions we have inherited from the nineteenth century— the need to order and classify the world, to artificially separate into discrete units entities that, if studied together, would teach us far more about the status and function of our own subject positions in the world. But renewed connections to the past can emancipate us, provided they are used to elaborate empowering myths for living in the present and for affirming our belief in the future. The purpose of my work is to put into practice my belief in the interconnectedness of the various traditions I analyze. I hope the textual scrutiny that forms the basis of the following chapters in this book illustrates this commitment.

To establish nonhierarchical connections is to encourage lateral relations: instead of living within the bounds created by a linear view of history and society, we become free to interact on an equal footing with all the traditions that determine our present predicament. On a textual level, we can choose authors across time and space and read them together for new insights. Although my book is organized diachronically from Augustine to Marie-Thérèse Humbert, that orderly historical progression is perhaps not the best way to read it. While Chapters 1 and 2, on Augustine and Nietzsche, clearly form a unit and can profitably be read together, each of the following chapters on the women writers can and should be juxtaposed with either chapter of Part I, since each of the women borrows from or revises the earlier, male writers. Part II also forms a unit, but I have purposely interwoven elements of one chapter with those of another, so as to bring out affinities between them. I will introduce each chapter in detail later and suggest concrete sequences my reader might want to follow. For now, let me simply state that for me *métissage* is a praxis and cannot be subsumed under a fully elaborated theoretical system. *Métissage* is a form of *bricolage*, in the sense used by Claude Lévi-Strauss, but as an aesthetic concept it encompasses far more: it brings together biology and history, anthropology and philosophy, linguistics and literature. Above all, it is a reading practice that allows me to bring out the interreferential nature of a particular set of texts, which I believe to be of fundamental importance for the understanding of many postcolonial cultures. If, as Teresa de Lauretis has pointed out, identity is a strategy, then *métissage* is the fertile ground of our heterogeneous and heteronomous identities as postcolonial subjects.[11] The reactionary potential of a separatist search for a unitary and naturalized identity is a well-known danger on which I shall not dwell here. Only a well-understood feminist politics of solidarity can protect us from such a danger.[12]

Solidarity calls for a particular form of resistance with built-in political ambiguities. These ambiguities allow gendered subjects to negotiate a space within the world's dominant cultures in which the "secretive and multiple manifestations of Diversity," in Edouard Glissant's words, will not be anticipated, accommodated, and eventually neutralized.[13] A politics of solidarity thus implies the accep-

[11]Teresa de Lauretis, "Issues, Terms and Contexts," *Feminist Studies / Critical Studies*, ed. de Lauretis (Bloomington: Indiana University Press, 1986), p. 9.

[12]See for example Sandra Harding, *The Science Question in Feminism* (Ithaca: Cornell University Press, 1986), chap. 7; and Frantz Fanon's critique of negritude as I discuss it briefly in Chapters 2 and 3.

[13]Glissant, p. 12, trans. mod.

tance of *métissage* as the only racial ground on which liberation struggles can be fought. For the five women writers discussed here, the possibility of emancipation is indeed linked to an implicit understanding of *métissage* as a concept of solidarity which demystifies all essentialist glorifications of unitary origins, be they racial, sexual, geographic, or cultural.

As Glissant explains, "To advocate *métissage* is to presuppose the negation of *métissage* as a category, while sanctioning it as an absolute fact which the human imagination has always wished to deny or disguise (in Western tradition)."[14] But denial has never prevented symbiotic transcultural exchanges among groups interacting in systematically creative states of tension. Racial and cultural "mixing" has always been a fact of reality, however fearfully unacknowledged, especially by the proponents of "racial purity." It is in large part because of the scientific racism of the nineteenth century that hybridization became coded as a negative category. At that time, science created the idea of the "pure race," an extremely fallacious and aberrant form of human classification, born of the West's monotheistic obsession with the "One" and the "Same." As a result of colonial encounters and confrontations, the troubling question of miscegenation began to feed the European imagination with phantasms of monstrosity and degeneracy. Nineteenth-century scientists firmly believed that the white race had to be kept pure for its own protection, for it might otherwise become "degenerate." As historian of science Nancy Stepan has shown, a wide-ranging literature on the threat of degeneracy expressed "the fervent desire of white physicians and biologists to foreclose a multiracial society . . . and to insist on the necessity of distance" between the races. Identifying race as species, polygenists inferred that crosses between different races—as with different species of animals—would either be infertile or yield infertile hybrids. Monogenists and polygenists alike claimed that "the fate of races when they transgressed their boundaries was a 'degeneration' that could be so extreme as to cause racial extinction."[15] Clearly, experience showed even then that human "races" did not constitute "species," which might fit this scientific

[14]Ibid., p. 251, trans. mod.
[15]Nancy Stepan, "Biological Degeneration: Races and Proper Places," in *Degeneration: The Dark Side of Progress*, ed. J. Edward Chamberlin and Sander Gilman (New York: Columbia University Press, 1985), 100, 99.

model of "hybridization." But the loathing of nineteenth-century society for interracial mixing or "un-natural unions" led many scientists to conceptualize "hybridization" as monstrosity, decadence, and deterioration: like the mule, the mulatto was believed to be "a degenerate, unnatural offspring, doomed by nature to work out its own destruction."[16] Thus also, as Lévi-Strauss reminds us in *Race et histoire*, for Count Arthur de Gobineau, the father of racist theories, and author of the infamous *Essai sur l'inégalité des races humaines*, "The flaw of degeneracy was linked . . . to the phenomenon of hybridization [*métissage*] rather than to the relative position of each race in a scale of values common to all." If each race remained in its proper place, the deterioration of the species would be minimized.[17]

[16]Josiah C. Nott, "The Mulatto, a Hybrid," *American Journal of Medical Science* 5 1843), 256, cited in Stepan, p. 107.

[17]Claude Lévi-Strauss, *Race et histoire* (Paris: Gonthier, 1961), p. 10, my translation. If we take the most extreme and aberrant case, South Africa, we discover "a crazy game of musical chairs" (*Time* March 9, 1987, p. 54). "Everyone in South Africa is classified by race, placed at birth into one of nine racial categories that determine where he can live and work." But people can also petition to "have their classification changed if they can prove they were put in a wrong group." Every year the Home Affairs Ministry announces by decree who fits into which category subsequent to the petitions filed that year. Thus, the *Time* report says, in 1986 "nine whites became colored, 506 coloreds became white, two whites became Malay, 14 Malays became white, nine Indians became white, seven Chinese became white, one Griqua became white, 40 coloreds became black, 666 blacks became colored, 87 coloreds became Indian, 67 Indians became coloreds, 26 coloreds became Malay, 50 Malays became Indian, 61 Indians became Malay, four coloreds became Griqua, four Griquas became colored, two Griquas became black, 18 blacks became Griquas, twelve coloreds became Chinese, ten blacks became Indian, two blacks became other Asian, two other coloreds became Indian, and one other colored became black." The bottom line is that roughly 1,600 people changed "color," so to speak, were of "indeterminate status" and could thus be said to belong to the gray area where ethnic/racial identity is allowed to be fluid. "According to [Minister Stoffel] Botha," the report adds ironically, "no blacks applied to become white and no whites became black." In other words, at either end of the spectrum, the binary categories are still safely in place, and the established order of apartheid prevails for the majority. One could see the intermediate classifications as so many protective barriers—a kind of cordon sanitaire—aimed at preventing transgressive boundary crossings between the "white" and "black" areas. However absurd and unreal this juridical codification may seem, it serves in effect to legitimate the status quo—the mere fact that one can change one's label undermines the very possibility of according the label any kind of strictly *biological* validity: it simply reinforces the *ideological* presuppositions of apartheid. As Glissant has pointed out, "To assert that all peoples are mixed [*métissés*], that *métissage* has value, is to deconstruct a 'hybrid' [*métis*] category which might exist as a middle ground in its own right between two 'pure' extremes. It is only in those countries where exploitation is barbaric (South Africa for instance) that this intermediate category has been officially recognized" (p. 25, trans. mod.).

In my view, one of the most misunderstood factors of this nineteenth-century obsession with "races and proper places" has to do with an archaic, unconscious fear of conquest by the other, which is mediated by the female body. The French writer Théophile Gautier unwittingly displays an interesting example of such fears in one of his newspaper columns of 1845. His imagination is busy creating myths of "Orientalism," fueled by the recent conquest of Algeria, and he writes: "How strange! We think we have conquered Algiers, and it is Algiers which has conquered us.—Our women are already wearing gold-threaded and multicolored scarves which used to belong to the slaves of the harems. . . . If this continues, France will soon become Mohamedan and we shall see the white domes of mosques swell up in our cities, and minarets mingle with steeples, just as in Spain under the Moors. We would willingly live until that day, for quite frankly, we prefer Oriental fashions to English ones."[18]

His stated preference for Oriental customs notwithstanding, Gautier was contributing to the European colonial myth about otherness, a myth that still dies hard. Today, conservative political rhetoric in many countries of Western Europe associates multiracialism with the specter of an imminent conquest of Europe by the Third World. The fear that underlies this discourse of "heterophobia," as Albert Memmi puts it, is deeply rooted, linked to some of man's most atavistic beliefs: the need to protect "our women" from being "taken" by the other, from becoming the instruments of miscegenation and *métissage*, perhaps even the willing instruments.[19] In Gautier's remarks, the interesting juxtaposition of "conquered," "our women," and "slaves of the harem" makes it clear that the (white) women's reproductive potential must be protected so as not to become the site of *métissage* inside the *métropole*. It is very easy, and indeed tempting, on a subliminal level to make some substitutions on Gautier's text: "and we shall see the white stomachs of our women swell up in our cities," whereas the phallic imagery, "and the minarets mingle with steeples," would simply seem to point paradigmatically to the ideological transformation of the con-

[18]Théophile Gautier, *La Presse*, Jan. 6, 1845, quoted in Gautier, *Voyage pittoresque en Algérie*, ed. Madeleine Cottin (Geneva: Droz, 1973), p. 19.

[19]Albert Memmi, *Le Racisme: Description, définition, traitement* (Paris: Gallimard, 1982), p. 115. Note also the role played by Jean François Le Pen's National Front party in the 1988 French presidential election.

tent, but not of the form, of sexual domination.[20] What is at stake in
the conservative resistance to *métissage* is clearly a patriarchal desire
for self-reproduction, self-duplication, within a representational
space—female bodies—uncontaminated by the presence of the other. Control of that space is essential to its enduring "purity," to the
continuation of the paternal lineage, and to the safeguarding of
patriarchal authority. In such a context, it quickly becomes obvious
how subversive the very idea of *métissage*—biological and cultural—
can be.

Métissage and Language

It is my suspicion that our common and current perception of
what constitutes a "race" can be tested by the terms we use to define
various "subcategories" within those races and by the way language
responds to and accommodates the fact of *métissage*. There is always
a certain cultural relativism at work in those terms; because language is molded by the politics and ideology of a community, it
influences—in turn—the way a given community comes to think
about the world. I would go so far as to argue that in the absence of
scientific or experiential grounding, it is language that conditions
our concept of race and that the boundaries of that concept change
according to cultural, social, and linguistic realities.[21]

The analysis of French, English, Portuguese, or Spanish terms
used to define racial categories reveals that those words do not
readily translate into one another because they do not cover the
same reality, hence have only local significance and are not inter-
changeable: their semantic values and connotative fields do not
overlap.[22] In the French colonial context, for example, the *métis* con-

[20]In a column written for *Le Moniteur Universel*, June 7, 1861, Gautier himself compared the round domes of the mosques he saw in Algiers to white breasts full of milk.
Cited by Cottin, in *Voyage pittoresque*, p. 48.

[21]Twentieth-century science has shown that it is impossible to define with any kind
of accuracy the genetic frontiers that might permit the classification of humans into a
set of well-defined "races." See for example, Masatoshi Nei and Arun K. Roychou-
dhury, "Genetic Relationship and Evolution of Human Races," *Evolutionary Biology* 14
(1983); Albert Jacquard, "A la recherche d'un contenu pour le mot 'race': La réponse
du généticien," and François Jacob, "Biologie-Racisme-Hiérarchie," both in *Le Racisme: Mythes et sciences*, ed. Maurice Olender (Paris: Complexe, 1981). Both Jacquard
and Jacob emphasize that the attempt to classify and hierarchize human beings is the
consequence of an *ideological* parti pris.

[22]According to anthropologist Marvin Harris, the comparative study of race relations in Brazil and the United States illuminates important ambiguities in "culturally

stitutes a distinct but unstable racial category, which varies according to geography: in Canada, the word denotes a "half-breed" of French and Native American descent only. In the late eighteenth century, however, in the capital of the Senegal, St.-Louis, the *métis* were generally persons of French and African descent who then constituted one-fourth of the total population of the town. In the island colonies of the Indian Ocean and the West Indies—as in New Orleans—the *métis* are also called *créoles, mulâtres, cafres* and *cafrines,* although the term may apply indifferently to people who are ostensibly white (*créoles*) or black (*cafres*); the words have even wider semantic ranges in the local creole languages.

The very notion of *métissage,* then, is something culturally specific. The word does not exist in English: one can translate *métis* by "half-breed" or "mixed-blood" but these expressions always carry a negative connotation, precisely because they imply biological abnormality and reduce human reproduction to the level of animal breeding. "Mulatto" is sometimes used, but usually refers to a certain kind of fictional character, the "tragic mulatto," as in William Faulkner's *Go Down Moses* and *Light in August* or Mark Twain's *Puddin' Head Wilson.*[23] But here again, the connotations are totally negative and the referent is the animal world, namely, the generally sterile mule. In English, then, there is no real equivalent for the word *métis* and

---

controlled systems of 'racial' identity." His inventory of Portuguese lexical terms which define Brazilian "racial" types number 492, and do not correlate with precise usage: which is to say that there is no objective agreement among native Brazilians as to the "racial" status of a given person. Full siblings who look different phenotypically are identified by heterogeneous terms, and there is no such thing as a single "sociocentric racial identity," even within the same community or family. (Some of the 492 Portuguese expressions listed by Harris translate as: white African, white Negro, black Negro, black Indian, Indian mulatto, yellow white, white mulatto, white yellow, blond black, mestizo black, and so on. This highly subjective terminology is by no means static.) And Harris argues that Brazilian ambiguity could allow for a much broader base of support among oppressed groups, unlike the situation in the United States, where racial splits fragment the lower classes. "Referential Ambiguity in the Calculus of Brazilian Racial Identity," *Afro-American Anthropology: Contemporary Perspectives,* ed. Norman E. Whitten and John F. Szwed (New York: Free Press, 1970), 75.

[23] As Sondra O'Neale has argued, the mulatto figure is "the most discussed black female character in American literature." Such women are "perceived as totally Europeanized, not only in facial features but in acculturation, as well." "Inhibiting Midwives, Usurping Creators: The Struggling Emergence of Black Women in American Fiction," in *Feminist Studies / Critical Studies,* pp. 139–156 (147). It should be clear that what I am stressing in my use of the term *métissage* is quite different from the assimilationist tendencies criticized by O'Neale.

we could infer that for all English-speaking peoples the very concept of race is different from that of the French, Spanish, or Portuguese speakers. Indeed, in the United States, even an "octoroon" is technically supposed to be a "nonwhite," and those who "look" white but have (some) black "blood" were said to be able to "pass" for white. What does this tell us about the social construction of "race" within different linguistic contexts? That language, in effect, can create reality, since certain categories, such as *créole* and *métis*, are not part of any visible racial difference for the average English speaker. The Anglo-American consciousness seems unable to accommodate miscegenation positively through language. It is a serious blind spot of the English language which thus implies that persons of indeterminate "race" are freaks. It is another way of making invisible, of negating, the existence of nonwhites whose racial status remains ambiguous.

When we attempt to understand the full range of connotations of our racial terminologies, we are forced to reexamine the unconscious linguistic roots of racial prejudice and to face the fact that language predetermines perception. This is why a word like *métis* or *mestizo* is most useful: it derives etymologically from the Latin *mixtus*, "mixed," and its primary meaning refers to cloth made of two different fibers, usually cotton for the warp and flax for the woof: it is a neutral term, with no animal or sexual implication. It is not grounded in biological misnomers and has no moral judgments attached to it. It evacuates all connotations of "pedigreed" ascendance, unlike words like *octoroon* or *half-breed*.

Furthermore, its homonym in ancient Greek, *mētis*, is the allegorical "figure of a function or a power," a cunning intelligence like that of Odysseus, which opposes transparency and the metaphysics of identity and is thus closely related, in practice, to the meaning of *métissage* as I understand it here—and as Glissant uses it too. Within the Greek context, the reality of *mētis* as a form of *techne* projects itself on a plurality of practical levels but can never be subsumed under a single, identifiable system of diametric dichotomies. It is a form of savoir faire which resists symbolization within a coherent or homogeneous conceptual system since it is also the power to undo the logic and the clarity of concepts.

And as Marcel Détienne and Jean Pierre Vernant point out, Mētis is also a proper name: that of the wife of Zeus, who swallowed her when she was about to give birth to Athena. Mētis is subjugated by Zeus, who appropriates her power of transformation, "thereby guaranteeing his paternal authority for eternity."[24] We may thus appropriate the term for our own feminist pantheon, thanks to the fortuitous nature of this link between the Greek representation of subjugated female power and the elusive semantic field of the French term *métis*: the very polyvalence of the word dictates and legitimates my own heterogeneous approach in this book.

Finally, the use of *métissage* as an analytical tool forces us to re-evaluate certain key concepts of literary history as well, for even Leopold Sédar Senghor, whose name is synonymous with the term *négritude*, also claims to be a defender of *métissage* and considered himself a pan-African *métis*.[25] Negritude has borne the brunt of much criticism because of the essentialistic racial ideology implicit in the term, although both Senghor and Aimé Césaire have argued that the criticism was based in a reductive appropriation of the concept of negritude, which came to be interpreted as a purely reactive gesture against white supremacy, without regard for the polysemic potential intended by its originators.[26]

By contrast, in Cuba, it is the concept of *mestizaje* which has long been used by politicians and poets alike (José Martí or Nicolás Guillén, for example) as an enabling metaphor of transculturation with revolutionary potential because it is capable of generating broad support, of enlisting and encouraging solidarity among different ethnic groups against a common enemy, namely the hegemonic discourse of racialism. As Cuban poet Nancy Morejón explains it, "*Transculturation* means the constant interaction, the transmutation between two or more cultural components with the unconscious goal of creating a third cultural entity—in other words, a culture—that is new and independent even though rooted in the preceding elements. Reciprocal influence is the determining factor here, for no single element superimposes itself on another; on the contrary, each

[24]See Marcel Détienne and Jean Pierre Vernant, *Les Ruses de l'intelligence: La Mētis des grecs* (Paris: Flammarion, 1974); and the review by Richard Klein, "The Mētis of Centaurs," *Diacritics* 16 (Summer 1986), 2–13 (4–5).

[25]See for example Senghor's Preface to Marie-Madeleine Marquet, *Le Métissage dans la poésie de Léopold S. Senghor* (Dakar: Nouvelles Editions Africaines, 1983).

[26]But see also the arguments against monolithic views of race put forth by René Depestre, "*Les Aspects créateurs du métissage culturel*," and Anthony Phelps, "Moi, Nègre d'Amérique . . . ," in *Notre Librairie* 74 (April–June 1984), 61–65 and 53–60.

one changes into the other so that both can be transformed into a third. Nothing seems immutable."[27]

In this constant and balanced form of interaction, reciprocal relations prevent the ossification of culture and encourage systematic change and exchange. By responding to such mutations, language reinforces a phenomenon of creative instability in which no "pure" or unitary origin can ever be posited. A linguistic and rhetorical approach to the complex question of *métissage* thus points to the ideological and fictional nature of our racial categories while underlining the relationship between language and culture. A linguistic approach shows how and why racial difference is a function of language itself. I suggest that any successful strategy of resistance to the totalizing languages of racism must be based in the attempt to create a counterideology by exposing our rhetorical conventions.

Now, this general strategy points us to Nietzsche and to his critique of monolithic Western modes of knowledge, for he can provide us with some important tools for analyzing the complicated and duplicitous use of language of which the human subject is capable. Indeed it is by positing a Nietzschean perspectivism on reality that we can perhaps focus on a positive—if somewhat utopian—view of writing as an enabling force in the creation of a plural self, one that thrives on ambiguity and multiplicity, on affirmation of differences, not on polarized and polarizing notions of identity, culture, race, or gender. For Zora Neale Hurston, Maya Angelou, Marie Cardinal, and Marie-Thérèse Humbert, it is this plurality of potentialities which eventually helps bring the personal in line with the political—the political understood as the building, rather than the burning (or jumping off), of bridges,—whereas for Maryse Condé, the autobiographical novel is a device for representing the unhappy consciousness at its most delusory. Victim of her own alienations and mimetic illusions, Condé's narrator serves as counterexample, as infertile and sterile hybrid, whose negativity is an insidious form of dependence on the racist discourses the author denounces.

Such a use of Nietzsche qualifies my epistemology as poststructuralist. In recent years that epistemology, and the "postmodern condition" it signals, has come under severe attack from those who defend various good old-fashioned forms of humanism. But it

[27]Nancy Morejón, *Nacion y mestizaje en Nicolás Guillén* (Havana: Unión, 1982), p. 23. My translation.

seems to me urgent to point out that the criticisms leveled against poststructuralist epistemologies have very disturbing parallels in the nineteenth-century polygenists' discourse of racial purity. In both cases, indeterminacy, hybridization, and fragmentation are feared because of the risks of "degeneration" of the human species, of the race, and of "traditional" literary culture. If *métissage* and *indeterminacy* are indeed synonymous metaphors for our postmodern condition, then the fundamental conservatism of those who fight against both should be obvious.[28]

As Darwin discovered, the more varied the life forms in a given environment, the greater their chances of thriving. Hybrid configurations and diversified descendants of original species have the edge in the struggle for survival. The paradigm of struggle, the *agon*, is thus not the most useful for understanding either the natural world or the process of filiation in literary tradition.[29] The paradigm of diversity is just as important, since, according to Darwin's principle of divergence,

> more living beings can be supported on the same area the more they diverge in structure, habits and constitution, of which we see proof by looking at the inhabitants of any small spot. . . . [D]uring the modification of the descendants of any one species, and during the incessant struggle of all species to increase in numbers, the more diversified these descendants become, the better will be their chance of succeeding in the battle for life. Thus the small differences distinguishing varieties of the same species, will steadily tend to increase till they come to equal the greater differences between species of the same genus, or even of distinct genera.[30]

Variety and heterogeneity lead to richer and more fulfilling lives for all those who share a given environment; multiplicity flourishes

[28]For a recent description of the eleven distinguishing traits of postmodern literary culture, see Ihab Hassan, "Making Sense: The Trials of Postmodern Discourse," *New Literary History* 18 (Winter 1987), 437–59.

[29]Despite Harold Bloom's ethnocentric views on the matter: see *The Anxiety of Influence: A Theory of Poetry* (New York: Oxford University Press, 1973) and *Agon: Towards a Theory of Revision* (New York: Oxford University Press, 1982).

[30]Charles Darwin, *The Origin of Species* (New York: Penguin Books, 1968), p. 170. For a detailed discussion of the principle of divergence, its history and importance, see David Kohn, "On the Origin of the Principle of Diversity," *Science* 213 (Sept. 4, 1981), 1105–8; and John Langdon Brooks, *Just before the Origin* (New York: Columbia University Press, 1984). I am indebted to David Hull for sharing these references and his wide knowledge of Darwin.

when the shackles of homogeneity and rigidity are broken. By contrast, to internalize patriarchal law is to create mutually exclusive categories of "reality" (male/female; white/black; primitive/civilized; autobiographical/fictional; etc.) and to forget that the production of discourses can function according to Darwinian divergence: that a given space (text) will support more life (generate more meanings) if occupied by diverse forms of life (languages). The authors in this study subvert all binary modes of thought by privileging (more or less explicitly) the intermediary spaces where boundaries become effaced and Manichean categories collapse into each other.

I have credited Darwin for giving scientific validity to the notion of heterogeneity. The United States is a country where grass-roots culture and the politics of small groups often exhibit this kind of Darwinian heterogeneity. Zora Neale Hurston's and Maya Angelou's works are lucid examples of that America, the one "blues critics" are helping to uncover and excavate from the historical myth of the melting pot.[31] Coming as I do from a "small spot," also visited by Darwin during his voyage on the *Beagle,* I have a vested interest in valorizing the principle of divergence. All too often it is excluded by a politics of knowledge, which values power and appropriates Darwinian theories of natural selection because they appear to give legitimacy to the strong. By contrast, and as Détienne and Vernant have shown, the Greek art of *mētis* is an art of transformation and transmutation, an aesthetics of the ruse that allows the weak to survive by escaping through duplicitous means the very system of power intent on destroying them. As I shall point out at the conclusion of my discussion of Maya Angelou's works, the art of *mētis* thus rejoins the signifying practices familiar to all oppressed peoples, in particular to the descendants of slaves in the New World. Such practices had to be learned by the slaves as survival tactics within a hostile environment that kept them subjugated, relegated them to the margins.

Reading the Writers

From Augustine to Marie-Thérèse Humbert, the seven writers in this book are examples of "divergent" individuals, living on bor-

[31]See Houston A. Baker, Jr., *Blues, Ideology and Afro-American Literature: A Vernacular Theory* (Chicago: University of Chicago Press, 1984), pp. 64–66.

derlines. They use linguistic and rhetorical structures that allow their plural selves to speak from within the straightjackets of borrowed discourses. The five women authors represent specific examples of creative *métissage* grounded in the historical and geopolitical realities that motivate and inspire them. In order to make clear the complex lineage that influences both their writing and my reading of their work, I have—as mentioned previously—found it necessary to go back to Augustine and Nietzsche. My point is not to use them as male paradigms or antimodels to be criticized and refuted: I want to examine how dimensions of their work that might be called feminine tend to be either ignored or coded in reference to a more "masculine" and hierarchical framework, even though these texts explicitly reject the possibility of such unproblematic appropriation by critics blind to the biases of their own disciplines and unreceptive to the subversive rhetorical features of language.

But dealing with Augustine and Nietzsche poses a problem opposite to that of the women writers. Far from being neglected, they have been buried under such a bulk of critical interpretation that it is sometimes difficult to approach their texts without preconceived notions colored by nineteenth-century misreadings of their work. What I have attempted to do in Chapters 1 and 2 amounts to a feminist reappropriation of the covertly maternal elements of both the *Confessions* and *Ecce Homo*. I contrast those with the metaphors of death and disease which permeate the authors' language and structure their narratives. I discuss the problematic status of orality in Augustine's text and the procreative symbolism of Nietzsche's. My reading of Augustine will thus lead to the deconstruction of the notion of gender as we commonly understand it in contemporary terms, and my use of Nietzsche will do the same with regard to the concepts of race and nationality.

Augustine's mother tongue was a North African patois, New Punic, spoken until about A.D. 550 in his hometown of Thagaste, near Carthage, a colony of the western Roman Empire. The classical Latin in which he wrote was a second language, learned in school. Instruction was dispensed by a grammarian who relied on corporal punishment to train his pupils. Augustine also learned Greek, but as he explains in the *Confessions*, that language was odious to him and so hard to understand that "[he] was constantly subjected to violent threats and cruel punishments to make [him] learn" it. Of his native language, he says that he learned it simply, without threats of punishments "while my nurses fondled me and everyone laughed and played happily with me."[32] For him, then, the language he would come to use as a writer—Latin—had done violence to his body and to his soul. This pain explains in part the ambiguous relationship he would maintain with all forms of discourse and his search for a silent resting point, a state of total metaphysical communion, where communication transcends language, is not circumscribed by it.

Nietzsche struggles with the languages of reason and unreason, the silences of hysteria and madness within the monologues of what Michel Foucault terms "the merciless language of non-madness."[33] He is acutely aware of the tyranny of rationalism, the conflicts of consciousness, and the symbolic structures that artificially order perception, feelings, selfhood. Nietzsche stages his life as *Ecce Homo*, a text of rupture and fragmentation. Operating in the space between being and becoming and as heir to Heraclitean and Darwinian notions of multiplicity, Nietzsche undercuts all our illusions about self-possession and self-appropriation: his "autobiography" is an interpretive reading of his corpus, a commentary on his linguistic selves. In many ways, Nietzsche reverses Augustine: the *imitatio Christi* collapses into the figure of the Antichrist, self-dissolution in the transcendent other becomes Dionysian metamorphosis. The last line of *Ecce Homo*, "Have I been understood?—*Dionysus versus the Crucified*—" is a proclamation and a promise of life against a Christian redemption in death. It is, however, the point at which writing ceases, since madness can only cancel out all possibilities of pursuing an oeuvre. In Foucault's words, "Nietzsche's last cry . . . is the very annihilation of the work of art, the point where it becomes impossible and where it must fall silent; the hammer has just fallen from the philosopher's hands."[34]

The five women writers also struggle with metaphors of death and disease or madness and silence as the ambivalent foci of their efforts at self-writing. Some of the women—Maya Angelou, Marie

---

[32]Augustine, *Confessions*, trans. R. S. Pine-Coffin (New York: Penguin Books, 1979), p. 35.

[33]Michel Foucault, *Madness and Civilization: A History of Insanity in the Age of Reason*, trans. Richard Howard (New York: Random House, 1965), p. ix.

[34]Ibid., p. 287.

Cardinal, and Marie-Thérèse Humbert—ultimately succeed in achieving a reaffirmation of life through the emancipatory potential of writing, with admittedly varying degrees of optimism and triumph. But for Zora Neale Hurston and Maryse Condé, who have experienced the lethal effects of historical contradictions, writing is an unrelenting search for a *different* past, to be exhumed from the rubble of patriarchal and racist obfuscations. The women's narratives thus dramatize relations of overwhelming indenture. As colonized subjects of patriarchy and racism, these authors are also acutely aware of and profoundly ambivalent about the literary and vernacular traditions within which they implicitly situate themselves as writers. This ambivalence is of particular interest to me because it reveals the damaging process of human internalization of negative stereotypes. I will try to uncover and analyze some of the (Nietzschean) dissimulating strategies these writers use to subvert generic or critical canons and to address social or cultural prejudices.

The women belong to widely different cultural backgrounds. Yet they share a profound concern for the rhetoric of selfhood, for the processes of self-reading and self-writing as facilitated or impeded by the styles and languages in which they are compelled to write. Two are Afro-Americans: Zora Neale Hurston and Maya Angelou, both raised in the South. Three are Francophone: Maryse Condé was raised in Guadeloupe, Marie Cardinal in Algeria, and Marie-Thérèse Humbert in Mauritius. But all are cultural *métis*, *créoles* whose socioideological horizons are marked by the concrete layerings or stratifications of diverse language systems. The textual space where these layers interact and enter into dialogue is the "auto-biographical" theme that will be my generic focus in this book.

Because the path of creativity is particularly tortuous for those who must straddle the interval between different and hierarchized cultural universes, each of the writers examined here has a different relationship to his/her chosen means of expression (the language in which s/he writes) as well as to the style and mode of discourse s/he chooses to adopt within the broader generic configurations of "autobiography." In other words, language is problematic for all of them, not simply because no one ever has a transparent relationship to a given linguistic frame of reference but more specifically because their frames of reference are cultural worlds apart. The space of writing in which these frames intersect positions the writing subject at the confluence of complex and sometimes conflicting creative impulses, which complicate both the writer's and the implied reader's relations in (and to) the text under scrutiny. Thus the denotative and connotative layers of the text can either undermine, contradict, and sabotage each other or reinforce and strengthen patterns of address which allow the subject to speak the language of the other—the implied reader—without risk of abandoning a privileged position within the semiotic field of the mother tongue. By implication, under the articulated, written, organized surface of the narrative there exists a certain energy that can alternatively disrupt the surface layer (as is the case with Condé, Cardinal, and Humbert) or pull together and unify seemingly contradictory or discontinuous narrative modes (as is the case with Augustine, Hurston and Angelou). Hence, I have chosen texts constituted by multilayered nestings, corresponding to their plural languages. These languages can only enter into dialogue when the interval between the textual layers is allowed to function as "third man," "demon," or "noise" to use Michel Serres's terminology.

For Serres, discourse—in whatever discipline—succeeds in producing meaning by exclusionary binary tactics: "The most profound dialectical problem is not the problem of the Other, who is a variety—or a variation—of the Same, it is the problem of the third man. We might call this third man the *demon*, the prosopopeia of noise." So that if we think of Western history and culture as one long dialogue between interlocutors who are united in one common goal—the search for knowledge or, as Serres has also said, "the hunt" for knowledge and the aggressive appropriation of truth and meaning by two partners in discourse who battle against "noise,"—then this "third man" is more often than not a "she-devil," a figure constructed variously as "woman" or as "*Third* World," the better to negate or abolish the multifarious differences among women, peoples, and countries not aligned with the dominant ideologies and conceptual systems of the West. The progressive historical marginalization of this "third" term is a direct consequence of the paradigm of struggle that Serres's metaphor of the hunt aptly summarizes: "Dialectic makes the two interlocutors play on the same side; they do battle together to produce a truth on which they can agree, that is, to produce a successful communication," and thus to expel or evacuate all interference from "the powers of noise" which become the excluded middle, the marginalized peoples, the silent but paradoxically "noisy" gender.[35]

In contrast to this dialectic of struggle in the autobiographical texts analyzed here a different kind of dialogue occurs *because* of the "noise" (the unfiltered, mumbled, "demonic" mother tongue) and thanks to interferences between contradictory strategies, not in spite of them. Starting with Augustine's *Confessions*, for example, we discover under the apparent structures of the text a different system of organization: I establish the presence of a form of coherence that belies the initial impression of discontinuity. And in *A l'autre bout de moi*, I show how the autobiographical novel, which seems to foreclose interpretation if we remain in the realm of linguistic coherence and read it as a "French" text, is inhabited by another tongue, which turns it into a palimpsest—a verbal rather than a visual one. Indeed, when a verbal sign hides another, to find the underlying structure of a given work, the most useful procedure is not to "look" for it but rather to "listen" for it, since speech acts are a matter of *parole* and not of static visual signs. Augustine and Nietzsche both offer clues, following which I develop the art of listening for "noise." In my approaches to Angelou and Cardinal, I then analyze the painful process of creativity for women writers who are also mothers and seem to have with words as complicated a relationship as they do with their children, thus reproducing their initial ambivalent relationships to their own parents and to the literary tradition that shapes their access to language. Following Hurston and Condé, I argue that the search for past connections must not be allowed to dissolve into negative mythic identifications but must be a thorough reinterpretation of the texts and of the other "noisy" voices of history. If, as critic, I can attempt to read the textual layers while occupying the interval where this otherness speaks, then perhaps I shall succeed in doing justice to strata that might otherwise go unnoticed, remaining masked under superficial and epidermic structures of address.

[35]See Michel Serres, *Hermes: Literature, Science, Philosophy*, ed. Josué V. Harari and David F. Bell (Baltimore: Johns Hopkins University Press, 1982), pp. 65–70 (67). In *The Parasite*, trans. Lawrence R. Schehr (Baltimore: Johns Hopkins University Press, 1983), Serres also develops the question of noise and the figures it assumes. In "The Algebra of Literature: The Wolf's Game," in *Textual Strategies: Perspectives in Post-Structuralist Criticism*, ed. Josué Harari (Ithaca: Cornell University Press, 1979), p. 276, he speaks of the "hunt" for knowledge.

The metaphors Marie Cardinal uses in her description of the Algerian civil war graphically summarize the tragedy of clashing colonial monolithic systems in their struggle to eliminate noise and heteroglossia. The hideous consequences of war on the lives of those who are caught under the wheels of history are a function of the abstract, mathematical itinerary traced by the discourses of power in their efforts to silence undesirable, hysterical, or "demonic" elements, that is, blood: "And yet, it was still the shameful agony of French Algeria. The degradation of everything was in the blood of civil war which ran into the gutters and overflowed onto the sidewalks, *following the geometric patterns in the cement of civilization.*"[36] When empirical considerations—such as pain or torture—are geometrically ordered so as not to disturb the intelligence-gathering powers in their search for "truth," war becomes a metaphor for all the great instruments of social codification which, in Deleuze's terms, fight against "nomad thought,"[37] or as Cardinal herself puts it, against the "divagations" that alone can free one from "the yoke of truth" (215). For Cardinal, the path to social self-consciousness is the crooked one of hysteria: only hysteria can transform the dominant codes through and by which we become self-aware as a collective body politic. Because wars need heroes and heroes must die, ancient patterns of honorable conduct and sacrificial victimization are repeated in all patriarchal conflicts. Laforest too was the victim of an unofficial and undeclared war between conflicting ideologies struggling to take possession of the colonized subject, to claim his linguistic soul to the "truths" of monolithic and Manichean points of view. Life, on the other hand, belongs in a different realm from truth, in that intermediate space where distinctions are effaced, divergence occurs, and one's fate can follow an unheroic, muddy, and noisy path: that is ultimately the perspective adopted by Cardinal.

Like Augustine, Angelou and Humbert write a rich and classical prose (English and French respectively) in a language that is not exactly their "mother tongue." Angelou grew up in the American South during the Depression and learned to read and write in a very religious community where the language of the Bible was familiar to

[36]Marie Cardinal, *The Words to Say It*, trans. Pat Goodheart (Cambridge, Mass.: VanVactor and Goodheart, 1984), p. 88, my italics. I have modified the translation.

[37]Gilles Deleuze, "Nomad Thought," in *The New Nietzsche: Contemporary Styles of Interpretation*, ed. David B. Allison (Cambridge, Mass.: MIT Press, 1985), pp. 142–49.

all. For her, to acquire a personal style was to combine the English literary tradition with old-fashioned southern idioms, biblical phrases and rural as well as urban dialects. Unlike other black American writers who choose to express themselves in dialect only, Angelou makes a conscious political decision to master "the King's English" in order to reach a wider audience but also, as she recognizes honestly, because "insecurity can make us spurn the persons and traditions we most enjoy."[38] But what she dispenses with on the level of language, she recuperates in the mythic dimensions of her narrative, which becomes a vast historical and allegorical fresco of the lives of black American women. The use of an eighteenth-century picaresque model, which she succeeds in subverting with humor and irony, is a distinctive feature of her style. She appropriates traditional patterns to her own distinctive ends, thus modifying our perception of what constitutes both "autobiography" and "fiction" in black and Anglo-American literatures.

For Humbert, writing is possible in the psychic space where three languages intersect. The Mauritian creole dialect of her native island seldom surfaces as such in the text or in the mouth of the characters, but it is crucial to a full understanding of the narrative layers and of the Nietzschean operation of self-dissimulation that her text performs on itself. Traces of English (the official political language of Mauritius) are frequent in a novel that rewrites Miranda's (and Caliban's and Ariel's) story in Shakespeare's *Tempest*. And finally, there is French, the "literary" language of Mauritius, which the Francophone population prides itself on cultivating and refining, the more so because it is by no means the language of the majority or the official language. On one level, Humbert's novel is a romantic melodrama with two traditional heroines, one tragic and one romantic, whose fates follow the patterns ascribed to such characters in the canonical texts of the genre. But under the surface structure of the narrative is a complex self-portrait that deconstructs the notion of "heroine," allowing the narrator to assume control and to reject the tradition of female passivity inscribed in the dominant scripts of her legacy.

Hurston and Condé are consumed by the need to find their past, to trace lineages that will empower them to live in the present, to

[38]Maya Angelou, *Singin' and Swingin' and Gettin' Merry like Christmas* (New York: Random House, 1976), p. 94.

rediscover the histories occluded by History. The impasse in which Condé's Véronica finds herself at the end of her stay in Africa is an allegory of the impasse of *départementalisation* in the French West Indies. As a figure for the failure of Antilleans to embrace their fate as *Caribbean* peoples (instead of "French" Antilleans), she epitomizes the cultural problems of her island. As Glissant points out, "The nation is not based on exclusion; it is a form of dis-alienated relationship with the other who in this way becomes our fellow man [qui ainsi devient autrui]."[39] Condé's disturbing pessimism is a reflection of the political morass of her people, who continue to live under the thumb of the *métropole*, thus entertaining an alienated relationship with the French other, who cannot, under those circumstances, become an *autrui*, that is, a peer and an equal.

So, unlike that of the other women writers, Hurston's and Condé's concern for the past remains linked to a certain pessimism about the future. Their narrators are the lost daughters, orphaned offspring, of an imaginary Africa. For Hurston, anthropological field research becomes a way to rediscover and study lost siblings, to learn about the transformations, transculturations, and cultural *métissages* at work in various areas of the New World. She succeeds in showing the value of "dialect" as a sophisticated means of expression, dispensing once and for all with sentimental or condescending attitudes toward so-called primitivism. But Condé's Véronica makes the trip back to Africa to discover the emptiness within, the false solutions of exile and nomadism. Her narrative presents the most disturbing questions about race and origin, sexuality and domination, intellectual honesty and political engagement. These are questions we must face with great urgency if we believe that intellectual work can have any kind of effect on reality, if we do not want our words to be "dust tracks on a road," aimless detours or strategies of deferral, and would rather choose to have them function as means of transforming our symbolic systems, for the symbolic is real, and in symbols lies our only hope for a better world. To reinterpret the world *is* to change it.

If Nietzsche and Augustine seem to write themselves into silence, the silence of madness or religion, by contrast, Angelou, Cardinal, and Humbert write in an attempt to break out of the prison house of

---

[39]Glissant, p. 463.

colonizing languages: writing becomes the only key to the (uto-pian?) creation of a different, heterogeneous, and multicolored fu-ture, a future in which the "principle of divergence" is recognized as valid and functional not only in nature but in all our cultural institu-tions as well, from language to politics. It is no accident that this emphasis on a life-affirming view of writing and creativity is com-mon to three women who are also mothers but whose articulation of the "maternal," as we shall see, is more problematic than Au-gustine's search for the kind of elusive plenitude that Julia Kristeva has termed the "Eternal Phallic Mother," although it will remain quite close to Nietzsche's writing of the (pro)creative body.[40] Au-gustine's search for plenitude and coherence leads him to empha-size wholeness and completeness, whereas for the women writers, it will become clear that the human individual is a fundamentally relational subject whose "autonomy" can only be a myth. In the context of our postcolonial history, this view inevitably implies a critique of the myth of economic and political independence of the so-called Third World nations whose survival depends on the "First" World's understanding of *inter*dependence, of "global relations [la Relation planétaire]."[41]

As the foregoing discussion suggests, permutations of all the chapters of this book are possible. Reading sequences might be the following: Augustine and Nietzsche, Augustine, Angelou, and the second half of Chapter 6, on Humbert; Nietzsche, Hurston, Cardinal and Humbert; Hurston, Angelou, and Condé; or Condé, Cardinal, and Humbert. But the reader should feel absolutely free to let her/himself be guided by the threads that seem most compelling and inspiring, as I have done in my own reading of the texts. Since reading is always appropriative, I should perhaps say a few words about my technique of appropriation, a technique I urge my own reader to employ with regard to my book. I try to derive my inter-pretive strategies from the texts themselves rather than to adopt a

---

[40]For a excellent feminist psychoanalytic approach to the issues that concern me here, see Shirley N. Garner et al., eds. *The (M)other Tongue: Essays in Feminist Psycho-analytic Interpretation* (Ithaca: Cornell University Press, 1985). I am more interested in the cross-cultural repressive linguistic mechanisms that "colonize" a writer's access to his/her (m)other tongue. I will be analyzing how this repressed linguistic layer resur-faces in the text, creating echoes of another discourse, another sensitivity under the apparent simplicity of the narrative.

[41]Glissant, p. 465.

single theoretical lens from the vast array of critical approaches available to the contemporary critic. This approach enables me to analyze the ways in which rhetorical structures produce meaning and to elucidate the process whereby text and context can ultimately be derived from the linguistic structures interacting on different levels of textual production. I then draw conclusions or elaborate theories on the basis of this close textual scrutiny. Theoretical commitments are of course indispensable. But I try never to impose a theoretical grid on the text; instead, I draw from it the means of theorizing its own process of production. This technique might be labeled a noncoercive feminist practice of reading, since it allows text and reader to enter a dialogue that does not follow the usual rules of linear, agonistic, and patriarchal discourses. To read noncoercively is to allow my self to be interwoven with the discursive strands of the text, to engage in a form of intercourse wherein I take my interpretive cues from the patterns that emerge as a result of this encounter—in other words, it is to enjoy an erotics of reading somewhat similar to Barthes's in *The Pleasure of the Text*.

Indeed, one does not enter into a fictional world without risk, the risk of being influenced by a specific point of view. Reading is a two-way street and by implicating myself in my reading, I am in turn transformed by that activity. I can never be a neutral observer of the structures of the texts I read, but my perspectives are also shaped, at least in part, by those present in the texts I discuss. Since I strongly believe that our lives are overdetermined by language and ideology, history and geography, my purpose in this book is to try to investigate how that larger context may be present *in* the text, in the interweavings of its languages, but sometimes in such a subtle way as to have been neglected by critical discourses that did not take this context into consideration or that simply tried to eliminate it.[42]

---

[42]The English version of Marie Cardinal, *Les Mots pour le dire* is an extreme case in point here, as will be shown in Chapter 6. A less extreme but nonetheless disturbing example of a critic who negates historical and geopolitical considerations is Christopher Miller, in *Blank Darkness: Africanist Discourse in French* (Chicago: University of Chicago Press, 1985). On p. 120, analyzing Baudelaire's language, Miller speculates at length about whether Baudelaire "invented" the term *cafrine* used in his poem "La Belle Dorothée" because such a term is not to be found in any of the major *French* dictionaries Miller has consulted. The term is a creole neologism, widely used in the islands of Reunion and Mauritius where Baudelaire spent time in 1841 and where he learned some Creole. Baudelaire's use of *cafrine* is a perfect example of the strong

Throughout my discussions, I rely on *métissage* as an aesthetic concept to illustrate the relationship between historical context and individual circumstances, the sociocultural construction of race and gender and traditional genre theory, the cross-cultural linguistic mechanisms that allow a writer to generate polysemic meanings from deceptively simple or seemingly linear narrative techniques. I thus establish the need for a kind of Geertzian "thick description" of those texts.[43] Indeed, the use women writers make of both Western literary (or religious) traditions and vernacular cultures (or dialects) contributes to a form of intertextual weaving or *mé-tissage* of styles. This, I believe, is a fundamentally emancipatory metaphor for the inevitably relational and interdependent nature of peoples, nations, and countries hoping to enter into a peaceful "Relation planétaire" at the threshold of the twenty-first century.

---

presence of that vernacular context *in the text*. Yet that context is ignored by a critic whose interest in discourse theory suffers from lack of historical grounding. As Derrida has put it: "The dialectic of language, of the tongue [*langue*], is dialectophagy." *Glas*, trans. John P. Leavey, Jr., and Richard Rand (Lincoln: University of Nebraska Press, 1986), p. 9.

[43]See Geertz, chap. 1.

Part I
Rereading the Past

One must have tradition in oneself, to hate it properly.
Theodor Adorno, *Minima Moralia*

This first section of the book will undertake a close reading of the *Confessions*, followed by an analysis of *Ecce Homo*. Its aim is to disclose some of the contradictions present both in the language of these autobiographies and in the critical reception they have elicited. In the case of Augustine, I am especially interested in showing that the dichotomy made by traditional criticism between form and content, artistic method and theological pronouncements, results in some misleading statements about the structural unity of the work. In a wonderfully clear and perceptive chapter of his *Augustine of Hippo*, Peter Brown, for example, defines book 10 of the *Confessions* as "the self-portrait of a convalescent," engaged in a meditation on the mystery of man's inner world, the sheer size of which was for him "a source of anxiety quite as much as of strength." Yet Brown avoids dealing with books 11–13 altogether and resorts to spatial metaphors that are very much in the spirit of Augustine's own prose but can hardly help clarify the function of a substantial part of the work (one-fourth of the whole, to be specific). Brown writes: "The remaining three books of the *Confessions* are a fitting ending to the self-revelation of such a man: like soft light creeping back over a rain-soaked landscape, the hard refrain of 'Command'—'Command what You wish'—gives way to 'Give'—'Give what I love: for I do love it.'" Augustine's progress in self-awareness, his "therapy of self-examination," as Brown puts it, does underscore a gradual movement from initial refusal or denial to greater acceptance of the word of God.[1] As Chapter 1 will argue, this movement is evident in the structure of the work itself. Analyzing this structure will bring into focus the nature of the reading process as it appears to be

[1] Peter Brown, *Augustine of Hippo* (Berkeley: University of California Press, 1969), 177–81.

encoded within some sections of the *Confessions*, permitting certain conclusions about Augustine's act of (self-)reading and illuminating the subtle process whereby "woman" comes to represent to Augustine an aspect of the self which must be effaced, erased, obliterated, because it is none other than the "sinning self." Interestingly for us here, at the same time as he is discovering that "woman" must be evacuated from the "converted self," Augustine is attributing to God the kind of receptive, nurturing, maternal, and nonauthoritarian qualities normally coded as feminine in Western culture. Augustine's perception of God moves from that of an authoritarian figure who can "Command" him to that of a more generous one who will "Give." In his relationship with the transcendent Other, Augustine moves from an oppositional stance to a deferring and accepting one. As we shall see in Part II, this is a trajectory that will have to be reversed in the case of women writers. They must first learn to reject a tradition of passive acceptance of the other before they can become the agents of their own discourses, the subjects of their own histories. Meanwhile, they will also incorporate into their stories a radical rereading of the tradition they implicitly aim to transform.

For both Augustine and Nietzsche, life and literature are very closely related, but whereas Augustine must transcend his narrative impulse to accede to eternal life, to become the reader of God's word, Nietzsche sees narrative as the redemption of the past and his self as the sum of his literary output. Augustine is always writing toward (that is, loving) his ideal, transcendental Other—God. By contrast, Nietzsche sees himself as his own ideal reader: "Und so erzähle ich mir mein Leben [And so I tell my life to myself]," as he will proclaim in *Ecce Homo*.[2] This is the kind of grand solipsistic and tautological gesture of which Nietzsche is fond. He thereby refuses to allow for any possibility of domestication or appropriation of his words by an other. This attitude points to a form of "reaction" which, as will be seen, remains importantly dependent upon the Christian mentality it seeks to undermine. Nietzsche will denounce Christian self-abnegation while using all sorts of false doubles and adopting doppelgänger roles that simultaneously affirm and condemn the principles he puts forward. His symbolic use of women's

<hr />

[2]Friedrich Nietzsche, *Sämtliche Werke* (Stuttgart: A. Kröner, 1964), 8:299; *On the Genealogy of Morals and Ecce Homo*, trans. Walter Kaufmann (New York: Vintage, 1969), p. 221.

procreative powers stems from what Margot Norris has called "Nietzsche's biocentric premises," his conviction that animal vigor, the realm of the biological, is the only "real." In their creatural role as biological mothers, women are opposed to "cultural man," who is but a pretext, a means, for women's instinctual drive to give birth. Culture, for Nietzsche, is engendered by an imaginary lack that provokes a mimetic response, an identification with the other. Maryse Condé's representation of the impasse of mimetic identifications can be profitably studied as a dramatic portrayal of the cultural dead ends resulting from such an imaginary lack. As Norris argues, for Nietzsche, "mimesis acquires a negative value as inimical to the animal's power and to the body's life."[3]

Nietzsche's critique of the fundamental alienation involved in any kind of imitative cultural behavior thus yields the basis for the examination in Part II of the ambivalence that *métis* women writers feel toward their variously conflicting colonial heritages. It is by returning to the physicality of their experiences, to the racial and sexual characteristics of their bodies, that these women become able to create culture as well. In essence, they ground culture in the body, thus erasing the traditional distinctions between culture and nature, the life of the mind and that of the body. They thus implicitly adopt the Nietzschean principle underscoring the experiential *and* performative aspects of literature: self-writing becomes self-invention.

[3]Margot Norris, *Beasts of the Modern Imagination: Darwin, Nietzsche, Kafka, Ernst, and Lawrence* (Baltimore: Johns Hopkins University Press, 1985), p. 5, and see pp. 53–100 especially.

1

Augustine's *Confessions:* Poetics of Harmony, or the Ideal Reader in the Text

Our noisy years seem moments in the being
Of the eternal silence
            Wordsworth, "Ode: Intimations of Immortality"

Toward the end of the *Confessions* (13:30, 31), Augustine makes a last reference to the Manichean doctrines he had espoused during his youth. From the vantage point of a now-acknowledged total dependence on the word of God, his youthful errors are dismissed as the blind ignorance and insane claims of a man not yet illuminated by the power of the word and the proper understanding of God's truth, the source of all harmony ("concordiam" [12:30]) and beauty. The Manicheans, those he calls *insani*, or "madmen," taught a form of materialistic dualism in the belief that good and evil (or light and darkness) were two separate substances, always in conflict. According to this doctrine, the creation of the world was the product of those conflicting forces, and the souls of men consisted of an element of light imprisoned in darkness. As Augustine makes clear in 13:30, Manicheans see God himself as subjected to determinism. God is not a free creator, since he was "compelled by necessity" to assemble the different parts of the universe, such as those had been created "elsewhere." The vocabulary used by Augustine in this very short chapter (sixteen lines) is of particular interest to the textual approach I shall be using here:

Opera tua, et multa eorum dicunt te fecisse *necessitate conpulsum,* sicut *fabricas* caelorum et conpositiones siderum, et hoc non de tuo, sed iam fuisse *alibi* creata et aliunde, quae tu *contraheres* et *conpaginares* atque *contexeres,* cum de hostibus victis mundana *moenia* molineris.

[They say that you were *compelled by necessity* to make many of your works, such as the *structure* of the heavens and the ordering of the stars; that you did not use your own materials but those which had already been made *elsewhere*, and that you merely *assembled them, pieced them together* and *wove them into one*, and that you erected a protective *rampart* made up of your defeated enemies.] [13:30; my italics][1]

Because of their belief in dualism, Manicheans cannot accept that the world, like God's book, is a harmonious creation. They see its textual fabric as a mere collection of borrowed elements hastily sewn together in order to create a frame, a rampart for protection against darkness and evil. Their views exemplify the need to compartmentalize, separate, and hierarchize reality, a need reenacted again and again throughout history by writers and philosophers intent on defining and classifying the polarities constitutive of Western culture: good/evil, light/darkness, male/female, and so on. In the *Confessions*, however, such a belief in dualism becomes unacceptable to Augustine the convert. For him, *all* of God's creation is good and beautiful as Genesis 1 asserts: "And you saw all that you made, O God, and found it very good." The last chapters of book 13 (32–38) go on to proclaim the glory of God's deeds, which reflect both his wholeness and his holiness. The fundamental Manichean conflict between the forces of good and evil is thus transcended by Augustine's adoption of a Neoplatonic Christian theology of unity and oneness.

As I show later in this chapter, the effacement of rigid boundaries leads Augustine to the progressive transformation and assimilation of what might be termed the feminine elements of his North African Roman Catholic culture. By integrating into one harmonious whole all the oppositional monads defined by Manicheanism, Augustine valorizes both of the opposing terms, making it possible to eschew the binary, exclusionary logic of rational thinking in favor of a more relational view of the world. It is such a relational view that subtends Augustine's structuring of his autobiography, foreshadowing the patterns of *métissage* in the writing of contemporary women authors. It is thus extremely appropriate to begin my book with a

---

[1]I use the Latin text from the Loeb Classical Library edition (Cambridge: Harvard University Press, 1977), vols. 1 and 2, and translations by R. S. Pine-Coffin (New York: Penguin Books, 1979). Citations in the text are to book and chapter. I modify the translation when necessary to provide a more precise rendering of the nuances of the Latin text, as I have done in this quotation. I shall indicate "trans. mod." when I do so.

detailed analysis of the *Confessions*, this founding document of Western autobiographical discourse, and to attempt to reread it in light of my own contemporary feminist commitment to eliminating the artificial boundaries that centuries of Manichean—indeed, phallogocentric—thinking have helped to erect. I need not rehearse here the Derridean critique of metaphysics, but let me simply state that my approach to Augustine seeks to free the *Confessions* from the philosophical and theological traditions that have appropriated it.

In dealing with the *Confessions*, a text doubly canonical in virtue of its literary qualities and theological statements, critics have generally been tempted either to focus on its status as *architexte* of Western autobiography and thus paradigm of a certain narrative mode and historical itinerary or to see it as doctrinal supplement to the larger body of Augustinian writings, which belong to a specific philosophical tradition based on Neoplatonic Christianity and Judaic exegesis.[2] Indeed, much Augustine criticism has tended to divide along those lines: secular reading of the narrative part, the first nine books, or philosophical/theological interpretation of the sacred doctrine using the rhetorical meditations of the last four books to clarify Augustine's notions of time, memory, origins, and beginnings.

Yet, if Augustine takes such pains to insist that God's text, the universe, is a harmonious whole, then I would like to suggest that Augustine's own text must have been structured so as to conform to similar standards of unity, goodness, and harmony. Why then the combination of nine narrative books (1–9) with one meditative section (10) and three exegetic books (11–13)? This question has perplexed, even troubled, all those who have tried to deal with the text. The structural unity of the work has been a subject of controversy for many critics and some editions of the *Confessions* even omit completely the last four books on the ground that "they do not form an integral part of the biography."[3]

It is certainly difficult for the modern reader to cope with the sudden shift in emphasis which occurs in book 10. The narrative collapses, human historical time gives way to a non-temporal, non-linear meditation on the nature of memory (book 10) and time (book

[2]I borrow the term *architexte* from Gérard Genette, *Introduction à l'architexte* (Paris: Seuil, 1979).

[3]Dom Roger Huddleston, ed. and trans., *The Confessions of St. Augustine* (London: Fontana Books, 1957), p. 13.

11), and to an exegesis of the first verses of Genesis 1 (books 11–13). This seemingly didactic aspect of the four "episcopal" books[4] easily leads the secular reader to reject them as doctrinal supplement and therefore not relevant to students of autobiographical narratives. One recent study by William S. Spengemann goes so far as to claim that "correlative changes in the form and doctrine of *The Confessions* do not permit us to see the three parts as elements in a single preconceived structure" and asserts that there is a "fundamental antipathy" between Augustine's theology and his artistic method.[5]

Even Paul Ricoeur, in the first volume of his *Time and Narrative,* focuses on the aporias of the experience of time in book 11 of the *Confessions* without ever relating his discussion to the first nine books; Augustine, he says, "inquires into the nature of time *without any apparent concern for grounding his inquiry on the narrative structure of the spiritual autobiography* developed in the first nine books." Thus Ricoeur dismisses the so-called spiritual autobiography as irrelevant to his purposes. There is, he says, an unbridgeable, radical discontinuity for Augustine between time and eternity. This ontological split is antithetical to narrative, because "narration is possible wherever eternity attracts and elevates time, not where it abolishes it." Even if the narration of the first nine books "accomplishes the itinerary whose conditions of possibility are reflected upon in Book 11," this accomplishment only emphasizes the inherent discontinuity present in the internal hierarchization of the work as a whole.[6]

That there are hierarchy and discontinuity among the various modes of discourse used by Augustine is clear. But I disagree with Ricoeur's reading of this fact as an unresolvable opposition: his critical discourse, I suggest, exactly mirrors and mimics the Manichean problematic discussed by Augustine, but Augustine is able to move beyond such binary sterility. For him, the problematic of time and eternity is analogous to that of good and evil and of the split subjectivity. The conflicting forces that make man an enigma to himself

---

[4]The term is Kenneth Burke's, in *The Rhetoric of Religion: Studies in Logology* (Berkeley: University of California Press, 1970), p. 136.

[5]William S. Spengemann, *The Forms of Autobiography* (New Haven: Yale University Press, 1980), pp. 6 and 25.

[6]Paul Ricoeur, *Time and Narrative* (Chicago: University of Chicago Press, 1948), 1:4 (my italics), 237 n. 38, 29.

signal, indeed, a fundamental dichotomy that can be analyzed and probed through memory and language—that is, the activity of self-reading and self-writing which constitutes the "spiritual autobiography"—but must then be accepted and transcended through a process of reading alterity, otherness—that is, reading God's word.

It is on this twofold process of reading—writing as self-reading and exegetic reading as redemption—that I want to focus in this chapter. For Augustine, the project of narrating his own life is doomed to a dead end and must be redeemed by his reading of the sacred texts. This reading is a mode of revelation or illumination quite different from the experience of ecstasy (that is, the vision at Ostia or the unsuccessful attempts at atemporal contemplation of the "One" in book 7, which momentarily abolish time and give him a taste of eternity). Reading as revelation is paradigmatic of the vertical filiation that elevates the soul out of the region of dissimilarity and allows it to be "converted," that is, "turned toward" God, in order to become filled with the word or with love. For love, like language, is both human and divine. Like the human self, it contains the seeds of good and evil, and when used to perverted or self-serving ends, it must be redeemed by a transcendent sublation that returns it to God's own "grammar" (to use Eugene Vance's term), so that the creation of all things, both good and bad, can be praised as what Hans Jauss calls "God's poiesis."[7] Containing both human and divine elements, both good and evil, the act of reading cannot be the final unification with God, but it is a necessary intermediate step, the only bridge between time and eternity, humanity and God. As such it is indispensable to the structure of Augustine's "autobiography."

Indeed, a close reading of the *Confessions* shows Augustine dealing repeatedly with questions of truth and harmony, form and hierarchy, thus, I suggest, unequivocally anticipating some of the objections raised by critics of his text. For instance, it is difficult not to interpret 13:30 (cited at the beginning of this chapter) as an implicit warning against fragmentation of his own text into parts that did not seem to belong together originally, the use of such words as *con-*

[7]Eugene Vance, "Augustine's *Confessions* and the Grammar of Selfhood," *Genre* 6 (March–June 1973), 1–28; Hans R. Jauss, *Aesthetic Experience and Literary Hermeneutics* (Minneapolis: University of Minnesota Press, 1982), p. 144.

traheres, conpaginares and *contexeres* being a case in point. To try to separate textually the good that coexists with evil or the theological meditation from the narrative mode that it puts under erasure is thus to fall prey to the same problematic Augustine was trying to put to rest. Augustine's text is harmonious because it lets the power of God's word unify and transform the merely human (and potentially evil) dimensions of his narrative efforts. It is for this reason that book 11 reverses of the textual mechanism that subtends the previous nine books: Genesis becomes the source of Augustine's interpretive discourse, the pretext for his own writing or interpretive reading of the story of creation.

Augustine's criticisms of the Manichean doctrine refer, by contrast, to a theory of artistic creation to be modeled on God's creation and thus, by implication, to a poetics of harmony, completeness, and totality. Augustine was rooted in a mature tradition influenced by Platonic ideas of transcendence and Aristotelian notions of organic cohesion. His awareness of form is evident throughout his text, which repeatedly emphasizes the relationship of the parts to the whole as Socrates had in Plato's *Phaedrus:* "Any discourse ought to be constructed like a living creature, with its own body, as it were; it must not lack either head or feet; it must have a middle and extremities so composed as to suit each other and the whole work."[8]

Plato's comparison of discourse to the body became canonical in Latin rhetoric. Clearly stated in the *Confessions* is Augustine's own concern for the appropriate links that may exist among the individual parts of a system, as well as between those parts and the system as a whole. The issue arises whether Augustine is dealing with the realm of corporeal beauty, that is, "the due balance between the whole of the body and any of its limbs [pars corporis ad universum suum]" (4:13), or with the sense data that momentarily satisfy the flesh but do not simultaneously partake of our full understanding of the whole ("in parte est et ignoras totum" [4:11]). This, for example, is the case with speech, in which individual syllables must follow one another in order for the hearer to understand the whole sentence. Although each syllable cannot be present to the ear at the

[8]As translated by Roger Hackforth, "Phaedrus" in *The Collected Dialogues of Plato,* ed. Edith Hamilton and Huntington Cairns (Princeton: Princeton University Press, 1961), 264c, p. 510.

same time, it is only when they can be perceived together as one (one word or sentence) that they make sense and are pleasurable ("plus delectant omnia quam singula, si possint sentiri omnia") [4:11].

Augustine raises the same questions when discussing either the relationship of individuals to society—"For any part that is out of keeping with the whole is corrupt" [Turpis enim omnis pars universo suo non congruens]" (3:8) (he is referring here to the members of a society who violate the law)—or the hierarchical relation of creatures to God the creator—"the sum of all creation is better than the higher things alone [sed meliora omnia quam sola superiora]" (7:13).

Finally, one of the concluding chapters (28) of book 13 summarizes these principles: God's attitude before his creation shows that his is a power of synthesis. He is able to look at the universe as a whole ("vidisti . . . omnia quae fecisti") and to see it all at once ("tamquam simul omnia"). It is only when taken together and all at once that the creation is revealed as "not merely good [but] very good [et bona et valde]." The same principles apply to every material thing of beauty, every kind of body ("quaeque pulchra corpora"): "For a thing which consists of several parts, each beautiful in itself, is far more beautiful than the individual parts [ipsa membra singula] which, properly combined and arranged, compose the whole, even though each part, taken seperately, is itself a thing of beauty." Be it God's or an artist's, any creation must, for Augustine, contain a unitary principle in order to be beautiful and good. As a student of literature and a professor of grammar and rhetoric, Augustine was always sensitive to questions of aesthetics and well aware of what constituted the classical canons of beauty in a literary form. The *Confessions* mention Homer, Virgil, Plato, Aristotle, and Horace. Augustine also talks about his love of the theater (3:2) and analyzes his own reactions to the emotions portrayed on the stage (as Rousseau would centuries later). Let us then look at the *Confessions* in terms of its implicit aesthetics. It must to a large extent conform to Augustine's own standards of beauty besides being a document of faith in and love for God. It is through such an approach that we can perhaps best understand the structure of the work as well as the problematics of writing and reading implied by that structure.

Death and Writing

"Do we love anything unless it is beautiful?" asks Augustine. "What, then, is beauty and in what does it consist? What is it that attracts us and wins us over to the things we love? Unless there were beauty and grace in them, they would be powerless to *win our hearts* [ad se moverent]" (4:13, my italics). These aesthetic questions were of great concern to Augustine; indeed, it was on this subject that he wrote his first book, a treatise called *De pulchro et apto* ("Of beauty and suitableness"), written shortly after he entered the poetry contest at Carthage and won first prize for his dramatic poem, in the year 377. This book, he tells us, has been "lost"; more likely, he did not consider it worth preserving, as it had no religious value, being a purely aesthetic and theoretical document. The *Confessions*, on the other hand, was written in 397–398, some twelve years after his mystical experience in the garden with Alypius (in 386) and subsequent conversion to Catholicism. The *Confessions* is not just a confession of sins, or *confessio peccati*, but also a *confessio fidei* and a *confessio laudis*, that is, a statement of faith in the greatness of God and a song of praise and gratitude for the Lord's love and power.[9]

Its purpose therefore is twofold: Augustine confesses his sins to God and lets others, his brothers, know of his trials and errors so that his conversion may be an example to them. As he explains in 10:3, "When others read of those past sins of mine, or hear about them, their hearts are stirred so that they no longer lie listless in despair, crying 'I cannot.'" And having confessed his sins, he is free to declare his faith and love, which become the main justification for writing books 11–13: "By setting them down, *I fire my own heart and the hearts of my readers with love of you*. . . . I have said before, and I shall say again, that I write this book for love of your love" (11:1; my italics).

How does Augustine "fire the hearts" of his readers with the love of God? And how does the *Confessions* "win our hearts" (to Augustine, if not to God)? To answer, "By the beauty of its language," is to state a paradox, since beautiful language is constantly assigned

---

[9]John C. Cooper, "Why Did Augustine Write Books XI–XIII of the *Confessions?*" *Augustinian Studies* 2 (1971), 37–46. Also Karl J. Weintraub, *The Value of the Individual: Self and Circumstance in Autobiography* (Chicago: University of Chicago Press, 1978), pp. 18–48.

a very negative connotation throughout the narrative books. What do these tensions and ambivalence reveal? The answers to these questions lie primarily in the essential themes of the *Confessions*, themes that can be unnecessarily blurred if undue emphasis is put on the "doctrinal" aspects of the last four books. For example, the narrator's changes of perspective throughout the three parts of the work suggest a reversal of the position of authority which is first imparted to that narrator in books 1–9. Indeed, in 11–13, purely human authority is completely eroded by the gradual surrender of the writer to the transcendental relatedness of all things in a healthy and unified whole.

In books 1–9, Augustine's discursive effort of narration is an inquiry into the divided nature of the self, the conflicts of consciousness, the processes of memory and the seduction of beauty and language. But his purpose is to make known both what he was as a sinner and, as he says, "what I am now, at this moment [in ipso tempore], as I set down my confessions" (10:3). His autobiographical project is thus to be understood within the framework of a dialogue both with God, the "physician of [his] soul [medice meus intime]" (10:3), who is always already in possession of the truth about Augustine, and with the many, "who wish to listen as I confess what I am in my heart into which they cannot pry by eye or ear or mind" (10:3) but whose otherness is mitigated by their willingness to open their ears and to believe him because they have charity.

If the work is to reveal both what he *was* and what he *is*, then its form must embody the difference between past and present and serve as a mirror of the different selves corresponding to the divided, discontinuous nature of Augustine's being before his ultimate surrender to the transcendent other. As Lawrence Rothfield has pointed out, "The Augustinian self . . . is dispersed through a space from which it takes its shape, fragmented in its very existence."[10] In the narrative books, this division is exemplified by the dual nature of narrator (the converted self) and protagonist (the sinning self). The narrator describes his past life from a point outside of it. He confesses the protagonist's sins, his restlessness, his lusting after material things of beauty, until finally, at the point of conversion,

---

[10]Lawrence Rothfield, "Autobiography and Perspective in *The Confessions* of St. Augustine," *Comparative Literature* 33 (Summer 1981), 213.

both instances of the self acquire the same degree of enlightenment and then gradually proceed in the rest of the work toward total communion with God. This can only be achieved at a point and time outside the autobiography, that is, in *death*. The open-ended nature of book 13 calls attention to this hypothetical moment when the symbiosis will be complete, the narrator having been granted salvation by his spiritual addressee, God.

Textually, this reversal of narratorial authority is clearly signaled by the increasing use of scriptural quotations. For although the *confessio fidei et laudis* is the chief concern of books 10–13, the narrative books, too, are studded with examples of Augustine's declaration of faith and love. Smoothly integrated in his own narrative style are a large number of scriptural citations. But that which is only intertext in books 1–9 becomes pure pretext in books 10–13. These citations function first to illustrate the points Augustine is making about the protagonist's lack of focus, his dispersion, or *distentio:* "This, too, was due to the sinfulness and vanity of life, since I was *flesh and blood, no better than a breath of wind that passes by and never returns*" (1:13; italics are quotations from Psalm 77).

Second, these scriptural verses are often meant as frames or boundaries for Augustine's own text, thus giving justification to what would otherwise be a gratuitous and illegitimate love of words: "Let my whole self be steeped in love of you and all my being cry *Lord, there is none like you!* . . . The words of your Scriptures were planted firmly in my heart and on all sides you were like a rampart to defend me" (8:1, italics from Psalm 34). Again we encounter the image of the frame, the rampart as protection against evil, except that instead of trying, in Manichean fashion, to separate the good that coexists with evil, Augustine's text lets the power of God's word unify, transform, and transfigure his writings. God's voice takes precedence over his own, and he writes so as to persuade the unbelievers "to be silent and to open a way to their hearts for [God's] word" (12:16). Augustine has become "infans [speechless]" again and he is now clinging ("tibi cohaerendo" [12:11], "adhaerere tibi semper" [13:2]) to God in and for eternity, to a God whose "maternal" symbolic dimensions are clear here. This maternal element is synonymous with a primary identification with, and absorption into, a place of rest, of absolute peace. The "I" is dissolved into the other or, as Julia Kristeva would say, into the "Eternal Phallic

Mother" who "rescues" the subject from fragmentation and brings him to bliss or *jouissance*:[11] "I shall not turn aside until you gather all that I am into that holy place of peace, rescuing me from this world where I am dismembered and deformed [dispersione et deformitate], and giving me new form and new strength for eternity" (12:16) Dismemberment, dispersion, deformity, or formlessness: such is the lot of the sinner. The narrative books correspond to this experience of disease and emptiness which generates the auto-biographical discourse and can be understood as an attempt to re-member the subject, to propel him into the wholeness of peace, "into a signifying or symbolic elsewhere where he exists as a sheltered exile."[12]

In his richly detailed study of the modalities of the self-portrait and its relation to ancient rhetoric, Michel Beaujour has argued that it is book 10 that articulates most clearly the experience of absence, the impossibility of self-description and self-unveiling, as attempted in books 1–9. Hence, Beaujour says, "the tenth book is a meditation on the process of remembering and forgetting, and on the memory of forgetfulness, but in it, Augustine says nothing about 'himself.' That is probably because the inaugurating experience of the self-portraitist is one of emptiness and absence."[13] But as I shall try to show, this experience of absence already informs all the first nine books, which constitute, in Beaujour's terms, the religious or spiritual autobiography, as opposed to what he terms the true "self-portrait," that is, book 10. It is this same experience of absence which determines the unfolding of the narrative and gives structural and thematic unity to the whole work. Indeed, it is precisely because Augustine's narrative is organized around an empty center, his empty self, that books 11–13 become essential to the completion of the self-portrait. Far from being mere doctrinal supplements, they are central to Augustine's ontology of the subject—the sinning then converted subject—whose mode of interaction with the world is first through a negative and decentered use of language (writing as a form of dispersion or *distentio*), then through a positive and dialogi-

[11]Julia Kristeva, *Desire in Language: A Semiotic Approach to Literature and Art*, trans. Tom Gora, Alice Jardine, and Leon Roudiez. (New York: Columbia University Press, 1980), pp. 191–208 (206).

[12]Ibid., p. 206.

[13]Michel Beaujour, *Miroirs d'encre* (Paris: Seuil, 1980), p. 9. All translations are mine.

cal one (reading as a form of paying attention or *intentio*). Paul Ricoeur understands the Augustinian contrast between *distentio* and *intentio* as strictly the dichotomy between time and eternity: for Ricoeur, Augustine's "paradoxes of the experience of time owe nothing to the activity of narrating a story."[14] What I am suggesting, by contrast, is that this pairing of opposites can just as profitably be understood to connote the subtle differences between writing and reading, narrating and analyzing, such as those activities are inscribed in different narrative segments of the *Confessions*.

When Augustine shows the vanity and complacency of a posture of self-reflection and self-analysis (10:39), it is to stress the futility of an exercise in pure narration (since these actions cannot give a center to his being). But having done this, Augustine must reveal in what way the converted self differs from the sinning self, and the only way to do so is to show the new self as filled with the word of God and thus fulfilling its spiritual destiny: the last four books thus complement the first nine. That is also why, for Eugene Vance, "it is only appropriate that Augustine should displace the narrative of the particular self and center his text instead on the arch-narrative of the Author-of-all, in whose image Augustine is made and in terms of whom all language signifies." Thus the *Confessions*, Vance adds, dramatizes Augustine's life in language, since the events he chooses to illustrate his progress to God include his acquisition of the power of speech (1:8), as well as his schooling in rhetoric and the parallel fornications he began to engage in (1:13–20; 2:1–10), until finally "the origins of self are forgotten for the origins of the universe."[15] Since in Augustine's vocabulary, and following biblical usage, to fornicate means "to break one's troth with God [(fornicabar abs te]" (Psalms 72:27, 73:27) through any misuse of language and all illicit pleasures of the flesh (1:13, 2:16, 4:2, 5:12), it becomes clear how language and all forms of narration are indeed central to the Augustinian notion of sin and to his experience of time and eternity. As Kenneth Burke has pointed out, Augustine himself makes an implicit comparison between the Latin words *fornix*, from which we derive "fornication," and *fornax* or "furnace":[16] "Cotidiana fornax nostra est humana lingua [the human tongue is a furnace in which

[14]Ricoeur, 1:52.
[15]Vance, pp. 13, 17.
[16]Burke, p. 140n.

the temper of our souls is daily tried" (10:37). To narrate is tantamount to sinning and narration must therefore be redeemed by exegetical analysis.

One of the paradigmatic acts of Augustine's life as a sinner is the famous episode of the stolen pears (2:4–10). Analyzing with great honesty and sincerity his own motivation for committing this theft, he comes to the conclusion that he would never have wanted to do it alone, that the seduction of the act was in the bond of companionship it tightened. He lucidly recognizes this as an instance of male bonding and, one might add, a rather sinister example of brotherhood, in which the "pear" is not sought for its own sake but as an excluded middle in the autoerotic fantasies of a gang of young males who have recently discovered the joys of their own virility. The pears, which are simply "thrown away to the pigs," are a forbidden fruit that can be read as metaphor for any object of sadistic power play. Kenneth Burke has argued that Augustine dwells on what is ostensibly a minor peccadillo precisely because it is for him the foremost and ultimate sin, "the complete perversion, or perfect parody, of his religious motives" and of the brotherhood of monastic life.[17] The "theft" affirms the individual's place within his community of friends, just as had "fornications" of another sort, fornications that are sometimes enjoyed (2:2) but may also be compulsively engaged in simply because Augustine does not want to appear less dissolute and depraved than his companions (2:3).

Here again, a close reading of the Latin text yields some very strong connotations of defilement in this act of "theft": "*Foeda* erat, et amavi eam; *amavi perire,* amavi defectum meum, non illud, ad quod deficiebam . . . sed *dedecus appetens* [It was a *shameful act,* but I loved it. *I loved my own perdition* and my own fault, not the thing for which I committed wrong . . . but *I longed for the shame itself*] (2:4, trans. mod.) The adjective *foedus,* -a, -um, generally translated vaguely as "evil" or "foul," derives in fact from the verb *foedare* which literally means "to defile, deform, or disfigure" and figuratively, "to dishonor or disgrace." Augustine is talking about defiling himself in committing this act, but his degree of self-defilement is a function of the other—the abject object of the act, made abject by the sinful intentions of the perpetrator: "I tasted nothing in them

[17]Ibid., p. 94.

[the pears] but my own sin which I relished and enjoyed. If any part of these fruits passed my lips, it was the villainy that gave it its flavour" (2:6; trans. mod.) Clearly here, the abjection is not seen as radically other, it is not something to be evacuated or purged from the self; rather, it seems to function as the place where communion and *jouissance*, or bliss, are glimpsed. It is the point of reconciliation, "the point where the scales are tipped towards pure spirituality," and sinfulness and saintliness merge. As Kristeva has noted, "One of the insights of Christianity, and not the least one, is to have gathered in a single move perversion and beauty as the lining and the cloth of one and the same economy."[18]

Augustine analyzes his narcissistic motivations with great lucidity. The episode of the pears can function as sign or reference mark for all other instances of negative object-identification Augustine describes. Pear tree in Latin is *pirus*: "arbor erat pirus" (2:4), and Augustine says: "amavi *perire*" (literally, "I loved to perish"). The close resemblance of the words *pirus* and *perire*, as well as the use of *appetens* (to long for) all point to a form of death wish, a desire for self-dissolution into an otherness that is attractive and pleasurable but also demeaning, degrading, and *disfiguring* because it is pleasurable. This is the ultimate perversion of divine love, divine *frui*, or *jouissance*, which gives life and *transfigures*. The converted narrator's didactic comments on the incident turn it into a paradigm of negative *frui*, negative orality (the flesh of the pears). This will be reversed into positive orality when the sole source of spiritual food becomes the word of God, the body of Christ. We are clearly dealing here with two sides of the same coin—the same psychic economy, as Kristeva succinctly puts it.

For Augustine, language is a form of orality which can be used to perverted ends, although language is also the power to create—as God's power is that of the word. This dual nature of language explains the divided structure of the *Confessions*. Language is both death dealing and life giving, and Augustine uses different modes of discourse as illustrations of the different stages of his spiritual evolution and as emblems of the different selves corresponding to these various stages. Each stage leads to a higher state of being, each

---

[18]Julia Kristeva, *Powers of Horror: An Essay on Abjection* (New York: Columbia University Press, 1982), pp. 127 and 125.

ever so much closer to God—hence the need to use a hierarchy of modes (narrative, meditative, and exegetic) to illustrate his soul's progress. But his various selves still have to be united by the process of writing, and it is the work, the book, in its very materiality and corporeality which allows Augustine to pull together these various facets of his being into an organic, synthetic whole. Only then can he offer himself—and the book as emblem of the self—as "gift [datum]" (13:26) to God, just as the universe with its hierarchy of creatures is God's gift to man. Thus the quest for truth and the search for the origins come together when Augustine has found God, since "to know God is to know our origins."[19]

But the question then becomes: *how* does one know God? For even if conversion brings faith, faith is not all: one must constantly struggle, through efforts of *will*, to maintain oneself in a state of grace.[20] What, then, is the posture of the converted self which allows for this familiarity with God? What talents, resources or attributes of the soul can promote a greater receptivity, or *disponibilité*, to the word of God?

As Beaujour indicates, the self has to undergo a certain kind of death in order to find God: "Augustine's self-portrait is the narrative of his pursuit of God, or rather, it is the itinerary of a man searching for God outside of himself, then within himself, destroying all the 'idols' he finds on his way: all perceptions, sensory images and contents of his memory which might be the source of anecdotal individualism."[21] Thus in book 10 all purely literary and personal use of language is subsumed under a rhetorical-philosophical meditation on the nature of body and soul, the "outer" man and the "inner" man. Since Augustine the convert is going to start looking for God within himself and since "we might say that the memory is a sort of stomach [venter] for the mind" (10:14), then book 10 amounts quite simply to the pumping out of Augustine's figurative stomach, the emptying of its poisons.

But this death of the embodied self had already begun in book 7:

[19]Vance, p. 16.

[20]In Augustinian terms, will is identical with love and analogous to the Holy Spirit. See for example a discussion of this topic in Hannah Arendt, *The Life of the Mind* (New York: Harcourt Brace Jovanovich, 1978), 2:99–104, based on the *Confessions* and *On the Trinity*. See also Eugene Vance, "The Functions and Limits of Autobiography in Augustine's *Confessions*," *Poetics Today* 5 (1984), 399–409 (408).

[21]Beaujour, p. 47.

before he can hear the voices in the garden, Augustine undergoes a kind of exorcism, and in 8:8 he reaches a paroxysm of indecision; "I was frantic. . . . I tore my hair and hammered my forehead with my fists; I locked my fingers and hugged my knees," because, he says, his "inner self was a house divided against itself." These images of violence culminate in deafness to sexual temptation. He still hears the voices of his mistresses ("nugae nugarum" [8:11]), but they have become very faint. Only then can he open his "inner ear," or soul, to a higher voice: the exorcism of his old flames from his old self prepares the ground for his intercourse with God (books 11–13). Following these dramatic events and the "tolle, lege" (8:12), Augustine is no longer a deaf corpse [surdis mortuis] (9:4); but he now loses the ability to speak. First a toothache, then breathing difficulties and lung pains force him to resign his professorship (9:4, 5). He thus gets progressively detached from the needs of his flesh, from the temptations of his intellect, and from the seductions of language and fornication. The meditation, or *exercitatio animi*, of book 10 therefore completes a process already underway in the narrative books: a killing of the body so the soul can be reborn.

Death, conversion and rebirth are the classic stages of spiritual evolution, and Augustine's *Confessions* exemplify this trajectory. The death of the self as it lives in darkness is the main theme of the narrative books. Conversion then leads to the cleansing or purification of book 10, in preparation for the act of reading and the dialogue with God, as mediated through the text of Genesis. These three stages (from external reality through internal reality to superior reality) correspond to the three structural parts of the *Confessions* but also point to a mimesis of the Catholic practice required of all the faithful: confession of sins, mortification and prayer, and holy communion. "And even when all is well with me, what am I but an infant suckling on your milk [sugens lac tuum] and feeding upon you [fruens te], the incorruptible food" (4:1, trans. mod.) as Augustine says, refering to "feeding" in the literal sense of eating the body of Christ during communion and in the figurative sense of reading and absorbing God's text. He has returned to a spiritual orality after the sinful orality that had filled his memory-stomach with the "idols" Beaujour mentions. In theological terms, these stages could also correspond to life on earth (1–9), in purgatory (10), and in heaven (11–13), purgatory being assimilated here to the Greek notion of *kenosis* or "being as emptying."[22]

Life on earth is life in death, and books 1–9 abound in examples of the deadly seductions that material things of beauty exert on the individual soul. Augustine loves the "fables and fictions" (3:2) of the theater because they can move him to sorrow. He loves poetry and knows the power and pleasure of language. In the words of Kenneth Burke, he is himself a "great verbalizer."[23] Adept at persuasion, he is a word monger ("venditorem verborum" [9:5]) who sells the services of his tongue in the markets of eloquence (9:2). He is well aware that pleasure subverts self-control and leads to deception, as happened with Alypius, who became "drunk with the fascination of bloodshed" (6:8) when he went to the gladiatorial games, presumptuously believing that he could shield himself from this terrible and blinding pleasure ("cum mira voluptate caecabatur" [4:7]). He had thought that he could remain master of himself but discovered how elusive self-control can be.

We later find an echo of this incident in 10:5. During his meditation on the "inner man," Augustine says, "there are some things in man which even his own spirit within him does not know." This Augustinian "inner man," which corresponds to the notion of "memory" or *memoria sui*, implies both the existence of a "subconscious" reality and the openness of the soul to a transcendent or metaphysical presence, distinct from the soul itself, as Etienne Gilson has shown.[24] What Gilson does not discuss, and what I would like to focus on here, are the various negative connotations associated with this notion of the "inner man." For example, there is another echo of the somewhat disturbing capacity of man's spirit or soul to be an enigma to itself in 13:32 and 34: "Just as in man's soul there are two forces, one which is dominant because it deliberates and one which obeys because it is subject to such guidance, in the same way, in the physical sense, woman has been made for man. In

---

[22]For an interesting discussion of *kenosis* in the context of "the anxiety of influence," see Harold Bloom, *The Anxiety of Influence* (New York: Oxford University Press, 1973), pp. 77–92.

[23]Burke, p. 83.

[24]Etienne Gilson, *Introduction à l'étude de Saint Augustin* (Paris: Jean Vrin, 1969), pp. 289–98.

her mind . . . she has a nature the equal of man's, but in sex she is physically subject to him in the same way as our natural impulses [appetitus actionis] need to be subjected to the reasoning power of the mind" and "You made rational action subject to the rule of the intellect, as woman is subject to man."[25]

In the hierarchy of creatures, woman is clearly associated with that part of the inner soul which can escape the control of intellect or reason (as happened to Alypius at the games). "Woman," then, is a construct, a projection on the external world of an inner and scary reality, which can exert a profound fascination ("voluptas") on the "reasonable" part of the soul. This inner reality is also revealing of man's divided consciousness, of his ability to see himself as an undefined or "confused reflection in a mirror [per speculum in aenigmate]" (8:1, 10:5, 12:13, 13:15), as goes the scriptural citation (I Cor. 13:12) so frequently used by Augustine.[26] This mirror image of a part of the self seems to be associated at times with the as-yet-unachieved metaphysical presence of God and at other times with these "appetites"—the instincts or the unconscious, in later terminology—which Augustine opposes to the reasoning power of the mind. The text thus constructs "woman" as an internal other, and a negative one, whereas God figures as the internal but positive Other: "man, made in your image and likeness, rules over all irrational creatures for the very reason that he was made in your image and resembles you, that is because he has the power of reason and understanding" (13:32, trans. mod.). If "woman" is a textually constructed reality, the negative other of man, then gender differences as traditionally conceptualized since Augustine are shot through with ideological misconceptions. These misconceptions continue to plague us today because hierarchichal distinctions have become naturalized through a process of condensation and reinforcement

---

[25]These two poles both correspond to active behavior: for Augustine, all human behavior is willed, "will is identical with . . . being" (12:28). There is no passivity, or rather, passivity is a willed choice. See the argument in 8:8–11.

[26]The phrase is traditionally translated as "through a glass, darkly." For a discussion of the *aenigma* as a kind of figure of speech in Latin literature and its influence on Augustine's theory of signification, see Marcia Colish, *The Mirror of Language: A Study in the Medieval Theory of Knowledge* (Lincoln: University of Nebraska Press, 1983), especially the preface and chap. 1. In Marie-Thérèse Humbert's novel, this image of the mirror will be used to refer to the troubled relation between Anne and her twin Nadège (see my discussion in Chapter 6).

which projects onto the external world fictional categories of the mind: masculine/feminine, mind/body, reason/unreason spirituality/sexuality, life/death, master race/ slave. This is the legacy that contemporary women autobiographers will have to face before they can start writing and rewriting their selves, thus inventing new and empowering traditions for their (literary) daughters, traditions that will draw upon many of the metaphors of death and loss, reconciliation and plenitude, darkness and light present in the *Confessions*.

In Augustine's imagery, woman is to man what the bitter sea is to the dry land, the sinning self to the converted self, the wicked souls to the faithful, and darkness to light (see 13:23, 24). Throughout the narrative books of the *Confessions*, this area of darkness is associated with language and literature, loss and death. It is out of this darkness that the soul must be reborn: "deus meus, illuminabis tenebras meas" says Augustine in 4:15, echoing the narration of God's spiritual creation in Genesis, as he will discuss it in 13:2 and 3: "In its [life's] formless state, it would not have been pleasing to you unless it became light. And it became light, not simply by existing, but by fixing its gaze upon you and clinging [cohaerendo] to you, the Light which shone upon it."

The divine light transforms formless matter into the living soul, which thus becomes a reflection of the transcendent Other, whose light it absorbs. What then of the negative other? The one associated with "woman," darkness, and literary language, that is, the fables and fictions that can have such a powerful effect on Augustine's emotions? To answer this question we need only look at the context in which literature is discussed.[27]

In 1:13–17 Augustine recalls his schooling in language and literature and his profound love of Latin poetry. He mentions the *Aeneid* in particular: how he had memorized the "wanderings of a hero named Aeneas" and "wept for Dido" (1:13). These fictional, epic characters and other "empty romances" delighted his boyhood, providing him with futile and enchanting dreams. Relating his skill at recitation, Augustine tells us how he had to learn Juno's speech (from the *Aeneid* 1:37–49), in order to repeat in prose Virgil's text. Of

[27]This is the place to acknowledge my pervasive and diffuse debt to Shoshana Felman's work. My reading of Augustine was *enabled* in many ways by her brilliant studies of language, madness, silence, and the feminine in *La Folie et la chose littéraire* (Paris: Seuil, 1978).

all the schoolboys who were assigned that task, he was the one who found "the best words to suit the meaning, and best expressed feelings of sorrow and anger appropriate to the majesty of the character he impersonated" (1:17). He won that contest and was praised for it. But distancing himself from that boy of great promise ("bonae spei"), who could so easily lose himself in the beauty of deceitful words, the narrator denounces the "wine of error," [vinum erroris] literature, which is poured out to the young by the "masters of eloquence," the teachers who train them in the art of persuasion and thus blind them to the higher truths of the Scriptures (1:16). Commenting on the Carthaginian custom of hanging curtains over the entrances of the schools where literature is taught, Augustine says:"[These curtains] are not so much symbols in honor of mystery as veils [or covers] concealing error [tegimentum erroris]" (1:13). Later, Augustine describes God's forgiveness for his sins with a similar metaphor: God has "drawn a veil " over his past life, "covered" his past sins and errors ("quae remisti et texisti" [10:13]).

Augustine's sinning self is thus equated with his literary self, who shed tears for Dido when she died. In Augustine's own life, death is a recurrent theme: he mentions the death of his father (3:4) and that of his friend Nebridius (9:3); the major part of book 9 is devoted to his mother, Monica, whose death concludes the autobiographical narrative; Augustine himself comes close to dying in 5:9 but regains his health, fortunately, for at that point in his life, his soul is still "diseased" or "mad," and he has no desire to be baptized.

This theme of death and loss culminates in book 4. The death of another dear friend (4:4) profoundly affects him. Life becomes dull and distasteful; he feels alien and absent. He is a puzzle, a mystery, a great riddle to himself: "factus eram ipse mihi magna questio." He is utterly lost without his friend and because he has not yet found himself in God. Augustine's grief foreshadows Montaigne's distress at the death of La Boétie, whose absence is literally inscribed in the text of the *Essais*, which announces the insertion of La Boétie's own works (in book 2, chap. 29) and then defers this insertion without explanation.

The grief Augustine feels at the loss of his "second self," the "half of his soul [dimidium animae suae]" (4:6), as he says, quoting Horace's *Odes* (1:3:8), is represented by a rare instance of non-biblical quotation in the Augustinian text. As Kenneth Burke has pointed out, "There is a good 'literary' reason why at this point Augustine's account of the motives behind his conversion incorporated a quotation not from the Bible but from a purely secular source in pagan poetry. . . . [The death of his friend] coincided with what we might call an attempt at an 'aesthetic' solution of his problems. About this period, Augustine also wrote some books ('two or three, I think,' a revealing lapse of memory on the part of a man with an exceptionally good memory) on beauty and fitness (*de pulchro et apto*)."[28] But *De pulchro et apto* was already "lost" when Augustine started writing the *Confessions*. He mentions this work in 4:13 and devotes that chapter and 4:14 to a discussion of principles of beauty and harmony. These pages are almost at the mathematical center of the pre-conversion part of the narrative (his conversion occurs in 8.12). It is thus interesting to note that that center is occupied by a nonexistent book that seems to metaphorize Augustine's absence to himself as well as the death of his loved one. The aesthetic phase and the experience of death are clearly made to appear homologous.

The issue, then, is not just loss or "lapse of memory," as Burke puts it. If Augustine the sinner is also Augustine the lover of poetry, then how better to convey this fact than by mentioning *De pulchro et apto* at the empty center of the story of his life before conversion, a story that deals with language and loss, literature and death? In so doing, he gives us by analogy an image of himself as a man without God, a soul devoid of purpose. For if the apparent loss of memory seems to censure the remembrance of the treatise on beauty, it is most certainly a censorship that is willed, just as the meditation of book 10 wills the erasure, the veiling of all sensible and individual anecdotes—hence the mention of the treatise at the heart of this narrative, which is overlooked by Burke, although he does point out that the critical moment of conversion occurs at the center of the *Confessions* as a whole.[29]

We can now see why book 4 occupies a privileged place in the narrative part of the *Confessions*. It corresponds to the darkest years of Augustine's life, his most materialistic and pleasure oriented. It is also the "pivot [cardinem in arte]" (4:15) upon which turns the story of Augustine's life of sin. The opening paragraph sets the tone for the whole of book 4: "During the space of those nine years, from the

[28]Burke, p. 74.
[29]Ibid., p. 62.

nineteenth to the twenty-eighth year of my life, I was seduced my-self and I seduced others [seducebamur et seducebamus]." He and his friends used the liberal arts to deceive but only managed to feel "void and empty everywhere [ubique vani]."

The combination of the numbers nine and four seems to have a special importance here, which can help us understand the struc-ture of the *Confessions* as a whole. Book 4 corresponds to Au-gustine's nine years of life from nineteen to twenty-eight. Each of the four succeeding books corresponds to one of the four years of his life between the ages of twenty-nine and thirty-two, when his conversion occurs. This episode is followed by book 9, which is really the book of Monica, his human mediator and redemptor, in whose company he has the famous vision at Ostia. It is during this vision "that Augustine completes the process whereby the Holy Spirit attains final incorporation into his psychic economy," as Burke puts it.[30] Shortly thereafter, Monica dies, on the ninth day of her illness at the end of the ninth book of the *confessio peccati*. Augustine makes a point of stating that he is now thirty-three years old, thus identifying himself with Christ. Interestingly, it is through the death of the *mother's* body that Augustine can be resuscitated in spirit: the death of the mother is the culmination of his narrative of a life of sin and marks his liberation from earthly and bodily connections. It is necessary for the earthly mother to die in order for Augustine to get closer to God, whose attributes are both phallic and maternal. It is only now that the writing of the body can give way to the reading of the transcendent Other.

The temporal and rectilinear discourse (books 1–9) is followed by the eternal and circular speculations or meditations about memory and time, origins and beginnings (10–13). The first nine books would thus seem to correspond to the purification rites of ancient religions which are transformed into the Catholic practice of the novena, the series of pious exercises or privations performed for nine consecutive days or weeks, as a form of mortification.[31] Books

[30]Ibid., p. 117.

[31]In Zoroastrianism and Manicheanism, the number nine was believed to have special symbolic purification powers, and many rites were performed nine times during purification ceremonies. In Christian religious symbolism, the number four is also important: the fourth sacrament is that of Repentance; there are four Gospels, just as there are four elements and four points on the compass, etc. See *Encyclopaedia Britannica* (Chicago, 1986), article on "Rites and Ceremonies," 26:816–89.

1–9 include Augustine's nine years of sin, which culminate in the aesthetic phase of book 4, followed by the four years of looking for God in the wrong places after his best friend's death and being seduced by Manicheanism, until finally the "tolle, lege" of 8:12 steers him in the right direction, that of the Scriptures. This, and Monica's death, literally cleanse him in preparation for the spiritual exercises of the last four books and the inner search for God. There are many other instances of Augustine's special awareness of numbers throughout the *Confessions*, too tedious to discuss or enumerate. Here, the number nine seems to be associated with the literal experience of death (Monica's) and the process of mortification the sinner must undergo before acceding to eternal life. The self that is located within the textual space of the first nine books is thus the self that was trapped in sin—in death—and scattered, dispersed, fragmented because it was too concerned with visible phenomena. The process of writing can be viewed as the exercise in mortification which illustrates, while transcending, the spiritual death of the sinner.

Reading and Redemption

To understand the epistemological ground on which the distinction between writing and reading gets formulated in the *Confessions*, it is necessary once more to discuss passages in which Augustine outlines his aesthetic principles, opposing visual to aural knowledge. In his discussion of material forms of beauty, Augustine defines two classes of visible, corporeal objects (4:15): those beautiful in themselves and those properly proportioned in relation to something else. In both cases, he emphasizes that they are pleasing to the *eye*. His volumes on beauty and harmony he calls "corporeal fictions" or "material inventions [corporalia figmenta]," which "obstructed the ears of [his] inner self" because they dealt with visible beauty and thus conflicted with his real intentions, which were to listen to the voice of the bridegroom of his soul. Drawn out of himself, he is perverted by visual stimuli, pulled down into the void, the abyss.

He concludes book 4 with a passage on the perversion of the souls who are turned away ("aversi," "perversi," "revertamur," "ut non evertamur") from God; by contrast, the last lines of book 8 twice

emphasize conversion ("convertisti"), first in the sense of a transmutation into a higher level of divine understanding, then as a
transformation of sadness into spiritual joy. The emptiness of his life
is thus associated with his dispersion and lack of focus, his being too
oral (i.e., too verbal or inquisitive) and too visual (i.e., too concerned
with appearances).

It is indeed this concern with visible reputation which leads him
to follow his gang of companions on the road to lustful games, and
to dedicate *De pulchro et apto* to Hierius, a brilliant orator whom
Augustine admired because he was immensely popular. Augustine
goes through a phase of identification with this man, who becomes
an objective persona and role model for him during his years in
Rome (4:14). Augustine envies and praises him for his active use of
his tongue and his skillfulness in language.

As a textual figure, Hierius comes into direct contrast with the
bishop Ambrose, who is also a remarkable preacher but who fascinates Augustine because of his silent reading. Ambrose's spiritual,
non-oral nature is underlined by his nondiscursive spirituality of
silence. When he read, "his eyes scanned the page and his heart
explored the meaning, but his voice was silent and his tongue was
still [vox autem et lingua quiescebant]" (6:3). Ambrose's silent contemplation of the written word and his complete absorption in his
reading discourage any attempt by Augustine to question him.

Ambrose is described as the one who strives unerringly to understand the spiritual meaning of texts, as opposed to obeying the letter
of the law. His mode of being is in itself an allegorical representation
of the process of redemption and salvation. Augustine becomes
fascinated by this man who could be so absorbed in silence and he
begins to learn to use his *ears*. "I paid the closest attention to the
words he used"; "I was delighted by his charming delivery;" "I was
all ears;" "I also began to sense the truth of what he said, though
only gradually" (5:13, 14). Initially contemptuous of the content of
Ambrose's speech, Augustine is slowly drawn to a level beyond the
mere rhetorical appearances of his style. He becomes open, receptive, *disponible* to the "sober intoxication of [God's] wine," to the
words of another who now brings him to mystical ecstasy, spiritual
jouissance. Through the mediating role of Ambrose, God's "holy oracle," Augustine begins to achieve communion with God, to reach
the point of spiritual reconciliation, beginning a process that gradu-

ally teaches Augustine to turn inward rather than to disperse himself in meaningless questions about the nature of God and an arrogant use of his tongue and his rhetorical skills (6:3).

Inquisitiveness, or the sin of *curiositas*, thus becomes textually equated with the overvaluation of the visual at the expense of a proper auditory course of initiation into a truth that is revealed providentially to the receptive intelligence. As Pierre Courcelle indicates, the sin of curiosity is allegorized in the myth of Psyche, whose misadventures are those of the soul overly curious to know the face of God, a myth recounted in one of the earliest biographical narratives, Apuleius's *Golden Ass*, a possible intertext of the *Confessions*.[32] Psyche is an early instance of a fictional figure assigned a negative value because of a narcissistic desire to *know*, that is, to see and to *appropriate*. By contrast, the staging of Ambrose as the receptive reader par excellence is the first link in a chain of signifiers which creates a self-generating system of figuration, a figural embedding or *mise en abyme* of the reading process and its effect.[33]

An analysis of the narrative structure of the *Confessions* can yield significant insights into this Augustinian project of valorizing aural forms of knowledge. The tools of the structuralist method allow us to analyze and describe the signifying chain of homologous relations constituted by these instances of figural embedding, and through certain criteria developed by recent research in narratology we can use this signifying chain to understand the function of the last three books of the *Confessions* as an integral part of the autobiography because they show Augustine engaged in the act of performing a reading, an exegetic reading of the most sacred of texts in order to disclose its spiritual meaning to his readers.

Indeed, the manner in which reading is dramatized in book 8

[32]Pierre Courcelle, *Les "Confessions" de St Augustin dans la tradition littéraire: Antécédents et postérité* (Paris: Etudes Augustiniennes, 1963), pp. 106–8. Augustine had read *The Golden Ass* and comments on it in *The City of God* (18:18).

[33]For a detailed discussion of the *mise en abyme*, see Lucien Dällenbach, *Le Récit spéculaire* (Paris: Seuil, 1977). The term refers to a process whereby a mirror image of all or part of a picture is reflected within its frame. In textual terms, a segment of the text reflects the content, the form, the mode of production of the text, as well as the relationship between writer and reader. For Ross Chambers, "'Figural' embedding . . . consists of the incorporation into the narrative of a 'figure' that is representative in some sense . . . of the production and reception of narrative." See *Story and Situation: Narrative Seduction and the Power of Fiction* (Minneapolis: University of Minesota Press, 1984), p. 33.

mirrors both what Augustine does in books 11–13 and what I myself, as reader of the *Confessions*, feel programmed, even compelled
to do—by textual constraints—when dealing with those last three
books. For example, in 8:6 the conversation among Augustine
Alypius, and Ponticianus is triggered by "a book lying on a table."
This book, which happens to be Paul's Epistles, occasions Ponticianus to narrate two related and interdependent stories of conversion: first, that of Antony, the Egyptian monk who, having chanced
upon a reading of the Gospel, heeded the admonition inscribed
therein, gave his possessions to the poor, and became a follower of
Christ; second, that of Ponticianus's friend, who remains name-
less—purposely so, I think, because he figures as the "hypothetical
ideal reader" of Augustine's own text. I shall just call him X. His
story is related in great detail in the *Confessions*. Augustine actually
quotes his words, presumably as reported by Ponticianus, and we
learn that X once "found a book containing the life of Antony" and
was profoundly affected by it. It made him realize the precarious-
ness of a life in the service of the state and emperor, and he chose
instead to follow the example of Antony: "After saying this, he
turned back to the book, labouring under the pain of the new life
that was taking birth in him. He read on and in his heart, where you
alone could see, a change was taking place. *His mind was being di-
vested of the world*" (8:6; my italics). Here, reading favors *kenosis*,
which empties the soul, the memory or "inner man," of all sensory
and material perceptions in order to make room for God's word.
And as already mentioned, this is exactly how book 10 functions in
the *Confessions* as a whole.

These two stories—Antony's and X's—figure as *mises en abyme* of
the effect of reading. Antony's foreshadows Augustine's own conversion in the garden with Alypius (8:12), for although Augustine
had clearly learned the facts of Antony's conversion during the dialogue related in 8:6, he waits until after the "tolle, lege" of 8:12 to
reveal those facts to his own reader, thereby calling attention to the
specular relationship (as mediated through Ponticianus's tale) between the *Confessions* and the book of Antony's life: "For I had heard
the story of Antony, and I remembered how he had happened to go
into a church while the Gospel was being read. . . . So I hurried
back to the place where Alypius was sitting, for when I stood up to

move away I had put down the book containing Paul's Epistles. I seized it and opened it, and in silence I read the first passage on which my eyes fell . . . *it was as though the light of confidence flooded into my heart and all the darkness of doubt was dispelled*" (my italics). Now we see that reading also favors the illumination and enlightenment that mark the vertical discontinuity of the soul, its elevation to a different level of temporality (but not the abolition of time, as in Plotinian ecstasy). The homology between the role played by the Gospel in Antony's life and the one played by the Epistles in Augustine's life is thus obvious:

$$\frac{\text{Gospel}}{\text{Epistles}} : \frac{\text{Book of Antony}}{\textit{Confessions}}$$

The second story, about Ponticianus's friend is an allegorical representation within the Augustinian text of its own ideal reader, the one whose heart would be changed, whose mind would be freed, and who would be brought face to face with himself upon reading/hearing the *Confessions*, just as Augustine had been revealed to himself and had seen his own face in the story of the friend: "You were setting me before my own eyes [ante faciem meam] so that I could see how sordid I was, how deformed and squalid" (8:7). Augustine becomes able to *see* his own sins because he has learned to listen with an open heart. But as he adds, he is not ready to follow the example of the Roman civil servant: "I had prayed to you for chastity and said 'Give me chastity and continence, but not yet.' For I was afraid that you would answer my prayer at once and cure me too soon of the disease of lust, which I wanted satisfied, not quelled" (8:7).

Augustine is not yet ready to give up his life of sin, his dispersion or *distentio*, but his "life of sin" is also a metaphor for the act of writing, of autobiographical narration, which he continues through four more chapters of book 8 and the thirteen chapters of book 9. To be truly converted right away would have meant giving up all decentered use of language as "fornication" and putting the literary and historical narration under erasure at that very moment. Unlike Antony and X, who give up everything immediately, Augustine will now start looking for God, his transcendental addressee, within himself: "Ego ad me," he says after the departure of Ponticianus.

Textually, we now have all the elements of the signifying chain as they configure the role of Augustine as reader of God's text:

God as transcendental source
$\downarrow$
Ambrose as oracle
$\downarrow$

$$\frac{\text{Gospel}}{\text{Epistles}} : \frac{\text{Book of Antony}}{\textit{Confessions}} : \frac{\text{Ponticianus's friend X}}{\text{Augustine and ideal reader X}}$$

$\uparrow$

Ambrose as reader

$\uparrow$

God as spiritual reader

This sketch shows the circular, tautological nature of the reading process in the *Confessions*. Ponticianus's tale is the thread that allows Augustine and his reader to interface and to weave identical tales of recognition and salvation. In the filigree of those tales it is the unknown face of God which slowly becomes defined, textually in the form of clusters of scriptural quotations and thematically as the presence that constitutes the narrator as self, as living soul—a presence that is never experienced directly but is always mediated through another person or a book. These triangular relationships are of course based on the concept of the Trinity, itself a model for the tripartite structure of the *Confessions*.

As is clear from the example of Ambrose's silent reading and the fact that Antony heard the Gospel being read, the ideal kind of reading encoded in the Augustinian text is a reading/hearing as opposed to a reading/seeing, that is, a reading receptive enough to suspend judgment and questions temporarily rather than a reading that would try to appropriate meaning rhetorically from appearances and first glances, as Hierius was known to do. Hearing correctly, though, leads to correct seeing: Augustine hears the child's voice in the garden before having the vision at Ostia; he hears about Ponticianus's friend before recognizing his own predicament and seeing his own face in Ponticianus's tale.

In the hierarchy of the senses, the ears precede the eyes because it is harder for Augustine to resist the temptations of visible beauty, as he explains in 10:34: he is easily entrapped or ensnared ("innecto," "inhaeseram") by the beautiful. Its seduction is quite literally a scandal, from the Greek *skandalon*, a trap. The canons of beauty in a literary form are dangerous because they give a pleasure that subverts self-control, leads to deception, and blinds the individual to the higher truths of the Scriptures. Beautiful sounds, on the other hand, seem to inspire feelings of devotion, and in that case, beauty is acceptable because it is subjected to a higher good, because it has a spiritual telos (10:33). (This theory of the curative effects of music had already been advanced by Aristotle and would become an important medieval *topos;* for Nietzsche, music will become the source of self-dispossession and *ecstasis*.)

In the *Confessions*, the narrative mode is acceptable because it is subjected to the exegetic mode, just as action is to reason, "woman" to man and darkness to light. Since the protagonist of the narrative had himself used beautiful language to perverted ends, either remaining in the realm of "corporeal fictions" or "purveying weapons" to students of rhetoric, Augustine the convert must redeem himself by putting his tongue and his pen at the service of God's word. Since correct reading (as opposed to writing *De pulchro et apto* or the story of his empty life as sinner) is what gives meaning and a center to the self, then it is only appropriate that the autobiography should include an instance of Augustine engaged in such a reading, in interpreting the Scriptures, the most sacred of texts, in order to disclose their meaning to his own readers. That he should choose to comment on Genesis, on the story of God's creation, is of particular interest to us here because this amounts to a further *mise en abyme* of the effect of reading: "But by what means did you make heaven and earth? . . . You spoke and created them in your Word, in your Son," writes Augustine (11:5, 9), and, "The peoples of your city, your angels. . . . have no need to look up at this firmament of ours or read its text to know your word. For ever they gaze upon your face and there, without *the aid of syllables inscribed in time*. . . . *They read your will: they choose it to be theirs:* they cherish it. . . . For you yourself are their book and you forever are" (13:15; my italics). Just as the universe was created out of nothingness, Augustine re-creates himself, the plenitude of his being, out of an experience of emptiness. This re-creation is mediated through the process of reading, which allows him to absorb in his human, historical, linear dimension the timelessness of eternal substance. The result of that re-creation is his own book, the *Confessions*. Writing allows Augustine to see himself as a whole being, both a sinner and a saved creature, constituting himself in the act of synthesizing the past and the present and offering them to God as his contribution to their dialogue. Books 11–13 thus appear to be allegories of the act of self-creation which had been the narrator's aim in books 1–9. He had looked at his own life as if it were the protagonist's book, and then he interpreted its succession of events in order to understand and transcend his own corporeality. The genesis of his evolution parallels God's act of spiritual creation as Augustine interprets it in 13:3. The conclusion of this upward journey is physical death and eternal life. But the act of writing the *Confessions*, meanwhile, allows Augustine to define his past in terms of the three modes of being which combine to "make one inseparable life": to be, to know, to will ("esse," "nosse," "velle" [8:11]). These three are inseparable, yet distinct, just as books 1–9 (existence), 10 (knowledge), and 11–13 (will) are inseparable within the body of the *Confessions*. Because the book is "an attempt to remember the subject along an initiatory path," as Beaujour writes,[34] it is also the act of synthesis, and the precondition of illumination, which allows Augustine to enter "the intellectual heaven, where the intellect is privileged to know all at once, not in part only, not as if it were looking at a confused reflection in a mirror [non in aenigmate, non per speculum], but as a whole, clearly, face to face [facie ad faciem]" (12:13).

The book is a reflection of Augustine in his completeness, a creature in the image of God, engaged in the act of creating and reading/listening all at once. Viewed from this perspective, the text lays bare the paradox of all Western discourse about the self. As Jean-François Lyotard has pointed out: "To have the text and its illustration, that is the pride and the sin. This hesitation [/oscillation] is that of Christianity itself, the de facto Christianity which subtends the ground of our Western problematics: to hearken to a voice, yet to have a philosophy of creation."[35] For Augustine, the text is God('s) and the illustration man('s). The process of reading is an integral

---

[34]Beaujour, p. 283.

[35]Jean-François Lyotard, *Discours, Figure* (Paris: Klincksieck, 1978), p. 10: "Voilà le péché et l'orgueil, avoir le texte et l'illustration. Cette hésitation est celle du christianisme même, du christianisme de fait qui occupe le sous-sol de nos problématiques, à nous occidentaux: écoute d'une parole mais philosophie de la création" (my translation).

part of that illustration, and it is that which helps constitute the narrator as living self or soul.

But when listening to the voice of an ideal other or when reading alterity, the self becomes other. This form of effacement precipitates the need to re-create a corporeal being as illustration of the text, possibly leading to a verbal reproduction that will repeat ad infinitum the initial experience of emptiness. Indeed, for Augustine, writing can only create an illusory sense of plenitude. But since emptiness and plenitude are both given, once man has acquired knowledge through illumination, it will only be a matter of subduing the embodied self through a process of loving/reading God. Narrative discontinuity is but the illustration of this vertical discontinuity between carnal life and eternal being, a discontinuity already configurated in the embedded episodes of book 8, which stage reading as "illumination," as the process that bridges the gap between man and God. Paul Ricoeur's complex hermeneutical approach to the problems of time and narrative would thus appear to be based on a reductive paradigm from book 11, a paradigm that does not take into consideration the internal aesthetics of the *Confessions* as a whole. That is why I would like to suggest that in the text of the *Confessions*, the philosophical problem of time is quite secondary to the structural problematic of reading and of its transfigurative effects as they are rhetorically constructed by textual strategies that urge us to see the whole work as harmonious. That this narrative discontinuity would later be perceived by critics as a paradoxical scission or schism in the process of redemption and salvation attests to the enduring binary dichotomies which Western culture has helped to perpetuate and rigidify. Nietzsche's critique of Christianity and metaphysics focuses on this scission, which was not yet unbridgeable for Augustine, since discontinuity only serves to illustrate his belief in the vertical filiation that traverses the activity of reading and transports the soul to a silent and transcendent resting point.

Discontinuity and split subjectivity are thus metaphors used throughout the *Confessions* to illustrate a dialectical relationship between self-reading and writing, writing being the antithesis, which must be sublated into a higher form of (exegetical) reading. Given that in this dialectic writing the life of the body is coded as a negative stage to be transcended, it becomes important to stress how this sublation functions as a *denial,* a denial of the self, of the embodied self born of an earthly mother, to be precise, since it is the life of the soul, of the mind, which will become the focus of Augustine's attention after his mother's death accomplishes his earthly transfiguration. Nietzsche fights against this tradition, which he accuses of spawning the "despisers of the body," the decadent moralists.[36] His autobiography is a reading of his written work, a double emphasis on the physical and the textual body: an effort to return the corpus to a valuable place in the unfolding of a life.

It is thanks in large part to Nietzsche's—and Freud's—understanding of the fallacy inherent in the mind/body, nature/culture dichotomy that the women authors discussed here are able to subvert in their own writings the commonplaces and stereotypes that have contributed to the devaluation of the female body and its (re)productive capabilities. To reread the past and thus to write freely of the changing boundaries of our racial and sexual bodies constitutes an important step in the complex process of female emancipation dealt with later in this book. This step helps women authors retrieve and verbalize lost traditions and effaced connections to maternal symbolic systems that do not partake of a phallic or divine essence. Only then will these authors be able to regain a sense of what "touch[ing] each other in the spirit" can be like, as Zora Neale Hurston puts it.[37]

[36]Friedrich Nietzsche, *Thus Spoke Zarathustra,* in *The Portable Nietzsche,* trans. Walter Kaufmann (New York: Viking Press, 1967), p. 147.

[37]Zora Neale Hurston, *Dust Tracks on a Road,* ed. Robert Hemenway, 2d ed. (Urbana: University of Illinois Press, 1984), p. 173.

2

Silence and Circularity in *Ecce Homo:* "Und so erzähle ich mir mein Leben"

> The master of laughter?
> The master of ominous silence?
> The master of hope and despair?
> The master of laziness? Master of the dance?
> It is I!
> Aimé Césaire, *Notebook of a Return to the Native Land*

> I am not a prisoner of history. I should not seek there for the meaning of my destiny.
> I should constantly remind myself that the real *leap* consists in introducing invention into existence.
> In the world through which I travel, I am endlessly creating myself.
> Frantz Fanon, *Black Skin, White Masks*

We have seen how Augustine writes himself into silence, the silence of religion, the eternal silence of God, whose words become his own. By losing himself in an ideal other who redeems the flaws of his material being, Augustine returns to the origin. His goal is to become the mirror image of God through the imitation of Christ. The idea that redemption means total absorption into the other implies a hierarchical system of relationships in which all possibilities of egalitarian relations or interactions, as Glissant might put it, are abolished and negated. In such a system, the self and the other can never interact as peers or equals; the self must always undergo sublation into the other, whose transcendent qualities will always be coded as the "positive" versions of those with which the self is endowed.

If the self must become other, must lose itself in the other's essence, all possibilities of transformation into a third term—as happens in the *métissage* and transculturation described by Glissant and Nancy Morejón—are blocked. What we have instead is assimilation, incorporation, and identification with a mirror image that, since it is the reverse of the self, functions as the locus of a deadly attraction, a narcissistic illusion. Maryse Condé's *Heremakhonon* illustrates that predicament. Her narrator internalizes the collective psychosis of her colonial culture and cannot conceive of attributing value to the unknown realities she encounters but cannot decode because they exist outside of the Manichean principles she has absorbed.

It is by rejecting the whole Western tradition of binary thinking, which contributes to the naturalization of such distinctions as male/female, master/slave, autonomous/dependent, writer/reader, that Nietzsche succeeds in reaffirming a principle of interconnectedness in which subjects and objects, self and other, are conditioned by their interactions in the world and thus become open to transformations of all sorts. To privilege autonomous subjectivity or original writing as the locus of the authentic self is a way of ignoring that subjectivity (and writing) is always already filled with the voices of others—hence Nietzsche's interest in the literariness of the self and in the dynamic self-fashioning that results from the description and interpretation of that self. As we shall see in *Ecce Homo*, however, such a self often remains caught in an alienating polarization against the other or in a negative identification with that other, while it is struggling to *procreate* a third term. For Nietzsche, the transvaluation of values can only be performed by an affirmative principle beyond resentment and negation, which says an unconditional "Yes" to life in all its forms.

Through the work of two famous Martinican critics of white Western supremacy, I can suggest one of the threads that runs through my own reading of Nietzsche: the nomadic thread of a search for Nietzsche's homeless voices, the ones echoed in Aimé Césaire's poetry and Frantz Fanon's politics. Césaire and Fanon were both influenced by Nietzsche, and their texts, like Nietzsche's aphorisms, have been subjected to reductive appropriations that did not take into account the indeterminacy, plurality, and heterogeneity of their messages. I do not intend to offer here a rereading of Césaire or Fanon. But I should explain that my approach to Nietzsche is colored by a Francophone creole perspective, as is theirs. It is for this reason that I wish to detour through negritude and its critics before I follow Nietzsche's wanderings through the microcosm of his own corpus, through the bulk of his literary output.

"The master of laughter?/The master of ominous silence?/. . . Master of the dance? It is I!": these are direct echoes of Zarathustra, the prophet of irony, who wanders through islands and mountains, attacking the constraints of reason. Aimé Césaire's poetry attempts to liberate expression through a Dionysian mingling of dance, death, and ritual. He aims to alter the language of the "master race" by using poetic structures borrowed from surrealism and imagery inspired by his native island. His lyric and dramatic hero is a kind of black *Übermensch*, understood as an exemplary sufferer who redeems his community through his sacrifices. Césaire had read Nietzsche and mentions him in the issues of his journal *Tropiques*, published in the 1940s.[1]

For Frantz Fanon, this Dionysian self-creation—"In the world through which I travel, I am endlessly creating myself"—is diametrically opposed to the concept of "race" as romanticized and mysticized in a certain idea of negritude, which Césaire himself was to end up denouncing as deterministic.[2] Fanon's search was for a form of authentic communication not based in reaction and *ressentiment* but emphasizing a continually broadening freedom and responsibility, an actualization of Nietzsche's philosophy of becoming and affirmation.

"Man is not merely a possibility of recapture or of negation. . . . Man is a *yes* that vibrates to cosmic harmonies. Uprooted, pursued, baffled, doomed to watch the dissolution of the truths that he has worked out for himself one after another, he has to give up projecting onto the world an antinomy that coexists with him," Fanon proclaims, echoing a Nietzschean affirmation of life for life's sake.[3]

[1]See, for instance, Aimé Césaire, "Maintenir la poésie," *Tropiques* 8–9 (Oct. 1943), in which he discusses the implicitly Nietzschean dimensions of Claudel, pp. 7–8 and "Poésie et connaissance," *Tropiques* 12 (Jan. 1945), in which he gives his view of what the beginnings of modern literature owe to Nietzsche: "1850—la revanche de Dionysos sur Apollon," p. 159. Also A. James Arnold, in his *Modernism and Negritude: The Poetry and Poetics of Aimé Césaire* (Cambridge: Harvard University Press, 1981), discusses the influence of Frobenius, Spengler, and Nietzsche on Césaire's poetics (pp. 37–44, 50–54); the internal differences between Senghor's and Césaire's views of negritude (pp. 33–34, 44); and the debate among critics of the concept, such as Maryse Condé, Stanislas Adotevi, and Roberto Fernández Retamar (pp. 45–47). The quotation is from *Aimé Césaire: The Collected Poetry*, trans. Clayton Eshleman and Annette Smith (Berkeley: University of California Press, 1983), p. 83.

[2]See Arnold, p. 44. In the interview Césaire gave to Lilyan Kesteloot in Dec. 1971, he says: "I am for negritude from a literary point of view and as a personal ethic, but I am against an ideology founded on negritude" (published in Lilyan Kesteloot and Barthélemy Kotchy, *Aimé Césaire, l'homme et l'oeuvre* [Paris: Présence Africaine, 1973], p. 235). The quotation is from Frantz Fanon, *Black Skin, White Masks*, trans. Charles L. Markmann (London: Pluto Press, 1986), p. 229.

[3]Fanon, Introduction to *Black Skin, White Masks*, p. 10. Fanon discusses Hegel and Nietzsche specifically in chap. 7.

Like Zarathustra, who says "Where one can no longer love, there one should *pass by*," Fanon reaffirms his belief in the human capacity for love and change, for becoming more self-aware politically, for inventing new strategies and new semiotic contents for tired old social concepts.[4]

To attempt to read Nietzsche's "autobiography" from the place where Césaire and Fanon regard Western culture critically is thus to adopt a stance that questions our inherited notions of race, language, and selfhood in ways that are themselves radically Nietzschean. The circularity of this approach is perhaps a necessary step toward deterritorializing some of Nietzsche's voices, the ones that are implicitly heeded by the women writers discussed in this book, because they too perform subversive operations on our traditional notions of race, gender, culture, language, and genre. Let us then use as starting point the following denunciation of territorial, racialist thinking:

> Among Europeans today there is no lack of those who are entitled to call themselves homeless in a distinctive and honorable sense: it is to them that I especially commend my secret wisdom and *gaya scienza* . . . We children of the future, how could we be at home in this today? . . . We "conserve" nothing; neither do we want to return to any past periods; . . .
>
> We who are homeless are too manifold and mixed racially and in our descent, being "modern man," and consequently do not feel tempted to participate in the mendacious racial self-admiration and racial indecency that parades in Germany today as a sign of a German way of thinking and that is doubly false and obscene among the people of the "historical sense."[5]

In this aphorism from *The Gay Science* Nietzsche leaves no doubt as to his feelings about nationalism and racism: he reaffirms his refusal to be linked in any way to the proto-Nazis of Germany or to

[4]Friedrich Nietzsche, *Thus Spoke Zarathustra*, pt. 3, in *The Portable Nietzsche*, trans. Walter Kaufmann (New York: Viking Press, 1967), p. 290, hereafter cited in the text as Z, with part and page number. See also Fanon, *Black Skin, White Masks*, p. 228: "Have I no other purpose on earth, then, but to avenge the Negro of the seventeenth century?" and p. 230: "No attempt must be made to encase man, for it is his destiny to be set free."

[5]Friedrich Nietzsche, *The Gay Science* (New York: Vintage Books, 1974), paragraph 377, p. 338. Hereafter cited by paragraph number and the abbreviation *GS*.

any other form of fanaticism. Posterity would not immediately re-
member him for this strong antinationalism, partly because of the
Procrustean editing his sister Elisabeth Förster-Nietzsche performed
on his writing, thus helping fashion an unprepossessing popular
legend.[6]

To be sure, Nietzsche's metaphors, flamboyant style, and apparently contradictory statements can, and have, led to devastating
misunderstandings. As both his French and American translators,
Pierre Klossowski and Walter Kaufmann, have remarked, Nietzsche
is too "explosive" a figure not to have provoked violent reactions in
France, England, and the United States in the wake of two world
wars that seemed to vindicate a militarist/imperialist interpretation
of his conception of power.[7] Recent readings of Nietzsche by critics
as diverse as Gilles Deleuze, Jacques Derrida, Rodolphe Gasché,
Sarah Kofman, Alexander Nehamas, Margot Norris, and Ofelia
Schutte (among others) have contributed to a more nuanced understanding of his ideas and their relevance to our contemporary concerns, our antisystematic approaches to language, literature, philosophy, ethics, and politics.[8]

Less well known (and understandably so, given Nietzsche's reception in the English-speaking world) is the influence Nietzsche
has had on a writer like Aimé Césaire, whose concept of negritude
was a salutary and historically necessary antithesis to white racism,
while it was *reactive* in the Nietzschean sense. Negritude has been

[6]See Walter Kaufmann, *Nietzsche: Philosopher, Psychologist, Antichrist* (Cleveland:
Meridian Books/World Publishing, 1956), p. 19.

[7]See especially Pierre Klossowski, *Un si funeste désir* (Paris: Gallimard, 1963), chaps.
1 and 7. "Explosive" is Kaufmann's word in *Nietzsche*, p. 20.

[8]Gilles Deleuze, "Nomad Thought," in *The New Nietzsche: Contemporary Styles of
Interpretation,* ed. David B. Allison (Cambridge: MIT Press, 1985), pp. 142–49, and
Nietzsche and Philosophy (New York: Columbia University Press, 1983); Jacques Der-
rida, *Spurs/Eperons: Nietzsche's Styles,* trans. Barbara Harlow (Chicago: University of
Chicago Press, 1979), and *The Ear of the Other: Otobiography, Transference, Translation,*
trans. Peggy Kamuf and Avital Ronnell (New York: Schocken Books, 1985); Rodolphe
Gasché, "Autobiography as *Gestalt*: Nietzsche's *Ecce Homo,*" in *Why Nietzsche Now?*
ed. Daniel T. O'Hara (Bloomington: Indiana University Press, 1958), pp. 271–90;
Sarah Kofman, "Metaphor, Symbol, Metamorphosis," in *The New Nietzsche,* pp. 201–
214; Alexander Nehamas, *Nietzsche: Life as Literature* (Cambridge: Harvard University
Press, 1985); Margot Norris, *Beasts of the Modern Imagination: Darwin, Nietzsche, Kafka,
Ernst, and Lawrence* (Baltimore: Johns Hopkins University Press, 1958); and Ofelia
Schutte, *Beyond Nihilism: Nietzsche without Masks* (Chicago: University of Chicago
Press, 1984).

attacked by Fanon and others for its totalizing (and essentialist) approach to "blackness," which does not take into account the historical and cultural differences among peoples. As Fanon reminds us, negritude's emphasis on searching for a homeland and for the "identity" of the black soul partakes of a mythical desire for a plenitude that is always already lost for all those who are "homeless" by virtue of the colonialist diaspora of the last three hundred years:

> And it is also true that those who are most responsible for this racialization of thought—or at least of patterns of thought—are and remain those Europeans who have never ceased to set up white culture over and against all other so-called non-cultures [d'opposer la culture blanche aux autres incultures]. . . .
> The Negroes of Chicago only resemble the Nigerians or the Tanganyikans in so far as they were all defined in relation to the whites. But once the first comparisons had been made and subjective feelings were assuaged, the American Negroes realized that the objective problems were fundamentally heterogeneous. . . .
> Negritude therefore finds its first limitation in the phenomena which take account of the historicization of mankind.[9]

If the desire and the search for plenitude were the only foci of Césaire's works, then one would be entitled to criticize their essentialist underpinnings. But the limits put on concepts like negritude are comparable, mutatis mutandis, to the misunderstandings that have surrounded Nietzsche's writings. For example, in a recent article, Sunday O. Anozie discusses Léopold S. Senghor's concept of negritude and criticizes what he calls "a totalizing, emotional, reductionist and therefore misleading concept" that contradicts Senghor's own statements about "the liberating character and force of reality," as well as his "desire to maintain a lively fluidity of existence." The debate seems uncannily familiar to anyone aware of the history of Nietzsche criticism and the semantic disputes that arose over a narrowly construed reading of terms such as "will to power" and "mas-

---

[9]Frantz Fanon, *The Wretched of the Earth*, trans. Constance Farrington (New York: Grove Press, 1968), pp. 212, 216, modified here from the French, *Les Damnés de la terre* (Paris: Maspéro, 1968), pp. 148–49. See also the introduction by Clayton Eshleman and Annette Smith, *Aimé Césaire: The Collected Poetry*, pp. 1–31.

ter morality," on the one hand, and negritude, "black conscious-ness," and "black aesthetism," on the other.[10]

Césaire and Fanon have a larger debt to Nietzschean views of culture than to any other Western conceptual apparatus, un-surprisingly so in light of the radical critique of Western ideology and dogmatism that Nietzsche's works incorporate: his thoughts on history, language, selflessness, and selfishness, as well as homeless-ness, are pertinent to "Third World" or minority writers who want to shake off the damaging traps of dialectical thinking and of a founding myth of origins. For being "homeless in a distinctive and honorable sense" is not just the existential condition par excellence of generations of postwar Europeans (since the Franco-Prussian War of 1870), as Nietzsche points out. It has also been the de facto experi-ence of millions of people since the beginning of the European colo-nial era, a fact often obscured and occluded by a historical discourse that focuses on European perspectives on (neo)colonialism rather than giving a voice to those "too manifold and mixed racially and in [their] descent" to be tempted by any form of patriotism or by "this most *anti-cultural* sickness and unreason there is, nationalism, this *névrose nationale* with which Europe is sick," as Nietzsche pro-claims in *Ecce Homo*, one of his most controversial works and, in Richard Samuel's terms, "perhaps the strangest autobiography ever written."[11]

Ecce Homo is divided into two prefaces and four sections: "Why I Am So Wise," "Why I Am So Clever," "Why I Write Such Good Books," and "Why I Am a Destiny." The first two sections focus on the accidents of fate and physiology, the influence of place and climate on the body, and the choices of personal hygiene; the third contains a microcosm of Nietzsche's whole literary corpus; and the fourth, a strident finale, is "a burst of apocalyptic rhetoric that deliv-

---

[10]Sunday O. Anozie, "Negritude, Structuralism, Deconstruction," in *Black Litera-ture and Literary Theory*, ed. Henry Louis Gates, Jr. (New York: Methuen, 1984), p. 121.

[11]Friedrich Nietzsche, *On the Genealogy of Morals and Ecce Homo* (New York: Vintage Books, 1969), p. 321. References will be given in the text, and the abbreviation *EH* used when necessary. Richard Samuel, "Friedrich Nietzsche's *Ecce Homo*: An Auto-biography?" in *Deutung und Bedeutung: Studies in German and Comparative Literature Presented to Karl-Werner Maurer*, ed. Brigitte Schuldermann et al. (The Hague: Mouton [De Proprietatibus Litterarum, Series Maior 25], 1973) p. 210.

ers no threat, extorts no repentance, urges no conversion," and thus reverses the Christlike gesture of the title page, in a grand and consciously self-deceptive manner, which proclaims itself to be the obverse of the *"folie circulaire"* (*EH* 334), or manic-depressive insanity of decadent Christian humanity.[12]

In this chapter, I want to discuss each of the sections, focusing on the intertextual references of Nietzsche's rhetoric as regards the physical body and the literary corpus in order to show how he gives us a "map" for reading his works, while he is producing evidence about the "fated" nature of creativity, its grounding in the body. I shall conclude with a discussion of his view of hyperbole and self-dissimulation as the sine qua non of literary redemption. As he puts it in *The Will to Power:* "The spell that fights on our behalf, the eye of Venus that charms and blinds even our opponents, is *the magic of the extreme*, the seduction that everything extreme exercises: we immoralists—we are the most extreme."[13] That is why he can claim to be, in schizophrenic fashion, "every name in history," Christ and the Antichrist, and why he uses a style that disorients because each layer hides another that subverts the meaning of the first: biography and myth, history and allegory, strident tone and subdued irony.[14]

Reading and Writing the (Dying) Body

Published in 1908, *Ecce Homo* was written in the last productive year of Nietzsche's life, 1888, just months before he collapsed from insanity and a paralysis of syphilitic origin. It is his last work and in the second preface, he claims to have begun writing it on his forty-fourth birthday, that is, on October 15, 1888. As Europe is diseased and decadent, so does Nietzsche feel that his life is on the decline, and he sets out to analyze how he is affected by his "dual heritage" [doppelte Herkunft]"[15] which makes him both "a *decadent* and a

---

[12]Norris, p. 99.

[13]Friedrich Nietzsche, *The Will to Power* (New York: Vintage Books, 1968), paragraph 749, p. 396, hereafter cited in the text by paragraph number.

[14]In Nietzsche's final letter to Jacob Burckhardt. See *Unpublished Letters*, trans. and ed. Kurt F. Leidecker (New York: Philosophical Library, 1959), p. 155. See also the discussion in Gilles Deleuze and Félix Guattari, *Anti-Oedipus: Capitalism and Schizophrenia* (Minneapolis: University of Minnesota Press, 1983), p. 21.

[15]German quotation is from *Ecce Homo*, in *Sämtliche Werke* (Stuttgart: A. Kröner, 1964), 8:299, hereafter cited in the text, abbreviated *SW*.

beginning" (224), a principle of death and a harbinger of life: in other words, the perfect overthrower of idols, the one who knows how to follow the *"crooked* path," *"the way up"* (315), that is, the path that leads to a new dawn for culture. Nietzsche takes it upon himself to perform for Europe the role that Oedipus had for Athens: to die as his old self, almost blind (223), in order to be reborn in his works, for the benefit of the "children of the future."

Thus on that fall day of 1888, "this perfect day, when everything is ripening and not just the grape turns brown, the eye of the sun just fell upon my life: I looked back, I looked forward, and never saw so many and such good things at once" (221). Nietzsche, godlike, contemplates his accomplishments, echoing Genesis 1:31 and Augustine's use of this scriptural phrase: "And you saw all that you made, O God, and found it very good."[16] But Nietzsche celebrates his forty-fourth birthday by "burying" the past, godlike but also devillike, for he has created things that are "too beautiful." In the subsection of *Ecce Homo* called *Beyond Good and Evil* (1886), he ironically talks about theology and the need to relax and recuperate after creating such a masterpiece as *Thus Spoke Zarathustra* (written during the three years preceding *Beyond Good and Evil*): "Theologically speaking—listen closely, for I rarely speak as a theologian—it was God himself who at the end of his days' work lay down as a serpent under the tree of knowledge: thus he recuperated from being God.—He had made everything too beautiful" [Er hatte alles zu schön gemacht]" (*EH* 311; *SW* 8:387).

So Nietzsche is "grateful, [dankbar]" (*EH* 221; *SW* 8:298) for his own accomplishments, that is, for his "whole life," and he proceeds to bury his forty-fourth year by canceling out the residue of physiological weakness, the cycle of ill health, recovery, relapse, and decay that has been his lot for the past several years. He says that he started to suffer from a debilitating loss of energy and vitality when he reached his thirty-sixth birthday, the age at which his own father had died, but he is fond of the symbolism of dates. Nietzsche is not to be trusted with the "truth" of those facts: he could not already be thirty-six in the spring of 1879 if he turned forty-four in the fall of 1888! But this mythic identification with his father sets the tone for

---

[16]Augustine, *Confessions*, trans. R. S. Pine-Coffin (New York: Penguin Books, 1979), 13:28, p. 340.

the rhetorical gestures of the "autobiography" which link him directly to Christ, the Son of God the Father, who dies as man in order to be resurrected as a divine, glorious body. Thus Nietzsche is "already dead," like his father, but with *Ecce Homo* his writings are in the process of being immortalized, remembered, catalogued: about two-thirds of the text is devoted to his own interpretive reading of his opus, from *The Birth of Tragedy* (1871) to *The Case of Wagner* (1888).

His dying body has given him, he says, "a subtler sense of smell for the signs of ascent and decline than any other human being" (222), because it has made him acutely aware of the torments of physical pain and the possibility of self-regeneration through his own instincts of self-preservation. He has also acquired the ability to ride that pain, to let it carry him to new heights of freedom, to give him wings (227), to allow him to fly, Zarathustra-like, "6000 feet beyond man and time" (295). In other words, although physically diminished, he has never been afflicted by those "pathological disturbances of the intellect" (223) which might hinder his thinking: quite the contrary, he has "possessed a dialectician's clarity" and coldness (222), these being the ultimate symptoms of decadence, as exhibited by Socrates. He has a privileged sense and sensitivity "for all signs of healthy instincts" (257) and can thus avoid all forms of fanaticism. "Even in periods of severe sickness I never became pathological" (257), he says, reaffirming his disdain for poses and pathos, self-pity and self-doubt.[17] Indeed, some of his best books—*The Antichrist, Dionysus Dithyrambs, Twilight of the Idols, Nietzsche contra Wagner, Ecce Homo*—were written in that forty-fourth year, and we may surmise that it is because the corpus is immortal that "whatever was life in [that year] has been saved, is immortal" (221). The body is on its decline, but the corpus is soaring.

What are we to make of this apparently contradictory state of wisdom, wherein he is both a decadent and its opposite, God and the devil, the father and the son, Socrates and Zarathustra? The

[17]This form of stoicism recalls Montaigne: "What matter if we twist our arms, provided we do not twist our thoughts? . . . In the attacks of the stone, let her [philosophy] preserve the soul's capacity for knowing itself, for following its accustomed course, combating the pain and enduring it, not prostrating itself shamefully at its feet; . . . I test myself in the thickest of the pain, and have always found that I was capable of speaking, thinking, and answering as sanely as at any other time." See "Of the Resemblance of Children to Fathers," *The Complete Works of Montaigne*, trans. Donald Frame, (Stanford: Stanford University Press, 1948), p. 577.

state of being wise is physiologically determined, most noticeably by his special "nose," which is acutely able to smell out lies ("Mein Genie ist in meinen Nüstern" [*SW* 8:400; *EH* 326]), and by his "fingers for *nuances*" which know the filigree art of grasping (*EH* 223). But his wisdom also allows him to assimilate all past historical figures into his doppelgänger role: "This *dual* series of experiences, this access to apparently separate worlds, is repeated in my nature in every aspect: I am a *Doppelgänger*, I have a "second" face in addition to the first. *And* perhaps also a third" (225).

Nietzsche created the myth of his own mixed ancestry : he liked to say that he had a Polish father and a German mother, that he considered himself "mixed racially" and thus fatally governed by the principle of contradiction: "The good fortune of my existence, its uniqueness perhaps, lies in its fatality: I am, to express it in the form of a riddle, already dead as my father, while as my mother I am still living and becoming old" (222). He consciously appropriates this double origin, the dead father and the living mother, and as Derrida has said, commenting on this passage: "Inasmuch as I *am and follow after* my father, I am the dead man and I am death. Inasmuch as I *am and follow after* my mother, I am life that perseveres, I am the living and the living feminine. I am my father, my mother and me. . . . The double birth explains who I am and how I determine my identity: as double and neutral."[18]

These are the three faces of Nietzsche: the opposing poles of the dialectic *and* the neutral third that nuances the first two; dead, alive, and decadent; male, female, and neutral; Dionysus, Ariadne, and the labyrinth; positive, negative, and "chance" or fate: "My formula for greatness in a human being is *amor fati*: that one wants nothing to be different, not forward, not backward, not in all eternity" (258). Although physiologically speaking he is unhealthy, his sickness has given him insight into the "instinct of self-restoration" (224), the necessity to reject all forms of reactive behavior, which can only poison existence, make one vulnerable to the ravages of *ressentiment*. To be resentful is to be decadent, diseased, to leave oneself open to more depletions of energy. The only way to recover is to "exploit bad accidents to [one's] advantage" (224), to become a principle of selection, active rather than reactive. Since death is inevitable, one

[18]Derrida, *The Ear of the Other*, p. 16.

might as well take it in stride: "I do not know any other way of associating with great tasks than *play*" (258). In the context of disease and death, it is worth recalling that the hour of final reckoning, the last ordeal of the Christian soul, is often conflated with the image of a terrible game man plays with the figure of death (often a game of chess, as in medieval iconography or, more recently, in Ingmar Bergman's movie *The Seventh Seal*).

Nietzsche thus begins *Ecce Homo* by showing his philosophy to be a function of the accidents of his parentage, his genetic and physiological disposition: "I turned my will to health, to *life*, into a philosophy." He recalls his most depressed and darkest year, 1879, the year he claims to have turned thirty-six, retired from his professorship at Basel, and "reached the lowest point of [his] vitality" (222), becoming a shadow of his former self. It also happens to be the year he wrote *The Wanderer and His Shadow*. Augustine's narrative of his life revolved around similar experiences of death: the deaths of his father, his son, his best friend, his mother are metaphors signifying his own progressive descent into the abyss of sin. This loss of physical being culminated in severe pneumonia and forced Augustine to resign his professorship at the age of thirty-three: the death of the embodied self is a necessary prelude to his rebirth and resurrection in Christ, as *infans* and child of God. Augustine consequently devotes the rest of his life to the *imitatio Christi* that will, from then on, generate and guarantee his immortality, his eternal life.

For Nietzsche, the loss of vitality and energy, the cycle of recovery and relapse serve the purpose of "nuancing" his perceptions from the perspective of the sick ["von der Kranken-Optik"] (*SW* 8:301), of making him an expert on "the instinct of decadence" (223). He loses and regains his eyesight, acquiring insight into "observation itself as well as all organs of observation" (223). He turns his physical disability into a source of knowledge: "Now I have know-how, have the know-how to *reverse perspectives:* the first reason why a 'revaluation of values' is perhaps possible for me alone" (223). He is diseased and healthy; he is the sum of opposite racial, genetic, and physiological tendencies; he can encompass in his body all positive stimuli for life because he is strong enough to use everything to his own best advantage ("daß ihm alles zum besten gereichen muß," [*EH* 225; *SW* 8:303). Using the same argument that nineteenth century science made against racial mixing, Nietzsche simply reverses its conclusions: rather than making him into a degenerate offspring, his mixed lineage has given him the advantage of being "the opposite of a decadent" (225), one who thrives on principles of affirmation, who says "the great Yes to life" (226).

What Nietzsche is in fact doing here is translating the traditional ontological-ethical dichotomy between appearance and essence, visible signs and noumenon, onto the purely biological level, rather than disposing of it completely: one can appear to be sick or morbid, yet "im Grunde gesund ist" (*SW* 8:302), just as Nietzsche took himself in hand, made himself healthy again, thus proving that he was not fated, predestined to be morbid "im Grunde [at bottom]" (224). This ostentatious, detailed, graphic display of the body and its physiological characteristics serves, as Margot Norris has shown, several important functions: "The action of taking charge of his health, of taking a kind of physiological responsibility for both the causes and cures of his illness, solves Nietzsche's crucial rhetorical problem of devising a way of speaking of his ill health without making an appeal for sympathy and pity. . . . [I]t gives him an active, rather than a passive, invalid role and thereby certifies the continued efficacy of his powers, and it denies the lack or weakness that invites the appropriation of the 'other' (doctors, relatives, friends)".[19]

This self-display is not meant to invite response; it is meant to ground the enterprise of self-writing in an act of antispiritualism, a radical reversal of an ancient occupation since Augustine. I mean the traditional Neoplatonic Christian inquiry into the "true" nature of man, which consists in the *memoria sui*, the "inner man" who can be known only when abstraction is made of the physical, external being. It is through the death of this embodied being that true conversion is attainable and possible for Augustine and all those who search for their transcendent self beyond the mere simulacrum of spatial and temporal representation, be it physical, verbal, or painterly. At the core of this search is the belief that the degree zero of man, the ultimate reality of "being" is the self made in the image of God, the *imago Dei*, or, for the humanist who does not adhere to the Christian logos, the original, rational, and universal notion of a "truth" of man, a Cartesian "vérité de l'être."

Interestingly enough, the first drafts of *Ecce Homo* present us with

---

[19]Norris, p. 87.

a clear departure from this traditional inquiry in vocabulary that ironically reverses the Christian representation of an essential self. According to Richard Samuel's research, Nietzsche considered, then abandoned several titles: *Der Spiegel* and *Versuch einer Selbstschilderung* [crossed out] *Selbsabstraction* [sic] and *Ecce Homo/In media vita* and *Fredericus Nietzsche/De vita sua*. As Michel Beaujour has pointed out, one cannot help but be struck by the medieval connotations of those discarded titles.[20] The mirror (*Spiegel*), the *speculum*, harks back to the Augustinian attempt (*Versuch*) at self-portrayal in book 10 of the *Confessions*, where self-depiction (*Selbstschilderung*) is really an effort at self-abstraction (*Selbstabstraktion*). This is a form of self-erasure, since the memory of particular and sensible details is negated with the express purpose of transcending the "idols" of particularism and individualism and reducing the self to an outline, a drawing in the manner of mere shadow theater. The religious paradigm is clearly adopted and inverted. It is then further refined by the use of Latin phrases. *In media vita* alludes to the medieval Christian view of birth into this world as the real death:—"Media vita in morte sumus [In the midst of life, we are in death]," says a prayer in the Roman missal of the Council of Trent;[21] *De vita sua* recalls the custom of representing the exemplary lives of the saints as models of Christian itineraries. The religious paradigm finally culminates in the direct reference to the suffering and displayed body of Christ during his Passion: "Ecce Homo " was Pontius Pilate's exclamation as he presented Jesus in his crown of thorns and purple robes to the Jews before the crucifixion. In Christian eschatology, Christ's crucified body is supposed to be the object of a perpetual and devoted contemplation on the part of the faithful, who can thus become imbued with a sense of their own physical mortality and eventual redemption and rebirth in Christ's resucitated body. In the Middle Ages, "Ecce homo" ("Behold the man"; "Voilà l'homme") is used as an iconographic title for pictorial representations of the crucifixion and

[20]Samuel, p. 210; Michel Beaujour, *Miroirs d'encre* (Paris: Seuil, 1980), pp. 320–21, my translations. Beaujour notes that the whole ambiguity of Nietzsche's enterprise is evident in the symbolic move from German to Latin in those discarded titles. Nietzsche's ostentatious display of his body is thus an imitation of Christ as well as the performance of a transsubstantiation from Christian idealism to a new form of idiosyncratic materialism.

[21]See Philippe Ariès, *The Hour of Our Death* (New York: Knopf, 1981), p. 13.

by artists doing self-portraits, including Fra Bartholomeo and Albrecht Dürer.

That Nietzsche should proceed to render in detail the physical reality of his bodily ailments further contributes to the ironic inversion of the paradigm: three-day migraines, vomiting of phlegm, difficulties with his digestive system, effects of alcohol, coffee, tea, cocoa, etc.(222, 238, 239); the effects of place and climate on his constitution (240–41); the usefulness of hashish (249); and finally, the importance of being self-protective like "a *hedgehog* " (253) instead of being the object of self-flagellation, like the saints, or anthropophagous appropriation by one's disciples, like Christ. For Nietzsche, resurrection and renewal are possible strictly through "good hygiene," never as a result of asceticism.

For example, when Zarathustra encounters the Magician (Z, pt. 4, 367), whose moanings and jeremiads irate him, he does not let himself be contaminated by pity at the sight of this suffering body: instead, he beats the distressed man, who proceeds to congratulate him for his hardness. Indeed, the Magician explains that he only intended to test Zarathustra's "greatness" by engaging in a "game," albeit a *serious* one, pretending to be "*the ascetic of the spirit*" (368) only in order to ascertain Zarathustra's ability to act with the cruelty required of all great men, those of whom one may say "Behold a great man!" (370). And in *Beyond Good and Evil* (¶209), Nietzsche collapses the figures of Christ, Goethe, Napoleon, and himself into one ironic, anti-German comment about the remark ("Voilà un homme!") Napoleon is supposed to have made when he met Goethe at Erfurt in 1808: "At long last we ought to understand deeply enough Napoleon's surprise when he came to see Goethe: it shows what people had associated with the 'German spirit' for centuries. 'Voilà un homme!'—that meant: 'But this is a *man!* And I had merely expected a German.' "[22]

Ecce Homo: Wie man wird, was man ist ["How one becomes what one is"]: Nietzsche's final title, viewed in the light of the foregoing remarks, multiplies the irony and the plurality of identifications he appropriates as his faces or masks: "I am granted an eye beyond all merely local, merely nationally conditioned perspectives: it is not

[22]Friedrich Nietzsche, *Beyond Good and Evil* (New York: Vintage Books, 1966), paragraph 209, p. 133, hereafter cited by paragraph number in the text.

difficult for me to be a 'good European.' On the other hand, I am perhaps more German than present-day Germans" (*EH* 225). The rhetorical strategy involved in canceling the origin while reaffirming its importance is analogous to the gestures inscribed in the first preface, wherein Nietzsche (dis)orients his reader by stating à la Rousseau that "it seems indispensable to me to say *who I am*" because, above all, he does not want to be mistaken "for someone else." Not having left himself "without testimony" (217), he is compelled to read and clarify his own fragmented authorship, lest he be mistaken for some "prophet" or "those gruesome hybrids of sickness and will to power whom people call founders of religions" (219). It is thus important for him to distinguish his own voice from Christ's or Zarathustra's, the writer from the written, the author from the reader, although in this case, the author's self-reading tautologically returns him to the source, while granting him the special privilege of being his own best reader: "It is a privilege without equal to be a listener here. Nobody is free to have ears for Zarathustra" (220). Only a detour through the labyrinth of the corpus enables one to acquire the proper "ear" for those "otobiographical" revelations.[23] In attempting to bypass the mimetic identification with such others as Christ and Goethe, Nietzsche articulates the need to avoid idealist notions of imitation and returns language to its material and physical site: the body. In so doing he insists on the materiality of the word, opposing it to abstract rationality and to the religious or philosophical logos.

Reading the Corpus

What then is this "privilege without equal" which allows one to decipher decadence, to hear the silence of "objection" ["Einwand]" (*EH* 229; *SW* 8:307) and yet to be beyond *ressentiment*? Clearly it is a privilege that can be shared only by those who have eyes to see, a nose to smell, fingers to grasp, and ears to hear, in other words who are not disoriented by the spiritual strivings of their cultural selves, "the bite of conscience," that *"evil eye"* of asceticism and education (*EH* 236). Unlike Nietzsche's contemporaries—readers who are deceived by their belief in a different kind of truth and thus "hear" nothing

---

[23]See Derrida, *The Ear of the Other.*

when they read his books—those who are "worthy of hearing" (265)
Zarathustra's riddles are the ones brave enough to "embark with
cunning sails on terrible seas" (264). We have a theory of reading
quite close to Augustine's here, a reading/hearing that is a form of
absolute receptivity to the "other", an attempt to understand the
complexities of the text, at the risk of losing one's own idiosyncratic
point of view, rather than the reductive—subjective—appropriation
of one of its layers. This is the kind of reading which allows one to
experience the text in a blissful way and to "hear meaning" as
Kristeva, following Lacan, has said: "jouissance = j'ouïs sens." For
Lacan, this *jouissance* is the ecstasy of the mystics, but for Barthes it
is a radical form of materialism which returns theory to the site of
physical pleasure.[24] For Nietzsche too it is a state of exquisite physical perception, one in which pain and pleasure are collapsed into
one another, or as Marie-Thérèse Humbert's narrator would put it,
Zarathustra-like, it is a feeling quite the obverse of pity, it is "this
hideous joy, so keen that it seemed closer to pain than to pleasure
[cette affreuse jouissance, dans son acuité plus proche de la douleur
que de la joie]."[25] It is thus an experience through which the temper
of the individual is tried, the body put to the test: "The world is poor
for anyone who has never been sick enough for this 'voluptuousness of hell': it is permitted, it is almost imperative, to employ a
formula of the mystics at this point" (*EH* 250).

We may recall Socrates' analysis of pleasure and pain in the *Phae-
do:* they form a pair of opposites attached to a single head, and
anyone visited by one of them is later bound to come face to face
with the other as well (60b5–c5). This Janus-like experience is at the
heart of all Nietzschean conceptual critiques, and we must bear in
mind that the yes-saying individual thus shares a common "head"
with the no-saying one, for better or for worse: Dionysus and Socrates, God and the devil are faces of the same Nietzsche. That is
why to read Nietzsche with one's ear tuned to the duplicitous operations of *jouissance* under the hyperbolic claims of the defensive self is

[24]See Jacques Lacan, *Le Séminaire: Livre XX—Encore* (Paris: Seuil, 1975), pp. 9–18;
Julia Kristeva, *Desire in Language: A Semiotic Approach to Literature and Art*, trans. Tom
Gora, Alice Jardine, and Léon Roudiez (New York: Columbia University Press, 1980).
The introduction by Léon S. Roudiez contains a useful glossary, pp. 12–20; Roland
Barthes, *The Pleasure of the Text* (New York: Hill and Wang, 1975).

[25]Marie-Thérèse Humbert, *A l'autre bout de moi* (Paris: Stock, 1979), p. 427, my
translation.

to be truly prepared for the "thoughts that come on dove's feet" (*EH* 219), the revelations that only the receptive reader will have the opportunity of discovering only if s/he can "grasp" the fact that the book is "a present," "a voice bridging centuries," "a halcyon tone" (219).

Thus when Nietzsche implies that his aim is both to establish the difference between him and his books:—"I am one thing, my writings are another matter" (259)—*and* the impossibility of being anything other than the corpus he creates, his literary selves, we can take him quite literally, for he is Zarathustra, Dionysus, the Antichrist, the immoralist: "I have chosen the word *immoralist* as a symbol and a badge of honor for myself; I am proud of having this word which distinguishes me from the whole of humanity" (331). This can be viewed as a parodic and transgressive gesture toward Montaigne, who says in the exhortation "To The Reader" of his *Essays*, "I am myself the matter of my book." For Nietzsche then proceeds to emulate "Montaigne's sportiveness" (243), his well-known need to be physically active in order to think clearly: "My thoughts fall asleep if I make them sit down. My mind will not budge unless my legs move it."[26] And compare this with Nietzsche's advice for thinking clearly: "*Sit* as little as possible; give no credence to any thought that was not born outdoors while one moved about freely—in which the muscles are not celebrating a feast, too. All prejudices come from the intestines" (239–40). But whereas Montaigne could say with confidence, "I have done what I wanted. Everyone recognizes me in my book, and my book in me,"[27] Nietzsche can only act like the hedgehog who is never sure of the intentions of the "other" and must keep on adopting masks as shields for self-protection and self-dissimulation, because of the "*smallness* of [his] contemporaries" (217) who first must be seduced into listening to him, then into going it alone because he does not want any disciples. Nietzsche attempts to create a space for himself which is the site of a profound contradiction: a space independent of the gaze of the other and of the voices of culture and society, which can only make him more vulnerable to the kind of imitation he vehemently rejects because of its universalizing potential.

---

[26]Montaigne, "Of Three Kinds of Association," *Complete Works*, p. 629.
[27]Montaigne, "On Some Verses of Virgil," ibid., p. 667.

In *Miroirs d'encre*, Michel Beaujour has argued that the dialectical relationship between the self and the book, the body and the corpus constitutes one of the foremost characteristics of the "genre" of "autoportrait," that is, the mode of self-description whereby a writer uses a set of rhetorical *topoi* as means of self-writing. Montaigne and Nietzsche are prime examples of authors who use fragmentary writing to convey the dispersion, the dissemination of the self in language. As I hope to have shown for Augustine and as I maintain about Hurston, Angelou, Cardinal, and Humbert, even a traditional, linear, and chronological narrative of "a life" can exhibit this tropological structure, especially in the case of women writers who seek modes of discourse which reflect by analogy the traditionally stratified nature of their lives as "heroines" and as women, lovers, daughters, sisters, mothers, writers, and so on. In the case of Nietzsche, the conflation of the "life" with the corpus occasions an exemplary transformation of the trope of the body into its literary counterpart, the corpus, thus undermining all philosophical claims to the universality of the description:

> Sick persons, actors, poets and athletes discuss their own bodies without aspiring to universalism. But the relation the self-portraitist entertains with his body is more complex, and more paradoxical, because although a self-portrait is not strictly limited to a description of the author's own body, neither can this be passed over in silence. The self-portrait is the only genre in which writing cannot avoid wondering about the site of its production, the incarnation of the word and the resurrection of the body. The self-portrait thus stands in opposition to the philosophical logos. It is situated somewhere between opinion and reason, between embodied individuality and commonplace. The question of the relation between *loci* and *bodies* is thus raised in a general way through the body-corpus metaphor as well as through the details of the symbols around which the self-portrait organizes its topics.

"*Ecce Homo*," writes Beaujour, "is the textual site where the corpus and the body of Nietzsche respectively change status."[28]

Indeed, in the section titled "Why I Write Such Good Books," Nietzsche gives us his interpretations of his writings but also explains in detail how external circumstances—place, climate, well-

---

[28]Beaujour, pp. 307–8, 324.

being—influenced his process of creativity, "fated" his body to become capable of inspiration and revelation (300). In other words, the
"autobiography" becomes strictly a retrospective look at the loci, the
geographical *topoi* and psycho-physiological predispositions that favored the hatching or emergence of the corpus. This is why Nietzsche finds it necessary to adopt the veil of the iconoclast, for example, when discussing the nature and purpose of "woman" in the
scheme of creation: for Nietzsche envies nothing more than wom-
en's ability to procreate, to maintain their "natural" physiological
superiority over men who are "always a mere means, pretext, tactic"
in women's instinctive drive to give birth (267). But this giving birth,
like all Nietzsche's extremist statements, must be understood literally *and* metaphorically. His maternal space is a "biocentric" locus of
energy and affirmation quite different from the phallic/symbolic
realm within which Augustine's being comes to a perfect rest.
Nietzsche's return—one might even say his reversion or regression—to such an elemental and prelinguistic site as the essential
source of inspiration for his own writings raises fundamental questions regarding the very possibility of cultural production. By thus
returning to the body, Nietzsche provides a link in the nineteenth
century between the (male) use of embodiment in Latin and Renaissance rhetoric and the emphasis of contemporary women writers on
their shared specificity, their culture-producing body languages. As
I shall discuss in my last chapter, on Humbert, creation and procreation, production and reproduction are, like pleasure and pain, merely dual aspects of the same process for Nietzsche, and he even
compares his own long period of conception before the creation and
production of *Thus Spoke Zarathustra* to the gestation period undergone by the female elephant—"we get eighteen months for the
pregnancy" (295). Finally, the author underwent a "sudden birth
that occurred in February 1883 under the most improbable circumstances," that is, exactly at the moment of Richard Wagner's death
in Venice. Notice also how Nietzsche emphasizes the "sudden and
profoundly decisive change in [his] taste" (295) at the onset of the
"pregnancy" in mid-1881, just as newly pregnant women are believed to experience new and sudden cravings. Nietzsche's musical
taste especially undergoes transformation, is followed by "a rebirth
of the art of *hearing*." Music is for Nietzsche what reading is for
Augustine. Just as Augustine undergoes illumination and trans-

figuration through a process of reading alterity which returns him to the state of *infans*—the speechless, totally dependent creature—thus making him *disponible* and all ears for the Other, Nietzsche develops a new art of hearing, but in his case it is the acute ability to listen to himself become the begetter of words and the words themselves: midwife, mother, and child.

Metaphors of pregnancy and birth are extremely common in Nietzsche, so common that Derrida, for one, has called him "le penseur de la grossesse [the thinker of pregnancy]."[29] Here again, we can say that he is emulating his "enemy," Socrates, who performed the ancient art of midwifery, except that Socrates helped other people with the birthing of their thoughts. Moreover, Socrates insists that only those individuals who can no longer give birth become midwives (*Theaetetus*, 149–51), whereas Nietzsche is the pregnant one and the midwife at the same time, a rather circular and solitary predicament. Caught between solipsism and universalism, Nietzsche stresses the tripartite *female* nature of his being, thus parodying the *male* Trinity: Father, Son, and Holy Spirit. But as he says, "On every metaphor you ride to every truth" (301), and in these images of pregnancy and midwifery lies his whole conception of creativity—a conception, therefore, that owes much to Socrates' discussion of the topic in the *Theaetetus*. The body is the source of the begetting—the work—and the self-reading is the maieutic interpretation, which helps in the total process of (pro)creation. This procreative self-interpretation is an effort to avoid the silence that would follow the experience of creating a new language for people who have no ear for it. For if "a book speaks of nothing but events that lie altogether beyond the possibility of any frequent or even rare experiences . . . nothing will be heard, but there will be the acoustic illusion that where nothing is heard, nothing is there" (*EH* 261). The originality of Nietzsche's experience, then, is that of giving the world a "first language for a new series of experiences" (261), a language that makes visible those very things for which we would not otherwise have eyes. That is why in the *Gay Science* (¶261) Nietzsche defines originality as the ability "*to see* something that has no name as yet and hence cannot be mentioned although it stares us all in the face. The way men usually are, it takes a name to make

[29]Derrida, *Spurs/Eperons: Nietzsche's Styles*, trans. Barbara Harlow (Chicago: University of Chicago Press, 1978), p. 64.

something visible for them.—Those with originality have for the most part also assigned names" (218).

If his readers cannot be trusted with the ability *to see* and give meaning to this new series of experiences with which his works confront them, then he must be both mother and father, must give birth *and* have the prerogative of naming, since this is the only way to avoid the silence of ignorance. He has the responsibility to put into words, narrate, explicate the means by which he has come to understand himself as the "first *tragic philosopher*" (273) or, put another way, *the* philosopher who can negate being and affirm becoming, in order to redeem the past and the future:

> Zarathustra once defines, quite strictly, his task—it is mine too—and there is no mistaking his meaning: he says Yes to the point of justifying, of redeeming all of the past. "I walk among men as among the fragments of the future—that future which I envisage. And this is all my creating and striving, that I create and carry together into One what is fragment and riddle and dreadful accident. And how could I bear to be a man if man were not also a creator and guesser of riddles and redeemer of accidents? *To redeem those who lived in the past* and to turn every 'it was' into a 'thus I willed it'—that alone should I call redemption" (*EH* 308–9).[30]

This form of redemption is the basic theme of *amor fati*, or eternal return, the inescapable links between past and future, which must be *named* to be recognized and affirmed. The difficulty is that even such a naming does not guarantee that Nietzsche will be heard or understood, for the solipsistic gesture involved in raising the stakes at every confrontation between opposing concepts (or historical figures or contemporary "good-natured canaille" [323]) is bound to devalue the intensity of the hyperbole. And indeed, the last section of *Ecce Homo*, "Why I Am a Destiny," ends on the hysterical repeti-

[30]With these words, Carl Pletsch has said, "Nietzsche illuminates not only his concept of personal life as *amor fati*, but his authorship as well. His writings are fragments, riddles, and dreadful accidents redeemed by his Dionysian mission of raising the chaos of life from falsehood to the status of opportunity . . . to impose his own meaning upon the chaos—the chaos of his writings as well as the chaos of life." See "The Self-Sufficient Text in Nietzsche and Kierkegaard," *Yale French Studies* 66 (1984), 181. What I want to underline more specifically here is that Nietzsche views the re-membering of fragments of the past as redemptive of chaos—past chaos and future chaos: anamnesis and utopia.

tion of the phrase "Have I been understood?" and with the infinite regression of the "*folie circulaire*" (334) against which Nietzsche raises his pen and his voice, but in the wake of which he must needs become the other face of the same Janus, his doppelgänger. Wishing as he does to overthrow the idols, he leaves himself open to the vampirism of those moralists who would suck "the blood of life itself" (334) from his corpus. His oppositional stance makes him fall back on the very ground he is attempting to undermine.

Wanting to distinguish himself from Socrates and the philosophical tradition of objectivity and universality, Nietzsche constantly resists any form of dogmatic self-effacement that might suggest that his writings offer some form of universal truth. Instead, he gives us strident or hyperbolic statements that force the reader to take stock of what is actually being said, to get some distance from it, to be provoked into thinking for him- or herself. This is the "essence" of perspectivism, in that it forces one to question the origin and the ground on which beliefs and opinions are based, to rediscover "that nethermost self which had, as it were, been buried and grown silent under the continual pressure of having to listen to other selves (and that is after all what reading means)" (*EH* 287–88). To read and listen to other thinkers who would do your thinking for you is thus to become selfless in the worst possible way, to lose all "instinct of self-defense" (253), all ability to nurture your own thoughts and to cultivate and protect your (pro)creation.

Already in "Why I Am So Clever," Nietzsche had given his view of what reading means for a thinker: it is "recreation from [his] own seriousness" but, by the same token, must be avoided when he is "hard at work" (242): "Has it been noted that in that profound tension to which pregnancy condemns the spirit, and at bottom the whole organism, chance and any kind of stimulus from the outside have too vehement an effect and strike too deep? . . . a kind of walling oneself in belongs among the foremost instinctive precautions of spiritual pregnancy. Should I permit an alien thought to scale the wall secretly?—And that is what reading would mean. The periods of work and fertility are followed by periods of recreation: come to me, pleasant, brilliant, clever books" (242). Creativity and reading are two closely related phenomena, as are cultural creativity and biological procreation. They must avoid competing or interfering with each other. Ideas and books offer themselves like "sea animals" brought up in a net or on a fishhook from the depths of memory (290). Each thought is to some degree determined by its place of birth, and that is why Nietzsche situates the "origin" of each of his books in the geographical space, the *topos* where he was inspired to write each one of the books. *The Birth of Tragedy* was begun before the walls of the city of Metz, "amid the thunder of the battle of Wörth" (270), when Nietzsche was working as a medical orderly; *Human, All Too Human* is linked to the first Bayreuther Festspiele; *Dawn*, to the coast of Genoa; *Thus Spoke Zarathustra*, to Sils-Maria, Rapallo, Genoa, Rome, and Nice and Eze (both of which had been part of Italy until 1860); *Twilight of the Idols*, to the Upper Engadine and Turin, where Nietzsche would reside from then on.

There is a specific geographical body linked to the creation of the corpus, and we will see in Marie Cardinal and Marie-Thérèse Humbert's works a specific assimilation of the female body *and* the textual corpus to Algeria and Mauritius, respectively. With Maya Angelou it is the nomadic and picaresque wanderings of the "heroine" which will be opposed to the enclosed and nurturing places where the "writer" becomes able to create: her grandmother's store and the library. For Condé's narrator, exile to France and Africa allegorizes the alienating impossibility of being grounded and nurtured by a specific physical, geographic environment and the mimetic illusions of false returns to mythic places of origin. Her predicament exemplifies the sterility of lost and severed connections. Anthropological field research allows Zora Neale Hurston to collect information on her lost "siblings" of the African diaspora and to reestablish lost connections. Using that information, she creates an autobiographical self that, Chapter 3 will argue, owes much to Nietzschean notions of genealogy and ethnicity.

Part II
Creating a Tradition

There is no theory that is not a fragment, carefully prepared, of some autobiography.

Paul Valéry

To read a narrative that depicts the journey of a female self striving to become the subject of her own discourse, the narrator of her
own story, is to witness the unfolding of an autobiographical project. To raise the question of referentiality and ask whether the text
points to an individual existence beyond the pages of the book is
to distort the picture: as Picasso once said about his portrait of
Gertrude Stein, although she was not exactly like it, she would
eventually become so. The ability to "defamiliarize" ordinary experience, forcing us to notice what we live with but ignore, has long
been considered an important characteristic of art. Such is the
Russian formalists' notion of *ostraneniye*, or "making strange," the
surrealists' dream of a heightened level of awareness, Nathalie
Sarraute's "era of suspicion." New ways of seeing can indeed emancipate us. Literature, like all art, can show us new means of con-
structing the world, for it is by changing the images and structures
through which we encode meaning that we can begin to develop
new scripts and assign new roles to the heroines of the stories we
recount in order to explain and understand our lives.

The female writer who struggles to articulate a personal vision
and to verbalize the vast areas of feminine experience which have
remained unexpressed, if not repressed, is engaged in an attempt to
excavate those elements of the female self which have been buried
under the cultural and patriarchal myths of selfhood. She perceives
these myths as alienating and radically other, and her aim is often
the retrieval of a more authentic image—one that may not ostensibly be "true" or "familiar" at first, since our ways of perceiving are so
subtly conditioned by our social and historical circumstance and
since our collective imagination is so overwhelmingly non-female.
Having no literary tradition that empowers her to speak, she seeks

to elaborate discursive patterns that will both reveal the "hidden face of Eve" and displace the traditional distinctions of rigidly defined literary genres. Formulating a problematics of female authorship is thus an urgent task for feminist writers and one that they approach with much ambivalence.[1]

Theorists of autobiography have traditionally assumed with Roy Pascal that we read autobiographies "not as factual truth, but as a wrestling with truth."[2] In their attempt at selective grouping of first-person narratives, however, theorists have largely failed to "take hold of autobiography's protean forms," as Avrom Fleishman puts it.[3] And feminist critics in particular have been quick to suggest that "any theoretical model *indifferent* to a problematics of genre as inflected by gender" must needs be regarded as suspect.[4] Since it is notoriously difficult for women to recognize ourselves in the traditional images that literature and society (sometimes including our own mothers) project or uphold as models, it should not be surprising for an autobiographical narrative to proclaim itself as fiction: for the narrator's process of reflection, narration, and self-integration within language is bound to unveil patterns of self-definition (and self-dissimulation) which may seem new and strange and with which we are not always consciously familiar. The self engendered on the page allows a writer to subject a great deal of her ordinary experience to new scrutiny and to show that the polarity fact/fiction does not establish and constitute absolute categories of feeling and perceiving reality. The narrative text epitomizes this duality in its splitting of the subject of discourse into a narrating self and an experiencing self which can never coincide exactly. Addressing the

[1] I borrow the quoted phrase from the book by Nawal El Saadawi, *The Hidden Face of Eve: Women in the Arab World* (London: Zed Press, 1980).

[2] Roy Pascal, *Design and Truth in Autobiography* (Cambridge: Harvard University Press, 1960), p. 75. But see also Elizabeth W. Bruss, *Autobiographical Acts: The Changing Situation of a Literary Genre* (Baltimore: Johns Hopkins University Press, 1976); James Olney, *Metaphors of Self: The Meaning of Autobiography* (Princeton: Princeton University Press, 1972), and Olney, ed. *Autobiography: Essays Theoretical and Critical* (Princeton: Princeton University Press, 1980); Philippe Lejeune, *Le Pacte autobiographique* (Paris: Seuil, 1975), and *Je est un autre* (Paris: Seuil, 1980).

[3] Avrom Fleishman, *Figures of Autobiography: The Language of Self-Writing in Victorian and Modern England* (Berkeley: University of California Press, 1983), p. 37.

[4] Nancy K. Miller, "Writing Fictions: Women's Autobiography in France," *Life/Lines: Theorizing Women's Autobiography*, ed. Bella Brodzki and Celeste Schenck (Ithaca: Cornell University Press, 1988), p. 47.

problematics of authorship, the female narrator gets caught in a duplicitous process: she exists in the text under circumstances of alienated communication because the text is the locus of her dialogue with a tradition she tacitly aims to subvert.[5] Describing the events that have helped her assume a given heritage, she communicates with a narratee who figures in a particular kind of relationship both with her as narrator and with their shared cultural environment. By examining the narrative structure through these constitutive relational patterns, we can elicit from the text a model of reading which does not betray its complicated and duplicitous messages.

For example, Maya Angelou dedicates her first volume of autobiographical writings to her son, focusing on the difficult relationship between writing and mothering which is at the center of all feminist inquiries into the nature of creativity. The conflict between these roles is all too often a source of paralyzing guilt for the creative artist, as Tillie Olsen, Adrienne Rich, and Alice Walker have convincingly shown.[6] Marie Cardinal, on the other hand, dedicates her novel to the "doctor who helped [her] be born," and he is the explicit listener of her life story.[7] As such, his role is clear, but the text also encodes his presence as a catalyst whose function is not only to facilitate access to the narrator's effaced, forgotten, joyful "Algerian" self but also to mediate the reader's understanding of the story being told in the book, the "histoire racontée à du papier."[8] Marie-Thérèse Humbert's narrator wrestles with an impossible relationship to a twin sister who is a figure for the effaced and repressed

[5]The problematics and anxieties of authorship are brilliantly analyzed by Sandra M. Gilbert and Susan Gubar in *The Madwoman in the Attic: The Woman Writer and the Nineteenth-Century Literary Imagination* (New Haven: Yale University Press, 1979), pp. 45–92.

[6]See Tillie Olsen, *Silences* (New York: Delacorte Press, 1978); Adrienne Rich, *Of Woman Born: Motherhood as Experience and Institution* (New York: Norton, 1976); and Alice Walker, *In Search of Our Mothers' Gardens* (New York: Harcourt Brace Jovanovich, 1983).

[7]Marie Cardinal, *Les Mots pour le dire* (Paris: Grasset et Fasquelle, 1975). English translation by Pat Goodheart, *The Words to Say It* (Cambridge, Mass.: VanVactor and Goodheart, 1983).

[8]*Les Mots pour le dire*, p. 266–67. The story as told to the paper: this phrase recalls Montaigne's "mémoire de papier," his well-known need to "parler au papier." See Michel de Montaigne, "De l'utile et de l'honneste," *Oeuvres complètes* (Paris: Gallimard/La Pléiade, 1962), p. 767, "Of the Useful and the Honorable," *The Complete Works of Montaigne*, trans. Donald Frame (Stanford: Stanford University Press, 1948), p. 599.

other in her. Through this double, whose untimely death releases her, she comes to an acceptance of her privileged position at the intersection of different colonial cultures and recognizes the values of creolization, *métissage*, and transculturation. Relationships with parental figures, lovers, siblings, or offspring provide the important structuring elements of the narratives of all of these writers, revealing complex modes of interaction between familial and social contexts, the personal and the political, the textual and the historical. The tradition these women writers have begun to create is informed both by the systematic recovery of occulted histories and the utopian visionary power with which they unsettle our all-too-complacent notions about the present and the future.

Zora Neale Hurston's training as an anthropologist influences the way she looks at the complex system of human relations that constitute culture. Her autobiography makes use of the formal descriptive paradigms of anthropological research, becoming a self-portrait of the fieldworker in search of her own roots, her own siblings, her lost ancestral traditions, her veiled maternal heritage. Unlike the fixation on the past of Maryse Condé's narrator, which turns into a pathological flight from the political realities of life in her own country, Hurston's focus on the New World shows her sophisticated understanding of the transformations ancient African culture has undergone through the slave trade. Condé's Véronica is an ambiguous victim who identifies with the oppressor, much as her Europeanized father admires the values of French culture. To rebel against her father's self-defeating dressage of the mind, she first uses the only weapon she has: her body. But she thus manages to exchange one form of colonization for another, and remains a profoundly ambivalent and recalcitrant daughter of Africa.[9]

As they recover the past, women writers have to confront the images and stereotypes that have limited their choices. They must retrace the narrow paths along which the female heroine of literature has been allowed to walk. But they must also attempt to find new and empowering directions for themselves and their literary heirs. For all these writers, the personal and the political, the text, its contexts, and its intertextual elements are always interrelated; that is

[9]See Jonathan Ngaté, "Maryse Condé and Africa: The Making of a Recalcitrant Daughter?" *A Current Bibliography on African Affairs* 19 (1986–87), 5–20.

why these writers do not attempt to create new directions out of totally new cloth: they understand that our perceptions of ourselves are strongly influenced by the past, and they seek to focus our attention on the different kinds of heroines the (male) literary tradition has provided. Weaving the threads of old stories into new images of their own, women make their texts into a *métissage* of voices and textures. Hurston rebels against the patriarchal folk customs of her village; Maya Angelou rewrites the picaresque tale from a black feminist point of view; Marie-Thérèse Humbert creates twin sisters who represent, on a superficial level, the conventional romantic and tragic heroines of Bildungsromane. Against the distortions of the languages we speak and the literature we have been trained to consider "good" by our literary fathers, Marie Cardinal articulates the difficult process of coming to language, of becoming a writing subject. She spells out the deadening internalization of patriarchal rules of literary production, which continues to plague women writers. By showing the arbitrary nature of these standards, she undermines the conventions of genre and the concept of *patrie*, or nationality. Hurston goes a step farther: by reclaiming the Afro-Asiatic roots of Greek mythology she subverts all narrow appeal to an unproblematic "Western" tradition. Condé's use of the techniques of free direct and indirect discourse allows her to dramatize the impasses of realist representations.

The alienation women writers experience in creating a new tradition is reinforced by the difficulty they have in defining their audience, a difficulty compounded in the case of *métis* women, who write in a standard language but hope to transmit a vision molded and enriched by their vernacular customs. On one level, Angelou, for example, writes for white readers; but on another, she gestures toward the black community and "signifies" upon an established Afro-American mode of presenting truths and untruths. Because of the nature of (white) literary patronage during the Harlem Renaissance, Hurston had to perform her own self-censorship, evidenced in the gaps and the unsaid of her autobiography. Condé's representation of the colonized mentality continues to unsettle readers everywhere. Véronica can be seen as a self-indulgent character with no political sophistication of any kind, but if *Heremakhonon* is read as a political allegory in which Véronica is a figure a for the collective unconscious of the people of Guadeloupe, the narrative takes on new dimensions and reveals a complex network of relationships of dominance. This network contributes to the infantilization of a people who do not have the right to self-determination despite a seemingly democratic system of government. Finally, with Humbert, we have a kind of nonresolution of the double vision, since her book can be read by different audiences either as best-selling romance or as complex self-portrait of the writer as web maker and storyteller.

As the following discussions show, all the women writers draw on many diverse heritages while remaining unsure about the relative value of their conflicting backgrounds. As they emancipate themselves from the established codes that constrain them, most go through a process of healing and reconciliation which takes them beyond *ressentiment*, thus allowing them to build bridges between cultures and to further the "pratique de *métissage*" for which Glissant calls.[10]

[10]Edouard Glissant, *Le Discours antillais* (Paris: Seuil, 1981), p. 462.

3
Autoethnography:
The An-Archic Style of
Dust Tracks on a Road

> One is an artist at the cost of regarding that which all non-
> artists call "form" as content, as "the matter itself." To be
> sure, then one belongs in a topsy-turvy world: for hence-
> forth content becomes something merely formal—our life
> included.
>
> Nietzsche, 1888

> The words do not count. . . . The tune is the unity of the
> thing.
>
> Zora Neale Hurston, 1942

> The greatness of a man is to be found not in his acts but in
> his style.
>
> Frantz Fanon, 1952

One need only glance at the table of contents of Hurston's autobiography to notice that it presents itself as a set of interactive
thematic *topoi* superimposed on a loosely chronological framework.
The seemingly linear progression from "My Birthplace" to "Looking
Things Over" is more deceptive in that regard than truly indicative
of a narrator's psychological development, quest for recognition, or
journey from innocence to experience as traditionally represented in
confessional autobiographies. The chapter titled "Seeing the World
as It Is," with which Hurston originally meant to conclude the
book,[1] is a philosophical essay on power, politics, and human relations on a planetary scale. It is the radical testament of a writer who
rejects *ressentiment* and, refusing to align herself with any "party,"
explains that it is because she does "not have much of a herd instinct" (344–45). Rather than recounting the events of her life,
Hurston is more interested in showing us who she is—or, to be
more precise, how she has become what she is— an individual who
ostensibly values her independence more than any kind of political

[1]See Robert Hemenway's comments in Appendix to *Dust Tracks on a Road*, ed.
Hemenway, 2d ed. (Urbana: University of Illinois Press, 1984), p. 288. All references
will be included in the text and flagged *DT* when necessary.

commitment to a cause, especially the cause of "Race Solidarity," as she puts it (327). Hers is a controversial and genealogical enterprise that has been much criticized, charged with accommodationism (xxxviii) and with disappointing the expectations of "frankness" and "truthfulness" which are all too often unquestioningly linked to this genre of self-writing.[2] Openly critical of *Dust Tracks* in his Introduction to the second edition, her biographer, Robert Hemenway, puts it thus: "Style . . . becomes a kind of camouflage, an escape from articulating the paradoxes of her personality" (xxxviii and see xxxiv–xxxv, for example).

An-archy and Community

In light of the skepticism with which contemporary literary theory has taught us to view any effort of self-representation in language, I would like to propose a different approach to the issue of Hurston's presumed insincerity and untrustworthiness.[3] It may perhaps be more useful to reconsider *Dust Tracks on a Road* not as autobiography but rather as self-portrait, in the sense redefined by Michel Beaujour—"des textes qui se tiennent par eux-mêmes, plutôt que la mimesis d'actions passées"[4]—and to try to elaborate a conceptual framework that would not conflict with Hurston's own avowed

[2]By *genealogical* I mean the reconstruction of the self through interpretations that integrate as many aspects of the past as are deemed *significant* by the agent of the narrative discourse. It is clear that Hurston considers cultural forms more significant than specific events. Thus, the self she fashions through language is not a fixed essence, partaking of an immutable and originary racial substance. Rather, it is a *process* of active self-discovery through self-invention by means of the folk narratives of ethnic interest. For a recent thorough and definitive analysis of these Nietzschean questions, see Alexander Nehamas, *Nietzsche: Life as Literature* (Cambridge: Harvard University Press, 1986). David Hoy has done an excellent and useful review of this book: see "Different Stories" in *London Review of Books*, Jan. 8, 1987, pp. 15–17. In the Afro-American context, genealogical revisionism is of course a common theme of literature. See Kimberly W. Benston, "'I Yam What I Yam': Naming and Unnaming in Afro-American Literature," *Black American Literature Forum* 16 (Spring 1982); as well as Jahnheinz Jahn, *Muntu: An Outline of the New African Culture* (New York: Grove Press, 1961), p. 125.

[3]For an overview of contemporary theories of autobiography, see Paul John Eakin, *Fictions in Autobiography: Studies in the Art of Self-Invention* (Princeton: Princeton University Press, 1985), chap. 4 in particular.

[4]Michel Beaujour, *Miroirs d'encre* (Paris: Seuil, 1980), p. 348: "texts which are self-contained rather than being the representation of past actions." All translations are mine.

methodology as essayist and anthropologist. Indeed, what I would like to suggest here is that *Dust Tracks* amounts to autoethnography, that is, the defining of one's subjective ethnicity as mediated through language, history, and ethnographical analysis; in short, that the book amounts to a kind of "figural anthropology" of the self.[5]

In a recent essay, James Clifford refers to the "allegory of salvage," which generally tended to dominate the representational practice of fieldworkers in the era of Boasian anthropology. For these fieldworkers, says Clifford, the preservation of disappearing cultures and vanishing lore was seen as the vital "redemption" of the "otherness" of primitive cultures from a global entropy: "The other is lost, in disintegrating time and place, but saved in the text."[6] This textualization of the object of representation incorporated a move from the oral-discursive field experience of the collector of folklore to his or her written version of that initial intersubjective moment—a transcription that is also a way of speaking *for* the other culture, a kind of ventriloquism. Having been trained under Boas, Hurston was supposed to be going in the field to do just that: to salvage her own "vanishing" Negro culture. Her position of fundamental liminality—being at once a participant in and an observer of her culture—would bring home to her the distorting effects of that problematic shift from orality to fixed, rigid textuality and thus would reinforce her skepticism about the anthropological project, in her assigned role as detached, objective interpreter and translator. Having shared in that rural culture during her childhood in Eatonville, she could not adopt the nostalgic pose common to those Western ethnographies that implicitly lament the loss of an Edenic, and pre-industrial past. Instead, her skepticism about the writing of culture would permeate the writing of the self, the autobiography, turning

[5]This phrase is used by Michel Serres in *The Parasite*, trans. Lawrence R. Schehr (Baltimore: Johns Hopkins University Press, 1982), p. 6. The French phrase is "une anthropologie figurée." See *Le Parasite* (Paris: Grasset, 1980), p. 13. See also Alexander Gelley, *Narrative Crossings: Theory and Pragmatics of Prose Fiction* (Baltimore: Johns Hopkins University Press, 1987), pp. 79–100, for a useful discussion of "parasitic talk" and narrative agency, cultural norms, and quotidian talk applied to Melville's *Confidence-Man*.

[6]James Clifford, "On Ethnographic Allegory," *Writing Culture: The Poetics and Politics of Ethnography*, ed. Clifford and George E. Marcus (Berkeley: University of California Press, 1986), pp. 98–121 (112).

it into the allegory of an ethnographic project that self-consciously moves from the general (the history of Eatonville) to the particular (Zora's life, her family and friends) and back to the general (religion, culture, and world politics in the 1940s). Unlike black spiritual auto-biographies, which exhibit a similar threefold pattern of death, conversion, and rebirth, as well as a strong sense of transcendent purpose, *Dust Tracks* does not seek to legitimate itself through appeal to what William L. Andrews has called a "powerful source of authorization," such as religion or another organized system of belief.[7] It is in that sense that *Dust Tracks* is a powerfully an-archic work, not anchored in any original and originating story of racial or sexual difference.

The tone of the work and its rhetorical strategy of exaggeration draw attention to its style and away from what it directly denotes. For example, the statement "There were no discrete nuances of life on Joe Clarke's porch . . . all emotions were naked and nakedly arrived at" (62) describes the men's reactions to instances of adultery (a folksy topic), but it also carries historical implications about the pioneer spirit in general, as the sentence that follows it makes clear: "This was the spirit of that whole new part of the state at the time, as it always is where men settle new lands" (62). Similarly, when Zora talks about her unhappy love affair, it is through vivid images that convey, with some irony, the universality of pain rather than deep personal anguish: "I freely admit that everywhere I set my feet down, there were tracks of blood. Blood from the very middle of my heart" (260). Regretting the "halcyon days" of childhood, she bemoans the gravity that pervades adulthood and makes us unable to "fly with the unseen things that soar" (78). And when she is discussing race, her denial—"No, instead of Race Pride being a virtue, it is a sapping vice" (325)—implicates us directly in that seemingly volatile statement instead of pointing us to the obvious historical context of the moment, that is, the rise of fascism, World War II, colonialism, the hypocrisy and self-satisfaction of "the blond brother" (343), and the preponderance of "instances of human self-bias" (281).

[7]See William L. Andrews, ed. *Sisters of the Spirit: Three Black Women's Autobiographies in the Nineteenth Century* (Bloomington: Indiana University Press, 1986), p. 13. To say that Hurston is not interested in *organized* resistance to patterns of social injustice is not to imply that she is not strongly critical of injustice. See pp. 336–45.

Clearly, *Dust Tracks* does not gesture toward a coherent tradition of introspective self-examination with soul-baring displays of emotion.

Paradoxically, despite its rich cultural content, the work does not authorize unproblematic recourse to culturally grounded interpretations. It is an orphan text that attempts to create its own genealogy by simultaneously appealing to and debunking the cultural traditions it helps to redefine. Hurston's chosen objects of study, for example, the folktales that come alive during the storytelling, or "lying," sessions she observes, are indeed never "fixed." Their content is not rigid and unchanging but varies according to the tale-telling situation. It is the contextual frame of reference, the situation of the telling, that determines how a tale is reinterpreted by each new teller; hence, for the anthropologist, there is no "essential" quality to be isolated in the content of those tales, but there is a formal structure that can and must be recognized if she is to make sense of, and do justice to, the data gathered. The chapter titled "Research" puts the matter clearly and succinctly:

> I enjoyed collecting folk-tales and I believed the people from whom I collected them enjoyed the telling of them, just as much as I did the hearing. Once they got started, the "lies" just rolled and story-tellers fought for a chance to talk. It was the same thing with the songs. *The one thing to be guarded against, in the interest of truth, was over-enthusiasm. For instance, if the song was going good, and the material ran out, the singer was apt to interpolate pieces of other songs into it.* The only way you can know when that happens, is to know your material so well that you can sense the violation. Even if you do not know the song that is being used for padding, you can tell the change in rhythm and tempo. *The words do not count. The subject matter in Negro folk-songs can be anything* and go from love to work, to travel, to food, to weather, to fight, to demanding the return of a wig by a woman who has turned unfaithful. *The tune is the unity of the thing.* And you have to know what you are doing when you begin to pass on that, because Negroes can fit in more words and leave out more and still keep the tune better than anyone I can think of. [197–98; my italics].

The whole issue of form and content, style and message is astutely condensed here. "Truth" is clearly a matter of degree and can easily be distorted by the over-enthusiasm of the performer. If *over-enthusi-*

asm can be seen as another word for hyperbole, then Hurston the writer is hereby cautioning her own reader to defer judgment about the explicit referentiality of her text. Why come to it with precon- ceived notions of autobiographical truth when the tendency to make hyperbolic and over-enthusiastic statements about her subject mat- ter is part of her "style" as a writer? Couldn't we see in this passage Hurston's own implicit theory of reading and thus use it to derive our interpretive practice from the text itself, instead of judging the work according to Procrustean notions of autobiographical form?

Hurston is fully aware of the gaps and discrepancies that can exist between intention and execution, reality and representation, reason and imagination, in short, between the words (or subject matter) and the tune, which is the source of unity for the singers on the porch. For her, too, the flow of creative energy is an imaginative transfiguration of literal truth/content through rhetorical proce- dures. The resulting text/performance thus transcends pedestrian notions of referentiality, for the staging of the event is part of the process of "passing on," of elaborating cultural forms, which are not static and inviolable but dynamically involved in the creation of culture itself. It is thus not surprising that Hurston should view the self, and especially the "racial self," as a fluid and changing concept, an arbitrary signifier with which she had better dispense if it is meant to inhibit (as any kind of reductive labeling might) the inher- ent plasticity of individuals.[8] Viewed from such an angle, *Dust*

---

[8]This is not the place to engage in a detailed analysis of the methods and assump- tions of Hurston's great teacher and mentor, "Papa" Franz Boas. Suffice it to say that as an anthropologist he was a firm believer in "the plasticity of human types": his research for his book *Changes in Bodily Forms of Descendants of Immigrants*, published in 1911, served to convince him that physical and mental characteristics were not simply inherited but profoundly modified by time and environment. Furthermore, the views expressed in his essay "The Race Problem in Modern Society," published in a work that was to be widely influential and of fundamental importance to the field of anthropology, *The Mind of Primitive Man*, could not fail to influence Zora Neale Hurston's own attitudes about the race problem in America, to reinforce her personal tendency toward individualism, and to strengthen her belief that human beings are infinitely variable and not classifiable into distinctive national or racial categories. As Boas puts it, "Our tendency to evaluate an individual according to the picture that we form of the class to which we assign him, although he may not feel any inner connection with that class, is a survival of primitive forms of thought. The character- istics of the members of the class are highly variable and the type that we construct from the most frequent characteristics supposed to belong to the class is never more than an abstraction hardly ever realized in a single individual, often not even a result

Tracks, far from being a "camouflage" and an "escape," does indeed *exemplify* the "paradoxes of her personality" by revealing a fluid and multidimensional self that refuses to allow itself to be framed and packaged for the benefit of those human, all-too-human mortals, "both black and white who [claim] special blessings on the basis of race" (235).

Indeed, in the case of the folkloric forms she studies, the plasticity of the "subject matter" of songs and tales is corroborated by her research experience in the field; if we can be justified in seeing the "subject" of the autobiography and the "subject matter" of folklore as homologous structures or *topoi* that reflect and mirror each other, then the dialogue between these homologies shapes the auto-biographical text while revealing the paradoxes of the genre. This dialogue serves to illuminate Hurston's combined identities as an-thropologist and writer as these simultaneously begin to emerge and to converge in *Dust Tracks.* In the process of articulating their differences, she actually establishes their inescapable similarities, prefiguring the practice of such theorists as Clifford Geertz or Victor Turner. As Hemenway rightly points out, "Zora never became a professional academic folklorist because such a vocation was alien to her exuberant sense of self, to her admittedly artistic, sometimes erratic temperament, and to her awareness of the esthetic content of black folklore."[9] But this psychologizing approach does not suffice to clarify the work and to explain Hurston's liminal position, her confident straddling of "high" (academic) and "low" (folk) cultures, the ease with which she brings to the theoretical enterprise of the academic collector of lore the insights and perceptivity of the teller of tales. What makes the autobiography interesting is that it unfolds the structures of meaning—the cultural "topics" that are discussed chapter by chapter (history, geography, mythology, kinship, educa-tion, work, travel, friendship, love, religion, politics, philosophy,

---

of observation, but an often heard tradition that determines our judgment" (344) (from a selection from *The Mind of Primitive Man,* 1911, reprinted in Ashley Montagu, *Frontiers of Anthropology* [New York: Putnam's, 1974], pp. 332–44.) Boas recognizes the role played by "tradition" and ideology in our construction of the world, and his work paves the way for what I would call Hurston's dynamic and contextual ap-proach to culture and to private forms of behavior.

[9]Robert Hemenway, *Zora Neale Hurston: A Literary Biography* (Urbana: University of Illinois Press, 1980), p. 213.

etc.)—through which the creative artist gives shape to her personal experiences as seen through the "spy-glass" of anthropology.[10]

Moving away from what might be the sterile analyses of a field-worker to the inspirational language of an artist, Hurston involves herself and her reader in a transformative process. She does not just record, describe, and represent; she transforms and is transformed by her autobiographical performance. To look at life from an aesthetic point of view and to celebrate her ethnic heritage are thus two complementary projects for her. Life is an aesthetic experience, a staged performance, reflected in the autobiography as well as the fictional writings, and literature is a means of recording with what Hemenway identifies as "a studied antiscientific approach" the lives and subjective realities of a particular people in a specific time and place.[11] It is this apparently antagonistic movement between life and literature, reality and its representation, orality and literacy, which informs the structural coherence of *Dust Tracks*, rather than the simply linear progression through the lived life. What the text puts in motion is a strategy of displacement regarding the expectations governing two modes of discourse: the "objective" exteriority is that of the autobiographer whose "inside search" does not bear out its promise of introspection, and the "intimate" tone is that of the anthropologist who implicates herself in her "research" by delving into Hoodoo, by performing initiation rites, and in an ironic and clever reversal of the ventriloquism of ethnography, by letting her informants inform *us* about Zora's persona in the field. As Big Sweet puts it, "You ain't like me. You don't even sleep with no mens. . . . I think it's nice for you to be like that. You just keep on writing down them lies" (189).

So, if Hurston sometimes seems to be aspiring toward some kind of "raceless ideal," it is not because she is interested in the "universality" of human experiences. Quite the contrary, she wants to expose, as Hemenway explains, "the inadequacy of sterile reason to deal with the phenomena of living."[12] And "race" in that context is

<hr>

[10]See Zora Neale Hurston, *Mules and Men* (Bloomington: Indiana University Press 1978), p. 3, hereinafter *MM*; and Barbara Johnson, "Thresholds of Difference: Structures of Address in Zora Neale Hurston," in *"Race," Writing, and Difference*, ed. Henry L. Gates, Jr. (Chicago: University of Chicago Press, 1985), pp. 317–28.

[11]Hemenway, p. 213.

[12]Ibid.

but a reasonable, pseudoscientific category for dealing with a basically fluid, diverse, and multifarious reality: "The stuff of my being is matter, ever changing, ever moving, but never lost" (279). Her philosophical position in *Dust Tracks* is in fact echoed more than twenty years later by Frantz Fanon in *The Wretched of the Earth:* "This historical necessity in which the men of African culture find themselves, that is, the necessity to racialize their claims and to speak more of African culture, than of national culture, will lead them up a blind alley." Warning that the undefined and vague entity "African culture" was a creation of European colonialism, Fanon chose to emphasize local historically and geographically specific contingencies, rather than "race" as a general and abstract concept: "And it is also true that those who are most responsible for this racialization of thought—or at least of our patterns of thought—are and remain those Europeans who have never ceased to set up white culture over and against all other so-called non-cultures [d'opposer la culture blanche aux autres incultures]."[13] Similarly, Hurston's interest in the folk communities of Eatonville, Polk County, Mobile, New Orleans, Nassau, Jamaica, and Haiti stemmed from the belief that the universal can only be known through the specific and that knowledge grounded in first-hand experience can yield more insights into the human condition and into the processes of acculturation, differentiation, and historicization to which human beings are subjected. I would thus argue that her unstated aim is identical to Fanon's later formulation: to destroy the white stereotype of black *inculture* not by privileging "blackness" as an oppositional category to "whiteness" in culture but by unequivocally showing the vitality and diversity of nonwhite cultures around the Caribbean and the coastal areas of the South, thereby dispensing completely with "white" as a concept and a point of reference. Unlike the proponents of the negritude movement, whose initial thrust was against white racism and prejudice, Hurston assumes the supremely confident posture of the anthropologist who need not *justify* the validity of her enterprise but can simply *affirm* by her study the existence of richly varied black cultures, thus delineating the semiotics of spaces where, in Houston

[13]Frantz Fanon, *The Wretched of the Earth,* trans. Constance Farrington (New York: Grove Press, 1968), p. 214. (I have modified the translation of both quotations.) *Les Damnés de la terre* (Paris: Maspéro, 1968), p. 146. The word *inculture* is practically untranslatable into English.

Baker's words, "white culture's representations are squeezed to zero volume, producing a new expressive order."[14]

What must not be overlooked, therefore, in the passage I quoted from "Research" is the emphasis Hurston puts on contextual considerations and the implicit distinctions she then draws between her own position as anthropologist observing the event and the role of the singers directly involved in the performance. For example, it is important for the anthropologist—and for the literary critic attempting to model her approach on Hurston's—to know the "material," that is, to be steeped in the historical, geographical, and vernacular contexts of the "songs" in order to be able to determine where "pieces of other songs" are "interpolated" and used as "padding" when the original material "ran out." Does Hurston imply that there is a certain autonomy of the original text which is violated by the interpolation of fragments of other songs? It would seem, rather, that as an anthropologist she feels that it is important to make those kinds of distinctions; yet she recognizes that for the singers the question is unimportant. The song goes on; the participants collectively "keep the tune" and do not worry about the singularity or inviolability of a given text or song. In other words, the question of intertextuality or of hybridization of content is not significant for the artists (they do not see it as a transgression of rules of identity), however important it may be for the observer who wants to be able to determine where one particular song ends and the next one starts. The question of boundaries is thus raised and examined by the anthropologist while the artist in her recognizes both the futility of such conceptual distinctions and how severely limiting it is to try to establish the "true" identity and originality of the subject matter— or of authorial subjectivity, permeated as it is by the polyphonic voices of the community, which resonate throughout the text and thereby reflect different narrative stances, different points of view on life and on Zora herself.[15] Indeed, since "no two moments are

[14]See Houston A. Baker, Jr., *Blues, Ideology, and Afro-American Literature: A Vernacular Theory* (Chicago: University of Chicago Press, 1984), p. 152.

[15]See Claudine Raynaud, "*Dust Tracks on a Road*: Autobiography as a 'Lying' Session," forthcoming in *Studies in Black American Literature* (Penkevill Annuals). Whereas Raynaud tends to see the autobiography as founding the self in a gesture of appropriation of the perennial proverbs and sayings of the community, I prefer to see in the text a continuing tension between philosophical skepticism about communal values and visionary creation.

any more alike than two snowflakes" (264), there is no inconsistency in presenting a multitude of personae and being nonetheless sincere. As a folk aphorism puts it, "Li'l flakes make de deepest snow," or what appears to be homogeneous is in fact a complicated layering of vastly disparate elements.

The chapter "Seeing the World as It Is" emphasizes Hurston's intentions and method: "I do not wish to close the frontiers of life upon my own self. I do not wish to deny myself the expansion of seeking into individual capabilities and depths by living in a space whose boundaries are race and nation" (330). Clearly, race and nation are singled out here as colonizing signs produced by an essentializing and controlling power ("Race Pride" 324–28) external to the inner self and bent on denying her access to "spaces" other than the ones to which she ostensibly belongs by virtue of her concrete situation. Her free-spirited call for "less race consciousness" (326) is to be understood in the context of her unabashed denunciation of "democracy" as just another name for selfish profiteering by the West at the expense of those "others" who live far away from the so-called democratic nations of Europe and America (338). These subversive and politically anarchic statements—which provoked the Procrustean editing of the autobiography—are the logical consequence of the ethnographer's skepticism. Because she remains radically *critical* without proposing positive and totalizing alternatives, she exemplifies a truly philosophical sensibility.[16] Her urge to ask questions rather than to propose solutions invites and provokes her readers to think beyond the commonplaces and received ideas of

[16]It might perhaps be appropriate to add here that Hurston shows a truly "metaphysical" turn of mind on top of her properly "exegetical" talents! See a reference to the debate between Robert Penn Warren and Sterling Brown in Henry L. Gates, Jr., *Figures in Black: Words, Signs, and the "Racial" Self* (New York: Oxford University Press, 1987), p. xix. And indeed, Fanon takes up the same relay: the last words of *Black Skin, White Masks*, trans. Charles L. Markmann (London: Pluto Press, 1986), (hereinafter BSWM) are "O my body, make me always a man who questions!" (232). It is not likely that Fanon either knew or read Hurston, although he was familiar with the work of Langston Hughes, but their accomplishments in *Dust Tracks on a Road* and *Black Skin, White Masks* derive from a parallel need to shake off the totalizing traps of historical determinism, and to do so in a style that is its own message, narrative and aphoristic in order to subvert the cultural commonplaces they both abhor. See also Chester J. Fontenot's study of Fanon and his useful discussion of form and content in *Black Skin, White Masks*, "Visionaries, Mystics and Revolutionaries: Narrative Postures in Black Fiction," in *Studies in Black American Literature*, ed. Joe Weixlmann and Chester J. Fontenot (Greenwood: Penkevill Annuals, 1983), 1:63–87.

our cultures, beyond those proverbial voices of the community, the vox populi, ouï-dire, Heideggerian *Gerede*, or Barthesian *bêtise*—always rendered in free indirect speech—which enunciate the webs of beliefs that structure local consciousness of self.[17] Reporting those quotidian voices, she establishes cultural context, but by her skeptical detachment, she undermines the gregarious values of the group, whether it is the folk community (involved in "specifying" [186, 304], in "adult double talk" [62], and whose verbal creativity is nonetheless celebrated) or the social consensus that articulates interdictions and contradictions of all sorts ("This book-reading business was a hold-back and an unrelieved evil" [117]; "Not only is the scholastic rating at Howard high, but tea is poured in the manner!" [156]; "If it was so honorable and glorious to be black, why was it the yellow-skinned people among us had so much prestige?" [226]). These "common" values are now made available for parody. She thus opens up a space of resistance between the individual (*auto-*) and the collective (*-ethno-*) where the writing (*-graphy*) of singularity cannot be foreclosed.

Yet, a nagging question remains: how can Hurston's historical, embodied self, subject to the determinants of time and place—an Afro-American woman confronting racism and a world war—represent the site of a privileged resistance to those webs of belief which might encourage resentment and fixation on an unjust and painful past? As she puts it:"To me, bitterness is the under-arm odor of wishful weakness. It is the graceless acknowledgment of defeat" (280). Since both the perpetrators and the immediate victims of slavery are long dead and since she has "no personal memory of those times, and no responsibility for them" (282), she affirms that she would rather "turn all [her] thoughts and energies on the present" (284). This affirmation of life against "the clutching hand of Time" (284) is a creative release from the imposition of origin and the prison of history. Zora becomes a joyful Zarathustra, whose world is no longer limited and bound by the reality principle and who advocates deliverance from the spirit of revenge. But can this visionary posture of the self-portraitist allow for a positive involvement in the

[17]For a detailed discussion of the philosophical and linguistic implications of the "discours indirect libre," see Gilles Deleuze and Félix Guattari, *Mille plateaux* (Paris: Minuit, 1980), pp. 95–109.

shaping of reality, present and future? How can it be reconciled with
the anthropological claim to locally specific knowledge and with the
historical novelist's success in drawing the suggestive allegorical
fresco of a mythic Afro-Mediterranean past in *Moses, Man of the
Mountain*?

Since Fanon, too, denounced revenge and fixation on the past as
"a crystallization of guilt" (*BSWM* 228), perhaps he can provide
some answer to the questions we ask of Hurston. If resentment is
the essence of negative potentiality for the self, it is clear why
Hurston rejects it outright. She wants the utmost freedom in "seeking into individual capabilities." Her refusal to adopt the "herd"
mentality for the sake of solidarity actually places her in a long
tradition of thinkers—Heraclitus, Montaigne, Nietzsche, Walter
Benjamin, Frantz Fanon, and Roland Barthes—all essayists or masters of hyperbolic aphorisms. Fanon, in particular, was well aware
of the peculiarly *racial* dilemma facing the children of the colonialist
diaspora: their marginality could not simply be articulated in terms
of binary categories of black versus white. Fanon's plea against racialist attitudes thus echoes Hurston's reformulation of freedom and
responsibility on a planetary scale:

> I as a man of color do not have the right to hope that in the white man
> there will be a crystallization of guilt toward the past of my race. [228].

> I find myself—I, a man—in a world where words wrap themselves
> in silence; in a world where the other endlessly hardens himself. . . .
> I am not a prisoner of history. I should not seek there for the mean-
> ing of my destiny.
> I should constantly remind myself that the real *leap* consists in intro-
> ducing invention into existence. [229]

> It is through the effort *to recapture the self and to scrutinize the self*, it is
> through the lasting tension of their freedom that men will be able to
> create the ideal conditions of existence for a human world. [231; my
> italics]

The wish to "create . . . ideal conditions of existence" is synonymous here with the fight against all petit bourgeois mental hab-
its that tend to favor manifestations of closure. Fanon wants to

demythologize history and to prevent it from being used as the source of "reactional" behavior because, as "Nietzsche had already pointed out" and as he himself elaborates, "there is always resentment in a *reaction*" (*BSWM* 222). While severely criticizing his fellow colonized intellectuals for simply reproducing the values of the colonizer in adopting racialist thinking, Fanon did not hesitate to state that the quest for disalienation must be mediated by the refusal to accept the "Tower of the Past" (*BSWM* 226) and the problems of the present as definitive, in other words, by the belief that only the poetry of the future can move and inspire human beings to action and to revolution. Unlike Fanon, Hurston did not develop the visionary perspective into a revolutionary one, but her mystical desire to be one with the universe stems from a similar utopian need for a "waking dream"[18] of the possible which might inspire us to see beyond the constraints of the here and now to the idealized vision of a perfect future, albeit, in *Dust Tracks*, a life after death in which the substance of her being is again "part and parcel of the world" and "one with the infinite" (279). Both Fanon and Hurston suggest that we urgently need to retrieve those past traditions that can become the source of reconciliation and wholeness, for it is more important to learn from those traditions than to dwell on pain and injustice.

For Hurston, "the effort to recapture . . . and to scrutinize the self" is a project grounded in the quicksand of linguistic performance and thus inseparable from what Beaujour has called "a type of memory, both very archaic and very modern, by which the events of an individual life are eclipsed by the recollection of an entire culture." As Michael M. J. Fischer has stressed, ethnic memory is not only past- but future-oriented, and the dynamics of interpersonal knowledge within the intercultural strands of memory are inseparable from Hurston's project of self-portraiture, since to recapture the past is literally to create a new field of knowledge within her academic discipline : "If science ever gets to the bottom of Voodoo in Haiti and Africa, it will be found that some important medical secrets, still unknown to medical science, give it its power, rather than

---

[18]The phrase is Ernst Bloch's. See Anson Rabinbach, "Unclaimed Heritage: Ernst Bloch's *Heritage of Our Times* and the Theory of Fascism," *New German Critique* 11 (Spring 1977), p. 7. Hurston was familiar with the German philosophical tradition of utopian thinking. She mentions Spinoza for example, *DT* 285. See also my comments in note 24.

the gestures of ceremony" (205).[19] By suggesting historically valid mythological connections between ancient deities and prophets such as Isis and Persephone, on the one hand, and Damballah, Thoth, and Moses, on the other, and between those figures and the "two-headed" magicians of Hoodoo (191), who know the creative power of words, Hurston leaves the door open for a historical revision both of Hoodoo religion and of antiquity, implying "two-headed" Egyptian and Greek origins for both Euro- and Afro-Americans. Because such a thesis would have been rejected by contemporary scholars, who then followed the "Aryan model" of antiquity, Hurston can only allude to it through literature.[20]

A comparison of the thematic similarities in Hurston's work does show that she was quite consciously using those ancient "personae" as multiple facets of her own self and of her own Afro-Mediterranean genealogy. One of her first published stories, "Drenched in Light," tells the story of Isis Watts, a protagonist who is clearly autobiographical, as is Isis Potts of *Jonah's Gourd Vine*.[21] This same persona is reintroduced in *Dust Tracks* under the name Persephone. The similarity of the protagonists suggests that the three narratives form a triptych: it is only by taking into consideration the mythological background of the protagonists' names that we can accurately understand the process of self-discovery through self-invention which characterizes Hurston's method. Tellingly, this process is a search for familial and maternal connections, for "mirrors" that can reflect positive aspects of the past instead of alienating images of subaltern faces.

[19]Beaujour, p. 26; see Michael M. J. Fischer, "Ethnicity and the Post-Modern Arts of Memory," *Writing Culture*, pp. 194–233 (201). Fischer uses "ethnic" autobiographical narrative as a means of allowing "multiple sets of voices to speak for themselves" thus effectively marginalizing his anthropological commentary on the ethnic group he studies.

[20]See Martin Bernal's revision of that model in *Black Athena: The Afroasiatic Roots of Classical Civilization* (London: Free Association Books, 1987). For Hurston's use of Damballah, Moses, and Thoth as facets of the same mythological persona, see her *Moses, Man of the Mountain* (Urbana: University of Illinois Press, 1984). See also Karla F. C. Holloway, *The Character of the Word* (New York: Greenwood Press, 1987), chap. 3, for a useful discussion of those figures.

[21]For the passages of *Jonah's Gourd Vine* which are useful here, I shall be quoting from *I Love Myself When I Am Laughing: A Zora Neale Hurston Reader*, ed. Alice Walker (New York: Feminist Press, 1979), pp. 189–96, hereinafter *ILM*. "Drenched in Light" is reprinted as "Isis" in *Spunk: The Selected Stories of Zora Neale Hurston* (Berkeley: Turtle Island Foundation, 1985), pp. 9–18.

History and Memory

It is thus significant that the only events of her "private" life on which Hurston dwells in *Dust Tracks* are those that have deep symbolic and cultural value: the death of the mother and subsequent dispersion of the siblings echo the collective memory of her people's separation from Africa-as-mother and their ineluctable diaspora. That is why Kossola/Cudjo Lewis's story emblematizes her own sense of bereavement and deprivation: "After seventy-five years, he still had that tragic sense of loss. That yearning for blood and cultural ties. That sense of mutilation. It gave me something to think about" (204). Coming at the end of the "Research" chapter, the embedded narrative of Kossola's life serves as a powerful counterpoint to Zora's own story of strife and reconciliation with her brothers (172–73). It is thanks to her research and professional travels that she becomes, like the legendary Isis of Egyptian mythology, the link that reunites, reconnects the dispersed siblings, who can now "touch each other in the spirit if not in the flesh." The imagery that describes the disintegration of the family unit is a clear reminder of the historical conditions of the Middle Passage:

> I felt the warm embrace of kin and kind for the first time since the night after my mother's funeral, when we had huddled about the organ all sodden and bewildered, with the walls of our home suddenly blown down. On September 18th, that house had been a hovering home. September 19th, it had turned into a bleak place of desolation with unknown dangers creeping upon us from unseen quarters that made of us a whimpering huddle, though then we could not see why. But now that was all over. [173]

As private experiences echo collective ones and punctuate the deployment of the self-portrait, a picture of the fieldworker as keeper of important knowledge, as go-between whose role is to facilitate the articulation of collective memory, emerges. By foregrounding the field research as the causal link to an empowering reunion with her scattered siblings, Hurston deploys much broader implications for the social lives of Afro-Americans. She implies that connections to the past must not be severed if we are to regain a sense of what it is like to "touch each other in the spirit" and also that a sense of history must not be allowed to degenerate into the remembrance of paralyzing images. That is why she also remarks that "any religion that satisfies the individual urge is valid for that person" (205). Since ancient traditions such as Hoodoo contain, as Hemenway says, "the old, old mysticism of the world in African terms," they are useful to a "thick description" of cultural nuances, and they help demarcate the historical context relevant to the study of folklore.[22]

Hurston's aim is to maintain the integrity of black culture without diluting it and to celebrate its values while remaining critical of those pressures from within the "family" which can mutilate individual aspirations—as her eldest brother Bob had been guilty of doing to her when she went to live with him, hoping that he would help put her through school, only to find herself playing the role of maid to his wife. It is this de facto lack of solidarity among "brothers" which Hurston observes and which forms the basis for her critique of a blanket endorsement of simpleminded, universal "Race Solidarity" (327) or of the pan-Africanism that in the thirties and forties must have sounded disturbingly like pan-Germanism, whose evil historical consequences were well understood. The text of *Dust Tracks* thus shuttles between appreciation and opprobrium, finding its impetus in the joyful affirmation of its contradictions. To recall the past in order to transcend it, Fanon will also point out, is the only emancipatory stance we can confidently adopt without risk of falling prey to reactionary forces.

Thus, the chapter titled "Religion" reveals Hurston's total indifference to the "consolation" traditional religion affords: "I am one with the infinite and need no other assurance" (279). Her style subverts the need for "organized creeds," which are but "collections of words around a wish" (278) and which Fanon will denounce as the motor of a "closed society . . . in which ideas and people are in a state of decay" (*BSWM* 224).[23] Comfortable in the knowledge that the whole world exists in a Heraclitean flux of becoming, Hurston affirms a principle of eternal change based in her observation of the radical fluidity of inorganic, organic, social, and cultural forces:

> I have achieved a certain peace within myself, but perhaps the seeking after the inner heart of truth will never cease in me. . . .
> So, having looked at the subject from many sides, studied beliefs by

[22]Hemenway, *Hurston*, p. 249. I use the phrase "thick description" after Clifford Geertz, *The Interpretation of Cultures* (New York: Basic Books, 1973), chap. 1.

[23]See Fontenot, p. 84 for a discussion of "open" and "closed" society as defined by Fanon. I have modified the translation of *BSWM*.

word of mouth and then *as they fit into great rigid forms, I find I know a great deal about form, but little or nothing about the mysteries I sought as a child. . . .*

But certain things have seemed to me to be true as I heard the tongues of those who had speech, and listened at the lips of books . . . .[277]

The springing of the yellow line of morning out of the misty deep of dawn, is glory enough for me. I know that nothing is destructible; things merely change forms. [279; my italics][24]

Poetic speech has now replaced the folk idiom, the artist, the anthropologist. The distinction between form and content ("mysteries") is made again but then put under erasure: "things merely change forms," and content is never lost; yet knowledge of content is determined by the "great rigid forms" that structure the universe while veiling the motley appearance of "matter." These allegories of death and rebirth, change and permanence, temporality and eternity, retroactively map the territory of the autobiographical text and the life it attempts to represent. By retracing those ephemeral "dust tracks" whose trajectory the table of contents surveys, Hurston seems to spiral out into infinity and the cosmos: "The cosmic Zora emerges," as she writes in "How It Feels to Be Colored Me" (*ILM* 155). Her journey, like that of the storytellers who never leave the porch, is an itinerary through language, "a journeying by way of narrating," as Alexander Gelley puts it. That is why it is impossible to make, on a theoretical level, "any clear-cut division between theme and form, between journey as geography and journey as narrative."[25] The "curve in the road" at which Hurston sees her first "vision" (93) is a mythical point of departure for the global adventure during which she will learn to take distance from the "tight chemise" and the "crib of negroism" (*MM* 3) that have shaped her. Distance alone can enable her to recognize and assemble the fragments of her changing folk culture in the New World, and because she is dealing with familiar territory, she does not run the risk of subjugating the "other" to her self, of making her subjects into mar-

[24]Hurston's Spinozist philosophy is evident here. See Benedict de Spinoza, *Ethics* (n.p.: Joseph Simon, 1981), pt. 1, proposition 8: "Every substance is necessarily infinite" (p. 32). As SPR Charter puts it in the introduction to this edition, "Spinoza attempted to unite the mind/body complexity and the realities of existence with the all-embracing actuality of Nature, and to do so organically—that is, without the imposition of man-made religious structures" (p. 3).

[25]Gelley, p. 31.

ionettes for the benefit of those patrons who are only interested in the static, "primitive" aspects of her research. Engaged in a truly dialogical enterprise and not in the delusions of Boasian "pure objectivity" to which she alludes ironically (174), she can negotiate the terms of her insertion within and without the ethnographic field and can even parody popular beliefs with impunity: the jokes come naturally with the territory of storytelling.

Similarly, the discursive enterprise of self-portraiture is a process of collecting and gathering, of assembling images and metaphors to portray a figural self, always already caught in entropy and in permanent danger of returning to "dust," of becoming again "part and parcel" of the universe. In what follows, then, I would like to examine briefly the textual mechanism that generates the journey of ethnic self-scrutiny, the slippage between particular and universal, individual and collective, daughter and mother(s), the self and its mythologies. In describing these displacements, I want to show how the collective functions as a silverless mirror, capable of absorbing the self into a duplicitous game in which one code, singularity, is set aslant by another, syncretic unity with the universe, thus preventing narrative closure.[26] The tensions at work in *Dust Tracks* between these two sets of expectations (local versus universal knowledge) are not simply resolvable through (ethnographic) narrative. They constitute what Stephen Tyler has called the proper domain of "post-modern ethnography," neither "the upward spiral into the Platonic . . . realm of conscious thought and faceless abstraction" nor the "descent 'beneath the surface' into the Plutonic 'other of separation.'" Hurston's approach to the study of culture indeed prefigures the future trend of the discipline as outlined by Tyler: "The ethnographic text will thus achieve its purposes not by revealing them, but by making purposes possible. It will be a text of the physical, the spoken, and the performed, an evocation of quotidian experience, a palpable reality that uses everyday speech to suggest what is ineffable, not through abstraction, but by means of the concrete. It will be a text to read not with the eyes alone, but with the ears in order to hear 'the voices of the pages.'"[27]

[26]What I call the silverless mirror here is to some extent assimilable to what Houston A. Baker, Jr., associates with the term "black (w)hole": "a *singularly* black route of escape" (p. 155). By analogy, it refers also to the covered looking-glass in the room of the dying mother (*DT* 88), to which I will return.

[27]See Stephen Tyler, "Post-Modern Ethnography: From Document of the Occult to Occult Document," in *Writing Culture*, pp. 133, 136.

Hurston, too, captures the voices of the people and relays them through the "lips of books," which do not "announce" their purpose but braid "palpable reality" with the incommensurable, the quotidian with the ineffable. She makes it possible to envisage purposive, enabling, and empowering structures of meaning which do not coerce the subject into historically and Eurocentrically determined racial metaphors of the self. She succeeds in tracing a map of her territory—a symbolic geography—by using the same accomodating principles that governed the expedient building of roads over the winding footpath between Orlando and Maitland: the metaphor of the road that curves effortlessly around "the numerous big pine trees and oaks" (7) reinforces a principle of flexibility, a respect for nature rather than the need to dominate it, a pliability connoting the plasticity of human forms, the capacity to undergo mutations, to endure and survive hardships in that middle passage from birth to death, from mud to dust.

The allegory of the voyage that is only a return to one's point of departure is already present in the first chapter, "My Birthplace." The "three frontier-seekers" who embark for Brazil only to return to the United States prefigure Hurston, who journeys through black folklore in order to rediscover the "geography . . . within" (115), the lost community of her childhood in "A pure Negro town!" (9). Her search for an originary plenitude is the universal biblical "return to dust" at the end of the road of life—not the romantic nostalgia for a prelapsarian time of innocence. In that respect, the death of her mother represents the first moment in a chain of destabilizing experiences that forever undermine her sense of belonging to a specific place: "That hour began my wanderings. Not so much in geography, but in time. Then not so much in time as in spirit. Mama died at sundown and changed a world. That is, the world which had been built out of her body and her heart. Even the physical aspects fell apart with a suddenness that was startling" (89). The death scene of the speechless mother becomes the motivation for writing, for the effort of self-fashioning, which is also an effort to stave off death. Hurston's wandering phase will be the result of this experience of absence and loss, which is repeated on different levels throughout the next chapters. The narrator attempts to fill the void of death by journeying *and* by narrating.

That is why it is interesting to note that the description of the

mother's death in *Dust Tracks* closely parallels the fictional rendering
of that scene in *Jonah's Gourd Vine*. Telling details are repeated almost word for word: "I could see the huge drop of sweat collected in
the hollow at Mama's elbow and it hurt me so" (*DT* 88) and " Isis
saw a pool of sweat standing in a hollow at the elbow" (*ILM* 195); "I
thought that she looked to me (*DT* 86). . . . I think she was trying to
say something, and I think she was trying to speak to me" (*DT* 88)
and "Isis thought her mother's eyes followed her and she strained
her ears to catch her words" (*ILM* 195). Isis is indeed the fictional
alter ego Hurston chooses for herself, the name of an ancient Egyptian goddess who wandered the world in search of her dismembered brother, a mythical representation of interiority as experience
of death. In Egyptian mythology, her brother, Osiris, is both the god
of fertility (like Demeter/Ceres in the Greco-Roman myth) and the
king and judge of the dead. He is also the companion of Thoth, god
of death and of writing, who presides with him in the underworld.
Hurston thus makes an implicit connection between the Osirian
mysteries, which were tied to the cult of the dead and of which Isis
was the high priestess, and the occult practices of Hoodoo, of which
Hurston herself became an initiate. Having flippantly named herself
the "queen of the niggerati" in one of her histrionic moments among
her New York friends,[28] Hurston then proceeded to develop (in the
autobiographical triptych) in a mythically accurate and artistically
sensible manner the theme of a life lived in the shadow of Isis/Per-
sephone, queens of the underworld, of the "dark realm" of otherness. The persona Isis—both the goddess and the fictional daughter
of Lucy Potts—is like the mirror that figures prominently in the
mother's death scene. She is an image of memory and interiority, an
"other" who focuses, crystallizes, and gives sharp contours to the
project of self-invention. She is an important thread in the process of
re-membering one's past and one's own mortality as one pays
homage to the dead and departed. Here, the folk custom of veiling
the mirror (so that the dead may rest in peace and not trouble the
living) is implicitly criticized: the dying mother suggests that the
mirror should not be veiled if the past and the faces of our mothers
in it are to leave their imprint on the memory of the living so that *we*
may live in peace with history and be thus able to "think back

[28]Holloway, p. 24.

through our mothers," as Virginia Woolf believed it was important for women to be able to do.[29]

What the death scene allegorizes, then, is Hurston's subtle and complex view of the relationship of individuals to culture and history: some elements of culture, because they are unexamined traditions, "village custom" (86), "mores" (89) upheld by the voices of patriarchy (the "village dames," or phallic women, and the father, who together prevent her from fulfilling her mother's wishes), are destructive and stultifying. The child's (Isis' and Zora's) experience of anxiety and guilt is the result of those unexamined cultural myths that thwart the mother's desire to remain imprinted on the daughter's memory. As Adrienne Rich has put it, "The loss of the daughter to the mother, the mother to the daughter, is the essential female tragedy."[30] The loss brought about by the patriarchal customs of the "village" is a painful enactment of separation and fragmentation, of lost connections to the mother as symbol of a veiled and occulted historical past. Albert Memmi and Frantz Fanon will both point out that our problem as colonized people (or gender) is that we all suffer from collective amnesia. The self-portrait Hurston draws in *Dust Tracks* is an anamnesis: not self-contemplation but a painstaking effort to be the voice of that occluded past, to fill the void of collective memory.

Indeed, Zora feels that her mother "depended on [her] for a voice" (87), and in *Dust Tracks* she chooses the mythical Persephone as alter ego. The Greek word for voice is *phone* and the scene of the mother's death is symbolic of the daughter's responsibility to articulate her story, to exhume it from the rubble of patriarchal obfuscation. Martin Bernal has pointed out that the Eleusinian story of Demeter searching for Persephone has its roots in the Egyptian myth of Isis and Osiris.[31] By identifying with Persephone in *Dust Tracks*, Hurston makes a brilliant and sophisticated rapprochement be-

---

[29]See Jane Marcus, "Thinking Back through Our Mothers," in *New Feminist Essays on Virginia Woolf* (Lincoln: University of Nebraska Press, 1981), pp. 1–30.

[30]Adrienne Rich, *Of Woman Born: Motherhood as Experience and Institution* (New York: Norton, 1976), p. 237. As Sandra M. Gilbert and Susan Gubar have amply demonstrated, the lack of a female tradition in which to insert her own words is the source of a great "anxiety of authorship" for the woman writer. See *The Madwoman in the Attic: The Woman Writer and the Nineteenth-Century Literary Imagination* (New Haven: Yale University Press, 1979), pp. 45–92.

[31]Bernal, pp. 69–73.

tween the two myths—a connection, says Bernal, that classicists who follow the "Aryan model" of antiquity have studiously avoided. Hurston approaches Afro-Mediterranean antiquity with the intuitions of the anthropologist who sees connections where traditional classical scholarship had not.

The displacement from Isis to Persephone as objective persona is significant in helping us understand Hurston's feeling of being an orphan, of being cut off from her origins, or *arche*. "Isis" is the wanderer who conducts her research, establishes spatiotemporal connections among the children of the diaspora, and re-members the scattered body of folk material so that siblings can again "touch each other." "Persephone," on the other hand, is not a rescuer but rather a lost daughter whose mother searches for her with passion. She is an ambiguous figure "with her loving and hellish aspects."[32] Ironically, it is Zora's reading of the Greco-Roman myth ("one of [her] favorites" [48]) during the visit of two white women at her school that attracts attention to her brilliance and configures her later "rescue" by other white mentors, friends who become surrogate mothers (like Helen in "Drenched in Light"). If, as Ronnie Scharfman has noted, "mirroring" and "mothering" are twin terms for defining the reciprocal nurturing bonds a female subject needs in order to feel anchored in the tradition linking her to her mother(s), then Zora's vain efforts to prevent the veiling of the mirror in the mother's room must be understood as an allegorical attempt to look into the mirror of her mother's soul, to retain severed connections, to recapture and to "read" the dark face of the mother in the silverless mirror of the past, and to become the voice that bridges generations.[33] Those efforts also prefigure her professional predicament as an adult. Persephone was the queen of Pluto's dark realm of the dead, but she also traveled back and forth between the underworld and "the sunlit earth" (49), like Hurston, who retrieves the voices of her black culture in order to call her readers, in Karla Holloway's words, "back to primal ground." Caught between the upper and the

---

[32]The words Bernal uses to describe Persephone (p. 70).

[33]See Ronnie Scharfman, "Mirroring and Mothering in Simone Schwarz-Bart's *Pluie et vent sur Télumée Miracle*, and Jean Rhys's *Wide Sargasso Sea*," *Yale French Studies* 62 (1981), 88–106. Scharfman discusses psychoanalytic object-relation theorists. My purpose here is to relate those issues to the larger historical and ethnographical contexts within which I situate *Dust Tracks*.

lower realms, the black and the white world, life and death, she bridges the tragic gap of separation by writing. As Beaujour has explained, "the self-portrait tries to reunite two separate worlds, that of the living and that of the dead."[34]

Her description of a ceremony in New Orleans in which she participates draws the obvious parallels: "I had to sit at the crossroads at midnight in complete darkness and meet the devil, and make a compact. There was a long, long hour as I sat flat on the ground there alone and invited the King of Hell" (192). Since we also know that fasting was an essential part of her initiation, the parallel with Persephone is even more convincing, for Persephone's fate was to be Pluto's queen for three months of each year because "she had bitten the pomegranate" (49). Cleansing by fasting is, of course, a common part of initiatory practices in many religions and underscores Hurston's philosophy of the universal oneness of religious symbols.

When the child's experience of absence in *Dust Tracks* becomes specifically racial, a new and negative dimension is added to the metaphor of the mirror. As Hurston puts it, "Jacksonville made me know that I was a little colored girl" (94). This discovery of the ethnic self as mirrored by the other, the white culture of Jacksonville, functions in the text as another moment of an-archic self-discovery. The image reflected in the mirror of white culture is like the photograph in which Janie, in *Their Eyes Were Watching God,* cannot recognize herself because she does not yet know that she is colored, that for the white family who calls her "Alphabet," she is different because she symbolizes namelessness, darkness, absence, and lack.[35] This is Janie's first experience of difference, seeing her face as a bad photograph, as a "negative" and a flaw in the developed picture she holds in her hand. This scene of nonrecognition, like the deathbed scene, is the primal motivation for the journey of self-discovery through language. Isis, Persephone, Thoth, and Osiris are thus the four poles that mark the perimeter of Hurston's cultural mythology of the self. Thoth's gift links writing to death and to immortality; here the threads of memory and narrative allow Janie to "[pull] in her

[34]Holloway, p. 113; Beaujour, p. 161.

[35]Zora Neale Hurston, *Their Eyes Were Watching God* (Urbana: University of Illinois Press, 1978), p. 21, hereinafter *TE*.

horizon like a great fish-net" (*TE* 286) in which the fragments of a faceless past are reassembled and given new names, new origins.

When we look at the allegory of the veiling of the mirror in *Dust Tracks* in the context of those similar scenes in the novels, a strong statement about the self and its enabling and distorting mirrors emerges. The idea that a mirror can be the vehicle of a negative self-image (depersonalization and loss) seems to be tied to two cultural myths perceived as destructive and debilitating by the child: the patriarchal folk belief about mirrors and death and the white culture's myths about blackness as radical otherness and absence. In both cases, reflections are void, absent, or distorted because they emanate from a reductionist context: the realities of a culture's myths about death and otherness become a burden and a distortion of the historical metaphors by which women must learn to live if we are to recapture the faces of our mothers in the mirrors of the past. It is by uncovering those mirrors that we can begin to articulate connections to ancient and empowering symbols of femaleness. Hence the anguish of the child at not being able to fend off the voices of white and black patriarchy, which rob her forever of the peace that comes from seeing the face(s)—and knowing the mythical name(s)—that connect her to a cultural tradition not grounded only in darkness and silence. Again Beaujour's formulation is valid: "The self-portrait is constructed around an empty center: vanished places and disrupted harmonies."[36] The experience of death generates the writing of a self-portrait through which appears, pentimento, the mother's lost face.

The child who leaves Eatonville after her mother's death experiences alterity and dislocation, distances herself forever from the illusory possibility of an unexamined and unmediated participation in the network of relations which constitutes culture. In effect, her avocation as anthropologist starts right then and there: her exile from Eatonville is the first step on the nomadic road of lore collecting, a road on which "the individual looks for soul-mates while simultaneously affirming [her] absolute difference from all others," Beaujour says. That is why the collective voice is so often relayed with irony and pathos: the self-portrait is the medium of subversion

[36]Beaujour, p. 22.

par excellence, which relativizes the fetishistic recourse to a foundational world beyond its discourse. It evokes the ethnic reality of which it partakes but, in so doing, puts into question the mimetic principles of description and classification which inform its writing. It thus simultaneously demystifies the writing of both the self (auto) and the culture (ethno) because it involves the self and its cultural contexts in a dialogue that transcends all possibility of reducing one to the other. Michel Beaujour expresses it thus: "Mirror of the subject and mirror of the world, mirror of the 'I' searching for a reflection of its self through the mirror of the universe: what might first appear as a simple correspondence, or a convenient analogy, proves under close scrutiny to be a homologous relation warranted by the rhetorical tradition and the history of literature."[37] Beaujour's formulation can be applied to *Dust Tracks* with an important modification: it is not the medieval rhetorical tradition that furnishes the topics of mimesis but the anthropological essay with its system of categories, which locate culture at the nexus of history and geography, religion and myth. What this formulation means for the "self-portrait," according to Beaujour, is that writing is engendered primarily by the *impossibility* of self-presence, by the realization that realist narratives are functionally distorting and that myths are more appropriately evocative and suggestive of a subject's liminal position in the world of discursive representation.

Here, a myth of ancient Afro-Mediterranean folklore establishes the parameters according to which Hurston will go on performing the role of daughter after her mother's death and until they can both be syncretically reunited. The faceless woman encountered on a porch in Jacksonville during a school walk, "who looked at a distance like Mama" (96), prefigures the last of her twelve "visions": the two women, one young (herself?), one old (the mother?), whose faces are averted as they are "arranging some queer-shaped flowers such as [she] had never seen" (58). This indirect allusion to the funeral flower—the white narcissus—is also the figure of the self reflected in the pool of language, the dark ("miroirs d'encre") medium of self-knowledge, the white symbol of death's attraction. It is an unformulated, unnamed, but richly suggestive allusion to the desire for the absent mother, which will be reenacted both in the

[37]Ibid., pp. 15, 31.

bonds of female friendships (the visitors at the school, Big Sweet, Fannie Hurst, Ethel Waters, the Dahoman Amazons) and in those of hatred or rivalry with other women (her stepmother and knife-toting "Lucy").[38] At once Persephone and Narcissus, the autobiographical narrator attempts to recapture the (m)other in the self and the self through the (m)other:[39]

> Once or twice I saw the old faceless woman standing outdoors beside a tall plant with that same off-shape white flower. She turned suddenly from it to welcome me. I knew what was going on in the house without going in, it was all so familiar to me.
> I never told anyone around me about these strange things. It was too different. They would laugh me off as a story-teller. Besides, I had a feeling of difference from my fellow men, and I did not want it to be found out. [58–59].

Her experiences of singularity and difference are intimately connected to her visions of death. Not surprisingly, the reference to "Pluto's dark realm" (48) and to the temporary reunification of Persephone with her mother turns the circumstances of her life upside down and transforms the past by reorienting it toward an unlived future in which the lost potentialities of love and daughterhood are given a second chance, and an elusive possibility of peace and transfiguration: "I stood in a world of vanished communion with my kind, which is worse than if it had never been. Nothing is so desolate as a place where life has been and gone. I stood on a soundless island in a tideless sea. Time was to prove the truth of my visions . . . bringing me nearer to the big house, with the kind women and the strange white flowers" (59).

[38]For an analysis of the "thematic consistency . . . found in these echoing episodes of female strength," see Raynaud. On this aspect of the text, I am in complete agreement with Raynaud.

[39]See Beaujour's informative discussion of the associations between Demeter, Persephone, and Narcissus in Greek mythology and the connections between these divinities and death. His argument is that narcissism as commonly understood in psychoanalytic terminology is a distorted and reductive interpretation of the myth and that far from being "narcissistic" in that sense, "the self-portrait tries to reunite two separate worlds, that of the living and that of the dead. . . . Through anamnesis, Narcissus . . . performs a poetic invention of 'childhood memories' which recreates a timeless paradise, at once personal treasure trove and cultural topic" (p. 161). See especially pp. 156–62.

If the mother is a figure for the "lost" potentialities of history and for the "dark" continent of Africa, it is not surprising that images of death and decay begin to pervade the daughter's self-recollection during those years of loneliness and wandering in which she feels "haunted" (116). Just like "Lazarus after his resurrection," she cannot experience her own self in a unified way, past and present, mind and body can never coincide completely: "I walked by my corpse. I smelt it and felt it. I smelt the corpses of those among whom I must live, though they did not. They were as much at home with theirs as death in a tomb" (117). Like the Zombies she will later study, she is one of the living dead whose childhood memories of that time—between ten and fourteen years of age—are the undeveloped photographic negative of the singular images of blankness which will keep recurring in later chapters. For instance, her first love affair, although it provides the closeness and warmth she had sorely missed ever since her mother's death, turns into an oppressive relationship that imprisons her in feelings of doubt and unreality that cannot be shared with the husband: "Somebody had turned a hose on the sun. What I had taken for eternity turned out to be a moment walking in its sleep. . . . A wind full of memories blew out of the past and brought a chilling fog" (251).

Numbed by the impossibility to communicate, drained of life, she buries herself in her work. The next time she falls in love, the pattern seems to repeat itself. She is thwarted by the conflicts caused by her career, the man's possessiveness, and his complaints that her "real self had escaped him." She is not permitted to have a life of her own, is restrained by limiting circumstances, "caught in a fiendish trap" (259). Love is never experienced as an empowering force— unlike friendship, this "mysterious and ocean-bottom thing" (321) without which life is not worth much: "To live without friends is like milking a bear to get cream for your morning coffee. It is a whole lot of trouble, and then not worth much after you get it" (248). In contrast to the flatness of her love life, her affective landscape is peopled with many picturesque and vivid portrayals of friends. The topic of "friendship" is a much richer and more satisfying one than "love," and the treatment it receives in *Dust Tracks* bears testimony to the importance self-portraitists have accorded to the interface with an other whose ambivalent companionship may be the spur that compels a writer to articulate the potentialities of his or her vision.[40] "Conversation is the ceremony of companionship" (248), Ethel Waters says to Zora and Zora's self-portrait is this conversation with the past, a ceremony for the dead mother(s), but one that simultaneously empowers the living.

The narrator also experiences singularity as separation from the realm of nature. After her departure to Jacksonville, her introduction to formal education goes together with another deprivation which adds to her grief and mourning: "the loving pine, the lakes, the wild violets in the woods and the animals [she] used to know" (95) are no longer part of her daily life. Orphaned for a second time when her father asks the school to "adopt" her and she is nonetheless sent home on the riverboat, she experiences a thrilling form of rebirth because she is again part and parcel of nature: "The water life, the smothering foliage that draped the river banks, the miles of purple hyacinths, all thrilled me anew. The wild thing was back in the jungle. The curtain of trees along the river shut out the world so that it seemed that the river and the chugging boat was all that there was, and that pleased me a lot" (109). The floating boat and the trees that "shut out the world" are like the protective layers of a womb; the boat's chugging motor connotes a maternal heartbeat, a reassuring companion that spells the return to an earlier form of peace and harmony. These layered allusions to the archaic times of a prenatal life and to the historical moments of preslavery days in Africa again configurate the mother as the sheltering presence whose disappearance generates the nomadic search for collective meanings that will establish a system of resonance between seemingly heterogeneous entities or "topics," such as daughterhood, friendship, nature, and antiquity—all of which can be seen as so many inaugurating moments of similarity within difference, of self-absorption in an enigmatic mirror, the Augustinian "per speculum in aenigmate," which can be contrasted and paralleled with death itself, the "face that reflects the face of all things, but neither changes itself, nor is mirrored anywhere" (DT 87).

Later on, working as a maid for the soprano of the traveling opera company, Zora becomes a kind of mascot for the whole company,

[40]Augustine, Montaigne (O un amy!), Gertrude Stein, Christopher Isherwood, Roland Barthes, to name but a few. See Réda Bensmaïa, The Barthes Effect: The Essay as Reflective Text (Minneapolis: University of Minnesota Press, 1987) pp. 62–89 especially.

and her writing career gets started: "I got a scrapbook . . . and wrote comments under each picture. . . . Then I got another idea. I would comment on daily doings and post the sheets on the callboard. . . . The results stayed strictly mine less than a week because members of the cast began to call me aside and tell me things to put in about others. . . . It was just my handwriting, mostly" (138–39). She becomes the repository of other people's words, a kind of transparent mind or ghost writer. She experiences another form of Zombiehood, mediated by the acquisition of language, by the absorption of other voices, just like all that "early reading," which had given her "great anguish through all [her] childhood and adolescence" because, as she puts it, "My soul was with the gods and my body in the village. People just would not act like gods" (56). Her experiences at school in Baltimore follow the same pattern: "And here I was, with my face looking like it had been chopped out of a knot of pine wood with a hatchet on somebody's off day, sitting up in the middle of all this pretty" (150–51). Undefined features, "a woman half in shadow," the self-portraitist draws a picture of herself which remains "a figure in bas relief," an intaglio, "the weaving of anthropology with thanatography."[41]

These echoing patterns of disfiguration and death give an improvisational rhythm to the text, the ebb and flow of musical counterpoint, and suspend meaning between suggestive similarities the reader is free to associate or not. One subtle parallel the text thus draws is between two gruesome events: the decapitation of Cousin Jimmie, "mother's favorite nephew" (85), unintentionally shot by a white man, who covered up the accident by making it look as though a train had killed him, and the similar fate that had befallen the son of Kossola/Cudjo, David, who was actually beheaded in a train accident. In both cases, it is the grief of the parental figures which resonates in the text, rather than a hypothetical repetition of real-life events. Indeed, framing as they do Hurston's vision of the two faceless women and Kossola's stories of famed Dahoman Amazons who sack cities and carry "clusters of human heads at their belts," the stories underscore a singularly repetitive pattern that

[41]The first two phrases are Fannie Hurst's in "A Personality Sketch," reprinted in *Zora Neale Hurston*, ed. Harold Bloom (New York: Chelsea House, 1986), pp. 24, 23; the third is Michel Beaujour's, p. 13. The first one is also the title of Mary Helen Washington's introduction to *ILM*.

would seem to point not to referents beyond the text but to the allegorical disfiguring of generation upon generation of black individuals whose plight is ignored or covered up, except in the memory of those who grieve for them as Cudjo's Takkoi King, beheaded by the Amazons, is mourned by his people (cf. 201).

The ephemeral quality of collective memory itself is reflected in the transient nature of Hurston's "first publication": "On the blackboard . . . I decided to write an allegory using the faculty members as characters" (153). The "allegory" is the source of much entertainment and laughter for her schoolmates, a successful rehearsal for her future tale telling and an important metaphoric hyphen between the immediacy of oral performance and the permanence of the written words. Like these allegorical portraits, which will be erased once they have served their purpose, her twelve visions, which were initially meant to structure the deployment of the autobiography, are soon forgotten because they do not need to be used. The tale teller dynamically reshapes her material as she goes along, the content of the visions becoming irrelevant since the essayistic form of the latter chapters ("My People! My People!" "Looking Things Over," "The Inside Light,") spontaneously generates a framework through which to communicate her philosophy.

As she ironically suggests about the experiences told by the religious congregation: "These visions are traditional. I knew them by heart as did the rest of the congregation, but still it was exciting to see *how the converts would handle them. Some of them made up new details. Some of them would forget a part and improvise clumsily or fill up the gap with shouting.* The audience knew, but everybody acted as if every word of it was new" (272; my italics). Inconsistencies are inherent to the performance of traditional cultural forms: it is precisely in the way they individually diverge from the set norms that the converts excite interest in the audience. The "origin" of the tradition must be acknowledged, but acknowledgment does not sanction simple repetition: each new performer "signifies" upon that origin by transforming it, and by allowing for infinite of permutations.[42] To approach a form genealogically, then, is to attempt to retrace its

[42]I am using the word *signifies* in the black traditional sense discussed in particular by Henry L. Gates, Jr., "The Blackness of Blackness: A Critique of the Sign and the Signifying Monkey," *Black Literature and Literary Theory* (New York: Methuen, 1984), pp. 285–321.

transformations back to an origin—*arche*—that will always prove elusive since every discrete manifestation is the interpellation of a previous one, which sets the stage for the next one, and so on ad infinitum. A particular form acquires value not from its timeless origin or essential qualities but because it is related to practices that inform a mode of life while dynamically shaping reality. Whether Hurston's twelve visions signify upon a particular religious tradition or the vernacular ritual of the "dozens" (cf. 187, 217) or both is of no importance since, in any case, she can make vicarious use of the cliches, parody some of them, ignore the rest, and "tell a story the way [she] wanted, or rather the way the story told itself to [her]" (206). Since "playing the dozens" or "specifying" is a form of invective and name calling that points genealogically to a fictitious origin—"they proceed to 'specify' until the tip-top branch of your family tree has been given a reading" (217)—we can readily infer that this "self-affirming form of discourse"[43] does not require foundational support in reality. It is by virtue of its perlocutionary function that it affirms the underlying gutsiness and creativity of the agent of discourse, drawing a portrait of the self as capable of enduring, diverging, and surviving because it adheres to the formal aspects of a dynamic and improvisational cultural tradition that allows the storyteller to "keep the tune" for the benefit of the collectivity, to lift the veil on the mirror of a different history, to be a "keeper of our memories" (*Moses* 350). Hurston's "exuberant sense of self"[44] allows her to adopt a thoroughly Nietzschean perspective on this "topsy-turvy world" of hers, and to value memory as a viable alternative to oppressive history.

In *Dust Tracks*, we have a powerful example of the braiding, or *métissage*, of cultural forms, since Persephone figures both as the voice of the dead mother and as the boundary crosser who links up two different worlds. Turning the mythical relation between Ceres and her daughter upside down, Hurston invents her own reading of the tradition, "signifying" upon that tradition in a specifically "black" way, diverging from the Greco-Roman text in the only way possible for the Afro-American self-portraitist. To rejoin her mother, Zora/Persephone must travel back to the underworld, to the "dark

[43]See Susan Willis, *Specifying: Black Women Writing the American Experience* (Madison: University of Wisconsin Press, 1987), p. 31.
[44]The phrase is Hemenway's in *Hurston*, p. 213.

realm" of her own people, to the friendship with Big Sweet, in order to learn to say what her dying mother could not, in order to name the chain of legendary female figures who can teach her to re-member and to speak the past.

4

Con Artists and Storytellers: Maya Angelou's Problematic Sense of Audience

> The story, though allegorical, is also historical; . . . and it is as reasonable to represent one kind of imprisonment by another, as it is to represent anything that really exists by that which exists not.
>
> Daniel Defoe, *Robinson Crusoe's Preface*
>
> My books. They had been my elevators out of the midden.
>
> Maya Angelou, *Gather Together in My Name*

As a literary foremother, Zora Neale Hurston meant a great deal to Maya Angelou the autobiographer. Urged by her editor to start work on a multivolume project about her life, Hurston said that she really did not *"want"* to write an autobiography, admitting that "it is too hard to reveal one's inner self." Like Hurston, Angelou affirms that she "really got roped into writing *The Caged Bird*," challenged by an editor who dared her to succeed in the difficult task of writing "an autobiography as literature."[1] That she wrote it *as literature* is the specific aspect of her work on which I shall focus in this chapter. Because the autobiographical project was a response to external pressures, it is in many ways directed to a white audience, but at the same time, it succeeds in gesturing toward the black community, which shares a long tradition among oppressed peoples of understanding duplicitous uses of language for survival. Thus a passage of *I Know Why the Caged Bird Sings* encapsulates the questions of "truth" and referentiality as well as Angelou's problematic sense of

[1] Maya Angelou, interview with Claudia Tate in *Black Women Writers at Work* (New York: Continuum, 1983), pp. 2, 6, hereinafter CT; Robert Hemenway, *Zora Neale Hurston: A Literary Biography* (Urbana: University of Illinois Press, 1980), pp. 275, 278. I shall be using the following editions and abbreviations of Angelou's works: *I Know Why the Caged Bird Sings* (New York: Random House, 1970): IK; *Gather Together in My Name* (New York: Random House, 1974): GT; *Singin' and Swingin' and Gettin' Merry like Christmas* (New York: Random House, 1976): SS; and *The Heart of a Woman* (New York: Random House, 1981): HW. This chapter was written before the publication of *All God's Children Need Traveling Shoes* (New York: Random House, 1986).

audience. In that passage, Angelou alludes to her grandmother's secretive and cautious ways with language:

Knowing Momma, I knew that I never knew Momma. Her African-bush secretiveness and suspiciousness had been compounded by slavery and confirmed by centuries of promises made and promises broken. We have a saying among Black Americans which describes Momma's caution. "If you ask a Negro where he's been, he'll tell you where he's going." To understand this important information, it is necessary to know who uses this *tactic* and on whom it works. *If an unaware person* is told a part of the truth (it is imperative that the answer embody truth), he is satisfied that his query has been answered. *If an aware person (one who himself uses the stratagem)* is given an answer which is truthful but bears only slightly if at all on the question, he knows that the information he seeks is of a private nature and will not be handed to him willingly. Thus direct denial, lying and the revelation of personal affairs are avoided. [164–65; my italics]

For Momma, the "signifying" of truths and untruths varies according to the status of her interlocutors, and it is in this differentiation between the "unaware" interlocutor and the "aware" that we can begin to understand Angelou's conception of "autobiographical" narration and the double audience she addresses in her writings: an audience split along racial and gender lines but also—and this is the important point here—split between those interlocutors, on the one hand, who share with the narrator an unquestioned sense of community and those, on the other hand, who have a relationship of power over that narrator.

Clearly, for Angelou, writing an autobiography has little to do with "the revelation of personal affairs," and like Hurston, she does not "reveal [her] inner self." Indeed, the passage about Momma can be read as an important example of the "self-situating" power of literary texts.[2] Momma's caution functions as an explicit warning to the reader, who is thus challenged to take note of the double-voiced nature of Angelou's text. Her narrator alternates between a constative and a performative use of language, simultaneously addressing a white and a black audience, "image making" (CT 1) and instructing, using allegory to talk about history and myths to refer to reality,

2See Ross Chambers, "An Address in the Country: Mallarmé and the Kinds of Literary Context," *French Forum* 11 (May 1986), 199–215 (199).

thus undermining the institutions that generate this alienated form of consciousness. Here, Angelou provides us with a model for reading and interpreting her narratives, just as Hurston had in her discussions of form and content, truth and hyperbole.

But unlike Hurston, whom we could see as strongly connected to other women in a network of friendly relationships, as well as to rich and solid folk traditions she helps to reclaim—that of "conjure women,"[3] for example—Angelou's narrator is a much more picaresque heroine, a modern-day Moll Flanders, who learns to survive by her wits. In that respect, she too is related to a black folk tradition, but one that is perhaps perceived as more "male": the shiftless trickster or con man, who relies on his ability to tell a good "story" to get out of sticky situations (Brer Rabbit, for instance). The narrator's mother also fits into this tradition. She is a consummate "business woman," runs her rooming house with a fist of steel, has "a roster of conquests" (IK 186) that testify to her independent nature. She is a Jill-of-all-trades who, by the fourth volume of the narrative, is said to have been "a surgical nurse, a realtor, had a barber's license and owned a hotel" (HW 28). The relationship between Maya and her mother has puzzled critics who have tried to approach the "autobiography" from the perspective of a "metaphysics of matrilinearism."[4] I prefer to see in the descriptions of Vivian Baxter's life and character the model of a streetwise, self-confident, "finger-snapping" woman (cf. IK 54). It is against this maternal persona and role model that Maya the narrator keeps measuring her accomplishments, only to find herself lacking. Her mother is so competent that she can only feel inadequate when she tries to emulate Vivian's indomitable individualism.

An example of Maya's imitative strategy is her attempt at running a whorehouse on the outskirts of San Diego. (GT chaps. 13–15). This episode ends, after her efforts at outsmarting the tough lesbian

---

[3]For an excellent study of the "conjure" folk tradition in black women writers, see *Conjuring: Black Women, Fiction, and the Literary Tradition*, ed. Marjorie Pryse and Hortense J. Spillers (Bloomington: Indiana University Press, 1985).

[4]See the article by Stephanie A. Demetrakopoulos, "The Metaphysics of Matrilinearism in Women's Autobiography: Studies of Mead's *Blackberry Winter*, Hellman's *Pentimento*, Angelou's *I Know Why the Caged Bird Sinks*, and Kingston's *Woman Warrior*," in *Women's Autobiography: Essays in Criticism*, ed. Estelle C. Jelinek (Bloomington: Indiana University Press, 1980), pp. 180–205. This critic discussed the Venus/Demeter archetypes in relation to the Vivian Baxter–Momma Henderson couple (p. 198).

whores who "work" for her prove unsuccessful, in her bewildered flight back to her grandmother's store in Arkansas. As the narrative develops, Maya gradually acquires her own survival techniques. These are, in a metaphoric way, closely linked to the development of her skills as "singer," "dancer," and "storyteller." In one of her San Francisco nightclub acts, for instance, she adopts the stage role of Scheherazade and succeeds, she says, because "I convinced myself that I was dancing to save my life" (*SS* 60). Her stated frame of reference is fiction and literature, and her style parodies that of such fictional autobiographies as *Moll Flanders*.

In this chapter, while focusing on Angelou's double-voiced technique of storytelling, I would like to emphasize three points. The chapter's first section shows how the narrator's love of books, always and everywhere, manages to pull her "out of the midden" (*GT* 90). As Tzvetan Todorov has said, "The desire to write does not come from life but from other writings."[5] Books are Angelou's "first life line" after the traumatic events of her childhood (*IK* 77) and will continue to inspire her throughout her career.[6] During her travels, for example, it is often through the prism of literature that she discovers and appreciates the peoples and places she visits: Verona through Shakespeare, Paris through Maupassant, London through Dickens. It thus seems appropriate, when analyzing her text, to use the literary paradigms she so cleverly manipulates. My second point concerns her use of the religious tradition: she inverts its messages, creating in the process nothing less than a feminist response to Augustine's *Confessions*. Finally, the third section shows how her problematic sense of audience is translated textually by an astute use of various embedded instances of alienated and nonalienated forms of human communication deriving from her folk traditions.

The Picaresque Heroine

Angelou's style owes as much to eighteenth- and nineteenth-century English narratives—those of Swift, Defoe, and Dickens in par-

[5]Tzvetan Todorov, *Literature and Its Theorists: A Personal View of Twentieth-Century Criticism*, trans. Catherine Porter (Ithaca: Cornell University Press, 1987), p. 165.

[6]Scanning the text for overt or covert references to well-known authors or fictional characters, I arbitrarily stopped counting at 100 at the end of the third volume, and I am not including in that figure the many folk poems, spirituals, composers, and songwriters also mentioned.

ticular—as it does to the black vernacular. It is truly a crossroads of influences and, at its best, weaves all these strands into a pattern in which, though they have become indistinguishable from one another, they give depth and detail to the narrative. George E. Kent has shown that "two areas of black life" subtend the development of Angelou's narrative, "the religious and the blues traditions." Her grandmother represents the religious influence: black fundamentalism, the Christian Methodist Episcopal church. Her mother, on the other hand, stands for the "blues-street" tradition, the fast life.[7] I agree with Kent's analysis but also believe there is a third term to add to this comparison: the literary tradition, all the fictional works the narrator reads avidly. This third tradition is represented figuratively in the text by two other strong women, Bertha Flowers and Martha Flowers (*IK* 77; *SS* 115). The text constructs these characters as fictional, boldly giving them almost identical names and stating that *flowers* is a recognizable slang word for "monthlies," or menstruation, in the black prostitutes' subculture (*GT* 39). When the narrator learns this "special" meaning of *flowers* from the two lesbian whores, she shows embarrassment and immediately resorts to "words" to conceal her feelings, to cope with her discomfort: "I knew that words, despite the old saying, never fail. And *my reading had given me words to spare.* I could and often did to myself or my baby, recite whole passages of Shakespeare, Paul Lawrence Dunbar poems, Kipling's 'If,' Countee Cullen, Langston Hughes, Longfellows's [*sic*] *Hiawatha*, Arna Bontemps. *Surely I had enough words to cover a moment's discomfort.* I had enough for hours if need be" (*GT* 40; my italics).

The flow of words is meant to cover a momentary discomfort, a discomfort due to an allusion to "flowers," which thus connotes an implicit comparison between women's creative and procreative powers. The juxtaposition between the slang word and "literary" words points back to the narrator's rediscovery of human language after her deflowering at the age of eight. It is thanks to the help of "Bertha Flowers," who teaches her to recite poetry, that she begins to talk again after a year of sensory numbness and dumbness, following the rape trial. This juxtaposition also points forward to her

[7]George E. Kent, "Maya Angelou's *I Know Why the Caged Bird Sings* and Black Autobiographical Tradition," *Kansas Quarterly* 7 (Summer 1975), 75.

friendship with "Martha Flowers," "a great soprano" and a member of the *Porgy and Bess* touring company, who will share her European experiences. Language and menstruation are thus brought into implicit parallel as flow, voice, words, songs all connote by association the fluid movements of music or text. There is a creative tension between Angelou's Nietzschean need to be free to "write with blood" and the narrative control she exerts on plot development.[8] What this tension denotes is her attempt to come to terms with the paradoxes and contradictions inherent in the concept of female creativity.

Indeed, the comparison between intellectual production and pregnancy, creativity and procreation, has been a commonplace of Western discourse since Socrates, who practiced intellectual *maieusis* on his students. What seems to be implied in Angelou's text is that menstruation is a far better paradigm for creativity, a paradigm Marie Cardinal will use with considerable effect in *The Words to Say It*. Are we to infer that Angelou is implying a conflict between writing and mothering? I would suggest not, in view of the role assigned to her mother, Vivian Baxter. Full of energy and self-confidence, she represents creativity in the "rhythm and blues" tradition, and Angelou uses images of liquids to describe her: "As I scrambled around the foot of the success ladder, Mother's life flowed radiant. Fluorescent-tipped waves on incoming tides" (*GT* 104).

The mother's energy flows unchecked and unselfconsciously. She has raw power, and her style is improvised like the ebb and flow of jazz. If this flow of creative rhythms is in counterpoint to the actual mothering of a real child, it is interesting to note again that Angelou the author dedicates her first volume to her son. Perhaps this is a perfect example of the ambivalence that occupies the center of all feminist problematics about writing: to produce the book, the woman must follow rhythms of creativity which may be in conflict with the mothering/nurturing role. To be sure, one can see Vivian Baxter as a nonnurturing, highly competitive, and goal-oriented mother. Yet she is the one who teaches Maya to trust her body, to follow her maternal instincts when her son Guy is born. *I Know Why the Caged Bird Sings* ends in the physical experience of giving birth to Guy.

[8]The phrase is Nietzsche's in *Thus Spoke Zarathustra*, pt. 1, in *The Portable Nietzsche*, trans. Walter Kaufmann (New York: Viking Press, 1967), p. 153.

"Famous for [her] awkwardness," the narrator "was afraid to touch him." But Vivian coaxes her into sleeping with the baby, although at first she "lay on the edge of the bed, stiff with fear, and vowed not to sleep all night long" (245). Eventually she relaxes and sleeps with her arm curled and the baby touching her side. This experience teaches Maya the same lesson that Milkman, the hero of Toni Morrison's *Song of Solomon*, learns facing death, that "if you surrendered to the air, you could *ride* it."[9]

Vivian puts it in a less poetic, more pragmatic way, teaching Maya that her body is a friend she can trust: "See, you don't have to think about doing the right thing. If you're for the right thing, then you do it without thinking" (246). What this remark implies is that the conflict between productive and reproductive roles is a false problem, a myth created by false anxieties; nonetheless it is a myth internalized by women writers, perhaps because there are as yet so few "creative mothers," like Vivian Baxter, who can show us how to "surrender to the air" *not* just in order to face death but so as to do "the right thing . . . without thinking," without being petrified by fear and guilt in the face of life, which is always change, flux, flow, tide, rhythm—like the music Vivian Baxter loves.

To the extent that Angelou feels strongly that a mother can never be fully independent—psychologically detached, that is—she constantly wrestles with this conflict. Her text embodies these tensions in its structure. During her year in Europe, she keeps having pangs of anxiety about her son, although she enjoys "every minute" of freedom: "Uncomfortable thoughts kept me awake. I had left my son to go gallivanting in strange countries and had enjoyed every minute except the times when I had thought about him" (*SS* 230). Hysterical from guilt and anxiety after her son becomes sick, she pays a useless visit to a psychiatrist, for whom, she imagines, she is only "another case of Negro paranoia" (235). Finally, she follows the advice of a friend and *writes* down her blessings: " I can hear / I can speak . . . I can dance / I can sing . . . I can write" (236). She regains her self-confidence, and her son simultaneously recovers: "Before my eyes a physical and mental metamorphosis began, as gradually and as inexorably as a seasonal change" (237). To write is to give herself the permission not to feel guilty. To write is to love her son in

9Toni Morrison, *Song of Solomon* (New York: Signet, 1977), p. 341.

a life-affirming way. The third volume ends on this image of rebirth for both mother and son: she writes and he "names" himself, as we shall see presently. There is no real conflict: it was only a societal myth about maternal neglect, an internalization of false dichotomies between mothering and smothering or mothering and working.

Angelou attempts to solve the conflict textually by creating metaphors that point to a reality beyond this form of deadly dualism. She creates a mythology of the "creative mother" so that other mothers writing do not have to "feel like a motherless child" (as the spiritual says) when attempting to be creative. For Nikki Giovanni, another contemporary black autobiographer, to "feel like a motherless child" is to be without a mythology of our own because we have "underestimated our strength." The power to create mythology is a characteristic of the "honkies" that Black women should imitate, she says. "The honkie is the best mythologist in creation. He's had practice because his whole wrap [sic] is to protect himself from his environment."[10]

Clearly stated here is the quintessential Western dichotomy between nature and culture. Learning to "ride the air," however, would mean learning to be nurtured by nature—as Colette knew well—learning to take pleasure in the materiality of the world (our children), as well as the materiality of the word (our writing), as Angelou discovers. We are not very far from Roland Barthes's statements in The Pleasure of the Text:

> If it were possible to imagine an aesthetic of textual pleasure, it would have to include writing aloud [l'écriture à haute voix]. . . . its aim is not the clarity of messages, the theater of emotions; what it searches for (in a perspective of bliss [jouissance]) are the pulsional incidents, the language lined with flesh, a text where we can hear the grain of the throat, the patina of consonants, the voluptuousness of vowels, a whole carnal stereophony: the articulation of the body, of the tongue, not that of meaning, of language. A certain art of singing can give an idea of this vocal writing.[11]

This "vocal writing" is familiar to Vivian who "sang the heavy blues . . . [and] talked with her whole body" (IK 54), and to Bertha

[10]Nikki Giovanni, Gemini (New York: Penguin Books, 1971), pp. 145, 124.

[11]Roland Barthes, The Pleasure of the Text, trans. Richard Miller (New York: Hill and Wang, 1975), pp. 66–67.

Flowers, who advises Maya: "Words mean more than what is set down on paper. It takes the human voice to infuse them with the shades of deeper meaning" (*IK* 82). It is also familiar to anyone who has ever told stories to a small child, stories that infuse words with meaning and let the child hear "the *grain* of the voice," as Barthes would say. Children who are learning to use language enjoy the density of words in precisely that playful way.

Angelou's own playfulness with words is evident in her choice of names for the characters. The names of the narrator, her brother, her mother, her son, and her lovers all bear interesting indications of a fictional and metaphoric use of language, closely resembling Defoe's in *Moll Flanders*. Maya Angelou, as she explains, is the stage name of Marguerite Johnson (*marguerite* being the French word for a flower, the daisy). Maya, she writes, is a name created for her in childhood when her brother started calling her first "my sister," then "my," "mya," and finally "Maya" (*IK* 57). Angelou is a corruption of her first husband's name, Angelos. Tosh Angelos is a Greek who shares her love of jazz (i.e., black) music and English (i.e., white) literature, but their marriage fails because "he wrapped us in a cocoon of safety" (*SS* 27), which was like another cage, a shield, a veil against reality. After her divorce, she finds a job as a dancer in a bar: "If men wanted to buy my drinks, I would accept and tell them [the truth]. . . . That, along with imaginative dancing, would erase the taint of criminality. *Art* would be my *shield* and honesty my spear" (*SS* 58; italics mine).

The narrator abandons one kind of shield—marriage—but adopts a new one—art and dance. Now, in the Hindustani language, *māyā* is the word for "veil," and in Vedantic philosophy it is synonymous with the power to produce illusions and appearances. The Goddess Mahāmāyā personifies the world of illusion, and she is the power that creates phenomena.[12] Might the author want to imply that the narrative is fiction and illusion, creations of Angelou, the author?

---

[12]"God Himself is Mahāmāyā, who deludes the world with her illusion and conjures up the magic of creation, preservation, and destruction. She has spread this veil of ignorance before our eyes," The Gospel of S'rī Rāmakrishna, p. 116, as quoted in Heinrich Zimmer, *Philosophies of India*, ed. Joseph Campbell (New York: Meridian Books, 1956), p. 569. I am not suggesting that Angelou uses Vedantic philosophy consciously. I am merely making connections which the polysemic nature of such proper nouns allows me to make as reader of her text.

That, like God, she has the power to (re)create the life story of the narrator, to show that she is an "angel," but in appearance only? . That she "sings" like an angel, perhaps? And dances, like Salome, a "Dance of the Seven Veils" (*SS* 45), creating a multilayered artistic illusion? The text clearly allows for all these interpretations. Furthermore, if "Maya" is a creator and a goddess, she is invested with powers comparable to those of the "conjure women" of black tradition, and we would thus be justified in reinscribing this text within that tradition. I do not intend to do this here, but I do want to point out that this possibility exists, especially when we consider that the Greek word *angelos, -ou* means "messenger." Maya thus figures as the creator, Angelou as her messenger, the one who brings her forth while remaining veiled (*maya angelou* means the veil of the messenger: an interesting combination of Indo-European roots).

Ironically, Vivian Baxter's name points to an eighteenth-century figure with whose writings Defoe was familiar, the Reverend Richard Baxter, whose preaching style and "technique of persuasion," writes Ian Watt, "depended almost entirely on the simplest of rhetorical devices, repetition."[13] Defoe and Angelou both rely heavily on the same device. In her texts repetition is most striking in the short summaries or recapitulations of past events that stud the narrative and serve as reminders to the reader before the onset of new developments. These are more and more frequent in the third and fourth volumes, becoming a leitmotiv, like the choral responses of church prayer and music, which are meant to create familiarity and audience participation.[14] This style of conscious repetition harks back to the advice Baxter gives as a preacher. Discussing Baxter and the influence he has had on Defoe, Ian Watt quotes the eighteenth century preacher: "If we speak anything briefly, they feel not what we say. Nay, I find if we do not purposely dress out the matter into such a length of words, and use some repetition of it, that they may hear it inculcated on them again, we do but overrun their understandings, and they presently lose us."[15]

All preachers, and those in the black church especially, use this

[13]Ian Watt, *The Rise of the Novel* (Berkeley: University of California Press, 1957), p. 102.

[14]See for example *IK* 230; *GT* 3; *SS* 8, 24, 25, 110, 179; *HW* 29, 34, 224, 263: These repetitions clearly underscore the picaresque themes.

[15]Watt, p. 102.

technique. Angelou follows Baxter's advice on a purely textual level: her narrative mimics and parodies this style. On metaphoric and symbolic levels, however, she constructs an interesting inversion of this paradigm: Vivian Baxter, fast living, impatient, with no interest in details and repetitions ("Vivian Baxter could and would deal with grand schemes and large plots, but please, pray God, spare her the details." [SS, 101]), is the female character she most admires and openly tries to emulate, as daughters emulate mothers. Vivian Baxter is a figurative inversion of her eighteenth century namesake— the preacher—as her "blues-street"[16] life makes clear. So, on the one hand, we have a religious style that allows us to insert Angelou's work back into the black *religious* context. On the other hand, we have a textual figure, Vivian, who is a model for the narrator and who embodies the free style of improvisation (with variation on and repetition of a single basic pattern) in black *music:* jazz and the blues. The link between these two poles is the literary tradition, which relays Richard Baxter, by means of Defoe's *Moll Flanders,* to the twentieth-century black female writer. The biological mother, Vivian Baxter, has a fictional counterpart in Moll, whose "autobiography" could be seen as the matrix that allows Angelou to produce and reproduce her own narrative discourse. As a central and polysemic narrative figure, Vivian embodies all the traditions whose combined influences are evident in Angelou's textual production.[17]

Furthermore, the anxieties Maya feels before her mother seem to metaphorize the author's relation to the British narrative tradition: meeting her mother in St. Louis, Maya is stunned by Vivian's beauty and presence. Her light skin, straight hair, and talented dancing

---

[16]Kent, p. 75.

[17]Ronnie Scharfman's statement that a "feminist aesthetic can shed new light on . . . the possible bonds between the text as mother, and the daughter-reader it produces" is highly appropriate here. See "Mirroring and Mothering in Simone Schwarz-Bart's *Pluie et vent sur Télumée Miracle* and Jean Rhys's *Wide Sargasso Sea,*" *Yale French Studies* 62 (1981), 88–106 (106). As I try to make clear, however, in Angelou's case, the mother-text is a "male" text, Daniel Defoe's *Moll Flanders.* As a fictional character, Moll Flanders, like Vivian Baxter, is a mediator for Maya: Moll mediates the (male) literary tradition, whereas Vivian relays the (male) black vernacular. Again, it is important to note that these are connections that I am making as a reader familiar with both English eighteenth-century narratives and traditional African and Afro-American cultures. The point is not whether Angelou *intended* to suggest the possibility of such playful associations. Rather, I contend that the dynamism of the text freely and ironically generates those meanings.

make her unreal to her children. "I could never put my finger on her realness" (*IK* 57), and she is "like a pretty kite that floated just above my head," (54) says Maya. She is an unattainable ideal, distant and out of reach for her "ugly" daughter. I would suggest that we can read in the descriptions of this too beautiful, almost white mother, the same "anxiety of authorship" that Angelou the writer may feel before her literary precursors, such as Daniel Defoe, for example, whose *Moll Flanders* she nonetheless tries to emulate.[18] This eighteenth century narrative, closer in language to many southern idioms than those are to contemporary standard English, offers a sympathetic yet inescapably alienating reading of an individualistic "heroine." Vivian Baxter is such an individualist, and in *Gather Together in My Name*, the narrator does attempt to adopt her mother's life-style. But in sharing ideals of beauty and independence which are beyond reach, the daughter only alienates herself. Similarly, the English literary tradition has a beauty and a power that attract Angelou the writer, yet must leave her feeling inadequate before her precursor's discursive models of staunch individualism.

Angelou gives other clues to help the reader understand her naming technique: her son's name in the second volume is Guy. Then in the third volume, he becomes "Clyde," without explanation. We could see this as one example of the kind of "casual attitude to . . . writing," as Ian Watt puts it, which goes far toward explaining the "inconsistencies in matters of detail which are very common in all [Defoe's] works."[19] Except that in Angelou's case, the matter of her son's name is hardly a "detail." At the end of the third volume, we are given the explanation that he himself has just decided to change his name to Guy. Clyde, he says, is "an O.K. name for a river, but my name is Guy" (238). At no point does the narrative explain or suggest why he was Guy throughout the second volume. What we can infer from the name Clyde however (the Clyde River of Scotland), is the idea of flowing waters, metaphoric female creation and procreation. Changing his name to Guy, this fatherless son appropriates the absent father's prerogative of naming and chooses a first name that is unmistakably "masculine": he thus sets himself

18On "anxiety of authorship," see Sandra M. Gilbert and Susan Gubar, *The Madwoman in the Attic: The Woman Writer and the Nineteenth-Century Literary Imagination* (New Haven: Yale University Press, 1979), pp. 45–92 especially.

19Watt, p. 99.

apart from the female creative principle. As Janheinz Jahn says in his study of African culture: "The new-born child becomes a *muntu* only when the father or the 'sorcerer' gives him a *name* and *pronounces* it. Before this the little body is a *kintu*, a thing; if it dies it is not even mourned. . . . A creature . . . which has its place in the community of men is produced, not by act of birth, but by the word-seed: it is designated."[20] Thus Clyde becomes a true member of the community after he has assumed the responsibility of naming himself. It marks the beginning of his separation and emancipation from the maternal realm. He is nine years old, and his show of independence connotes another separation, as in the act of birth, after a nine-month gestation. The child of her "immaculate pregnancy" (*IK* 245), he has now become a true "muntu" and designated himself as such: Guy, a guy, a man who rejects the erasure of his African past in much the same way that Malcolm X did by changing his name.

The names given to Maya's lovers and husbands suggest a duplicitous use of language and a conscious effort of fictional narration. *Tosh* in Scottish, means trim (and in black slang, to get or give "some trim" means to get laid [cf. *IK* 240]), as well as neat and proper. Tosh Angelos is a very proper and protective husband until marriage turns him into a louse. On the cruise ship that takes the opera company from Italy to Egypt, Maya meets the ship's doctor whose "eyes smoldered wonderful promises" (*SS* 201). He too is Greek: Geracimos Vlachos. But he says,"I am called Maki." He wants to marry her in order to emigrate to the United States, where he will be able to "make money" (214) practicing medicine. She flatly refuses. In the next volume, she marries a black South African freedom fighter. "His name was Vusumzi Make (pronounced Mah-kay)" (*HW* 104). He turns out to be pretentious and overbearing. In Cairo she soon becomes disillusioned with this fake "African King," who furnishes their apartment in "Louis XVI brocaded sofa and chairs . . . French antique furniture . . . Oriental rugs," (*HW* 214). Instead of experiencing the "African" way of life, she is burdened with all the external signs of European monarchy. The words *make* (Old English) and *maki* (Old Norse) are cognates: they both mean

[20]Janheinz Jahn, *Muntu: An Outline of the New African Culture* (New York: Grove Press, 1961), p. 125.

mate, consort, spouse. It is quite clear that these three characters are facets of the same type and that Angelou is playfully suggesting ironic similarities among them.

The theme of similarity within difference in their names seems to point to a philosophy of life at once similar and different from Moll's (and Vivian Baxter's): the economic individualism of Moll would have dictated that she marry Maki, the doctor, since his M.D. degree could be turned into real currency, real wealth. Also, Moll would have taken advantage of Make's lavish life-style, but Maya only finds it distasteful and alienating. Defoe is "not ashamed to make economic self-interest his major premise about human life," says Watt. Angelou's premise is more *engagé* and more modern. Like Defoe, she uses what Watt calls "an episodic but life-like plot sequence," but her aim is always to return to the familiar and nurturing domain of books and literature.[21] Like Moll, Angelou's narrator has definite ambitions, but whereas Moll wants to become a gentlewoman, Maya wants immortality and fame. She wants to join the "elite group of published writers" (*HW* 85): "I decided that one day I would be included in the family legend. . . . my name would be among the most illustrious. . . . I had written a juicy melodrama in which I was to be the star" (*GT* 28). Defoe writes with great sympathy for women's restricted roles in society, and Moll is a good example of a woman "smart enough" not to allow herself to be involuntarily restricted by a feminine role. Angelou's narrator struggles against similar social codes, and eventually finds the courage to stand her ground and define her territory, but it is the territory of a "too smart" woman (*GT* 166): libraries, books, and writing. In Cairo, she becomes a journalist (as Defoe was), and takes refuge in the newsroom of the *Arab Observer* and in its "library with hundreds of books in English" (*HW* 231). She achieves a measure of emancipation thanks to her intellectual talents and her love of books. It is quite an accomplishment for the little girl from Stamps, who grew up in the red dirt of the American South, "where children become bald from malnutrition" (*SS* 110). Her checkered existence finally comes to a resting point in Accra, where she lands a job as administrative assistant at the University of Ghana.

[21]Watt, pp. 127, 107.

Language and Silence

The title of Maya Angelou's first volume, *I Know Why the Caged Bird Sings*, introduces the major metaphors that will run through all four of her books: imprisonment and singing. In *Black Autobiography in America*, Stephen Butterfield compares this work with those of Richard Wright and Frederick Douglass. The male writers, he says, tend to portray their lives of struggle against the white oppressor and their efforts to destroy the "cage" of racism and slavery, "But, unlike *Black Boy* and *The Life and Times*, the subject of *I Know Why the Caged Bird Sings* is not really the struggle of the bird; it is the exploration of the cage, the gradual discovery of its boundaries, the loosening of certain bars that she can slip through when the keepers' backs are turned."[22]

Indeed Maya's "struggle" is of a different nature from that of the males: more personal and less public or social. There are no direct or violent confrontations with intense racial overtones. Her sense of humor is in sharp contrast to the seriousness of a Richard Wright. But I would suggest that, as the title of the volume implies, her subject is much more than the "exploration" or representation of this circumscribed domain. It is, rather, the investigation of the process through which the "bird" learns *how* to sing and the reasons *why* she does so in the face of adversity. To discuss the how and the why of the song, however, requires us to do a careful analysis of the textual layers and of their structuring moments.[23]

For example, the store where Maya and her brother live, "her favorite place to be" (13), the center of activity in Stamps and the source of food and surprises, is an important structuring image, whereas the rape trial is a central and structuring moment of the first volume. The store full of treasures is like a book that contains unexpected pleasures for the reader ("Alone and empty in the mornings, it looked like an unopened present from a stranger. Opening the front doors was pulling the ribbon off the unexpected gift [13]). The only place she calls "home" (GT 63), the store is a metaphor for

[22]Stephen Butterfield, *Black Autobiography in America* (Amherst: University of Massachusetts Press, 1974), pp. 207–8.

[23]Sidonie Ann Smith, "The Song of a Caged Bird: Maya Angelou's Quest after Self-Acceptance," *Southern Humanities Review* 7 (1973), 365–75, gives a detailed account of the various events that lead to the narrator's sense of always being out of place. My approach and conclusions differ from Smith's, however.

the storehouse of memory, which can be opened—as the "cage" will be opened—by the ribbon of language. It is a refuge like the libraries and the books she loves (and indeed she will seek refuge in a library after her rape). For Marie-Thérèse Humbert too the village store will function as a protective matrix, as a safe and enclosed space where the narrator can feel restored and reborn.

The way in which Angelou's text presents the events leading both to her rape and to the trial provides an interesting context to the whole notion of familial rape vs. social violation. The trial scene is the subject of chapter 13, but it is already symbolically implied in the opening scene of the book, where the experience of being on display—in church—is powerfully rendered. This opening scene is a classic example of the theme of woman-as-spectacle, woman unwillingly displaying herself. Here, it is a little girl thrust before a community of people gathered to worship God the Father. She had been looking forward to this day, dreaming that she was going to "look like a movie star" when she recited her poem in church: "What you looking at me for? / I didn't come to stay . . ." But on that Easter morning, she does not metamorphose into "one of the sweet little white girls who were everybody's dream of what was right with the world" (1). Instead, she is painfully aware of the gap between that dream and her actual physical appearance: she is wearing a dress that is "a plain ugly cut-down from a white woman's once-was-purple throwaway" (2); her "skinny legs" and skin that "look[s] dirty like mud" seem to be the focus of everyone's gaze. Not surprisingly, she loses all her aplomb, forgets her lines, hears only the "wiggling and giggling" (1) of the other children, runs out of church: "I stumbled and started to say something, or maybe to scream, but a green persimmon, or it could have been a lemon caught me between the legs and squeezed. I tasted the sour on my tongue and felt it in the back of my mouth. Then before I reached the door, the sting was burning down my legs and into my Sunday socks" (3). As she runs back home "peeing and crying," all she can think about is that (as the popular superstition goes) she must *not* hold back the flow of urine or "it would probably run right back up to my head and my poor head would burst like dropped watermelon, and all the brains and spit and tongue and eyes would roll all over the place" (3). The problem is that she will surely "get a whipping" for losing mental and physical control and be mercilessly teased by the "nasty chil-

dren" of the congregation. Her performance anxiety leads to complete failure, and failure results in harsh punishment imposed by
family (the whipping) and society (the laughter of her peers).

This scene encapsulates all the elements that have become identified with the ambiguities of female performance: having to live up to
an idealized image; feeling imprisoned in a body that does not correspond to the idealized image; dreaming of escaping from that
"cage"; dealing with the problematics of public speech when "other
things [are] more important," (1) such as the feeling of giving-
oneself-away-as-spectacle (an "ugly" spectacle at that) and the literal
numbness and dumbness that ensues. The flow of involuntary excretions is perceived as both releasing and threatening: if she holds
it back, she may "die from a busted head"'; (3) if she lets it flow, she
will surely be punished. To write or not to write is another facet of
the same predicament. Until abolition de jure, but until much later
de facto , it was a punishable crime to teach a black to read or write;
yet we also believe that a talented person may be "driven to a numb
and bleeding madness"[24] if creativity is constantly stifled and finds
no outlet. The bottom line remains painful: whatever her choices,
the consequences are going to be difficult. In this case, she runs
away from the public eye, choking back tears and laughter, her lines
unspoken, her pride wounded. Her body has had the upper hand,
its physical release from tension manifested in this uncontrolled
urge to urinate.

This opening scene squarely pits the mind against the body, the
mind biting the red dust of Arkansas because the body is such a
great liability. It is particularly significant that this episode, chrono-
logically out of sequence in the narrative, should set the tone for the
story. For this is clearly the tale of a woman who learns to "let the
words flow," to perform in public and sing "gloriously," and to find
the positive links between body and mind that will allow her to
break free of the cage of prejudice and self-hatred. As discussed
before, the book ends on another physical experience, the birth of
her son, which teaches her to trust her body's language and knowledge, to make it the source and the model of her creativity. This

[24]Alice Walker, "In Search of Our Mother's Gardens," reprinted in *The Norton
Anthology of Literature by Women*, ed. Sandra M. Gilbert and Susan Gubar (New York:
Norton, 1985), p. 2375.

trajectory is a familiar one in many women writers' autobiographies. The positive links that Angelou finds are literature and music.

Initially, however, she is literally brainwashed into silence by religion, family, and society. Grandmother Henderson is the primary agent—and model—of this silence. During cotton-picking season, she would get up everyday at four o'clock and "creak down to her knees, and chant in a sleep-filled voice: 'Our Father, thank you for letting me see this New Day. . . . Guide my feet this day along the straight and narrow, and help me *put a bridle on my tongue*,' "(5; my italics). Saying too much or saying the wrong thing is akin to being impudent, and "the impudent child was detested by God" (22). The consistent self-control that Momma can exert in stressful encounters (cf. 24–27) is in sharp contrast to Maya's frequent loss of control in church. There is another instance of hysterical laughter and uncontrolled urinating in chapter 6, and these episodes are severely punished. The hysteria, however, comes right after the narrator has been commenting on her increasing capacity for tuning out the world and wrapping herself in a cocoon of silence and private daydreams: "Turning off or tuning out people was my highly developed art. The custom of letting obedient children be seen but not heard was so agreeable to me that I went one step further: Obedient children should not see or hear if they chose not to do so" (34).

This is the first ominous hint we have of the state of catatonic indifference she will fall into after the rape trial. Raped by her mother's neglected lover, she identifies with her rapist, whose densely physical presence had released in the lonely child a sense of belonging, of affiliation and security. Yet her trust is betrayed by the man she wanted to love as a father. Her body has suffered excruciating pain, but that in itself is nothing new for a child used to repeated corporal punishment.[25] Her imaginary world of language and literature is stolen by the intrusion of phallic power. Her family, as a whole, fails her. Yet the "rape" is not over. She also has to confront society in the courtroom, and that encounter reduces her to total

---

[25] I am not trying to minimize the tragedy of sexual exploitation of the young by family members. I do want to emphasize (1) that it is different only in degree from other forms of physical abuse and torture and (2) that Angelou's text implies that the social attribution of a negative (polluting) value to the sexual nature of the offense is more damaging in the long run that the act of rape itself.

silence. It is during the trial that she finally internalizes the religious teachings of her childhood completely and consequently begins to perceive herself as evil: "I had sold myself to the Devil and there could be no escape" (73). The defendant's lawyer attempts to put the blame on her, and the child becomes convinced that she is responsible for the rape: "I didn't want to lie, but the lawyer wouldn't let me think, so *I used silence as a retreat* " (70; my italics). The child quickly learns how to decode the social system in order not to be victimized any further. She has no choice but to lie for survival's sake. On the familial and social level, the rapist has been punished, justice has been done. On a personal level, however, Maya's ordeal is just beginning: having sworn on the Bible to say the truth, she is now much more traumatized by the memory of the lie and by the belief that she is responsible for the man's death.

She begins to see herself, through society's eyes, as an ambiguous victim. She gets the message that she must, on some level, have done something wrong. Since the rapist is responsible for making her lie, he must be evil. Because of him, evil invades her too, she is hopelessly contaminated by those troublesome bodily fluids, which are polluting and taboo: "Obviously I had forfeited my place in heaven forever, and I was as gutless as the doll I had ripped to pieces ages ago. . . . *I could feel the evilness flowing through my body and waiting, pent up, to rush off my tongue if I tried to open my mouth.* I clamped my teeth shut, I'd hold it in. If it escaped, wouldn't it flood the world and all the innocent people?" (72; my italics). Language is a form of "evilness," waiting to escape from her inner self like those fluids and involuntary excretions that can be hard to control (urine or semen) or simply embarrassing ("flowers," or menstruation). Language is evil, polluting, uncontrollable, and most of all the source of undeserved and incomprehensible punishments. The little girl is thus in possession of another deadly secret: that every word she utters may allow her inner and evil reality to escape and to hurt or kill others. She has no choice but to remove herself from the community by refusing language:

> Just my breath, carrying my words out, might poison people and they'd curl up and die like the black fat slugs that only pretended.
> I had to stop talking.
> I discovered that to achieve perfect personal silence all I had to do

was to attach myself leechlike to sound. . . . I simply stood still—*in the midst of the riot of sound. After a minute or two, silence would rush into the room from its hiding place because I had eaten all the sounds* (73; my italics).

Her isolation and alienation are complete. She achieves control over yet other bodily functions, her tongue, her breath. She closes off all her orifices, paradoxically, by letting the outside world of sounds rush in, so that the inner reality of evil is prevented from rushing out. She achieves "perfect personal silence" by being totally open, or *disponible*, to the external world while keeping her inner world repressed or suppressed.[26]

The sequence of textual events Angelou establishes draws a close parallel between the experience of rape and the child's internalization of societal and religious standards. First, her body is appropriated by the father figure—precisely on Saturday, the day she would normally have exercised her freedom to read, to "breath[e] in the world" of literature (64). Then, in the courtroom, she is given a reflection of herself as evil, just as in the opening scene of the book she saw herself mirrored in the eyes of the church community as a shameful and "black ugly dream" (2) who was "sucking in air to breath out shame" (1). Now she sees herself as a sinful and dirty vessel. Her secret and imaginary world has been violated, contaminated, and she can no longer escape there. Performance anxiety made her speechless in church. Now she discovers that language can perform, create reality, that language *is* powerful performance because it can kill. Mr. Freeman dies, and Maya metaphorically cuts off her own tongue.

In the Greek legend of Philomela, Tereus, and Procne, it is Tereus the rapist who, after violating Philomela, rips out her tongue in order to prevent her from telling the truth to her sister Procne,

[26]On June 18, 1986, Maya Angelou was on the The Oprah Winfrey Show, ABC-TV, Channel 7, Chicago, talking about her most recent work, All God's Children Need Traveling Shoes. Discussing her childhood and the events surrounding the rape trial, as recounted in I Know, she said "From the age of seven-and-a-half till twelve, my whole body became one big ear: I memorized poetry but didn't speak . . . because my voice had killed that man." This image of "one big ear" is familiar to readers of Thus Spoke Zarathustra (see "On Redemption,", p. 249) and has inspired Derrida's commentary on Nietzsche's "Logic of the Living Feminine," in The Ear of the Other: Otobiography, Transference, Translation, trans. Peggy Kamuf and Avital Ronell (New York: Schocken Books, 1985), p. 3.

Tereus's wife. Philomela then sends to her sister a piece of embroidery on which she has woven her story.[27] Maya's self-inflicted punishment is similar to Philomela's. But it is as a result of her own absorption of patriarchal, social, and religious discourses that she stifles herself. She has become a docile and benumbed element of the oppressive system that controls her life, until the discovery of literature allows her to weave her own story. It is clear from her own remarks that Angelou the author identifies with Philomela: when she first becomes a showgirl and a dancer in San Francisco, she is attracted to a drummer who befriends her but loves only his wife Philomena, about whom he says: "—pretty name, ain't it? She can tell a story that would break your heart. Or else she can make you split your sides" (*SS* 58). Angelou's own narrative is a tragicomic tale of growing up black and female in America. She creates an allegory of the feminine condition which cuts across historical, social, and racial lines, using laughter and compassion to defuse the implicit violence of her subject matter.

We may recall that in the *Confessions*, Augustine discusses his access to human language. ("I ceased to be an infant unable to talk, and was now a boy with the power of speech [non enim eram infans. . . . sed iam puer loquens eram]" as a function of his initiation into the "stormy or tempestuous life of human society [procellosam societatem]." His acquisition of the power of speech as well as his schooling in rhetoric are paralleled with the "fornications" he began to engage in, meaning "lying and cheating," as well as other "perversions." Ultimately, his progress to God must include a gradual silencing of his tongue, a quieting of the "storm" of language. It is the example of Bishop Ambrose which teaches him a nondiscursive spirituality of silence ("his voice was silent and his tongue was still").[28] That is why his "autobiography" ends with an exegetic reading of Genesis, a reading that puts the narrative chapters under erasure and eliminates all further "personal" or "literary" use of language by the author. Augustine becomes filled with the otherness of God and transcends his corporeality as he reaches a spiritual

[27]See the *Oxford Classical Dictionary*, s.v. "Philomela."

[28]Augustine, *Confessions*, trans. R. S. Pine-Coffin (New York: Penguin Books, 1979), pp. 29, 114. The Latin is from the Loeb Classical Library edition (Cambridge: Harvard University Press, 1977). References to book and chapter are 1:8, 4:3, and on fornication, 1:3, 2:6, 4:2, 5:12.

resting point in the Word of God, and in the text of Genesis. From then on, his use of language is confined to its ontological purposes: words are signifiers used to convey the transcendental signified, God.

Angelou's narrator also wants "to achieve perfect personal silence" as a means of redemption from the "evilness flowing through [her] body." That is why she quiets her tongue and thus removes herself from human society. But she cannot find peace in God because she had already "sworn on the Bible that everything [she] said would be the truth, the whole truth, so help [her] God" (*IK* 71). And the God she knows is not a warm, loving black father; rather she imagines him looking like the policeman who announces to her family the death of Mr. Freeman: "Had they found out about the lie? . . . The man in our living room was taller than the sky and whiter than my image of God. He just didn't have the beard" (71). So she creeps into a cocoon of numbness and becomes almost catatonic, all her senses dulled: she hears people's voices as though muffled, cannot perceive colors very well, and forgets names. Meanwhile, her brother Bailey is becoming adept at using his "silver tongue" to shape words and "two-pronged sentences" (76) of sarcasm and jokes that enchant the rural community of Stamps, where they have both returned after the trial. Bailey is becoming the consumate con artist while the girl is sinking deeper into silence.

It is after a year in Stamps that she meets Mrs. Bertha Flowers, a very dark-skinned woman, whose color "was a rich black" (78). She is a maternal and nurturing figure like Momma, but her aristocratic demeanor and formal education make her an instant role model for Maya, the imaginative reader of English novels. This woman has a positive self-image and makes Maya "proud to be a Negro, just by being herself" (79). As a narrative figure, she is the opposite of the tall white godlike policeman, and she becomes Maya's savior, a sort of tribal deity who helps her reevaluate her position within the community as well as the community's virtues. Maya begins to compare the "uneducated" speech patterns of her grandmother unfavorably to Mrs. Flowers's perfect diction and elocution. The child begins to notice the "texture" of the human voice and simultaneously opens up to human language as Mrs. Flowers encourages her to read aloud and to try "to make a sentence sound in as many different ways as possible" (82). But she also teaches Maya that illiteracy is not ignorance and that in the "mother wit" of country people is "couched the collective wisdom of generations" (83). Thus, from the start, Maya is forestalled from a destructive temptation to hierarchize different cultural models or to devalue the "primitive" folk attitudes of her rural background—an insight which Angelou the writer surely owes to her familiarity with Hurston's work.

Mrs. Flowers recites *A Tale of Two Cities* and Maya hears poetry "for the first time" (84) in her life:

> "It was the best of times and the worst of times. . . ." Her voice slid in and curved down through and over the words. She was nearly singing. I wanted to look at the pages. Were they the same that I had read? Or were there notes, music, lined on the pages, as in a hymn book? Her sounds began cascading gently. I knew from listening to a thousand preachers that she was nearing the end of her reading, *and I hadn't really heard, heard to understand, a single word.* [84; my italics]

In contrast to the noise and "riot of sound" that make her deaf to the world and to herself, the narrator now discovers "vocal writing": the materiality of language, the self-referential nature of the poetic word, "the patina of consonants, the voluptuousness of vowels" as Barthes would suggest. She hears the sounds but does not understand their meaning, because meaning is not important. Language becomes an arbitrary system of signs not grounded in external reality, especially not in the transcendent meaningful reality of God but rather in the pure, playful immanence of sounds. The sensual joy of literature favors a process of ecstasis and self-dispossession as Maya escapes through imagination:

> I have tried often to search behind the sophistication of years for the enchantment I so easily found in those gifts. The essence escapes but its aura remains. To be allowed, no, invited, into the private lives of strangers, and to share their joys and fears, was a chance to exchange the Southern bitter wormwood for a cup of mead with Beowulf or a hot cup of tea and milk with Oliver Twist. When I said aloud, "It is a far, far better thing that I do, than I have ever done . . ." tears of love filled my eyes at my *selflessness.* [84; my italics]

Augustine too finds "selflessness" in reading: it is the process of reading which allows him to absorb in his human, historical, linear dimension the timelessness of eternal substance, the plenitude of intercourse and communion with God, and thus to return to his transcendent origins. His narrative and decentered use of language makes way for a selfless and silent disappearance into God's otherness which becomes his ideal self. And we may also recall here Nietzsche's warnings about "selflessness," which reading can favor, although it is also the source of great happiness: "Come to me pleasant, brilliant, clever books."[29] For Augustine, "selflessness" is deference to God; for Nietzsche, it is the alienation by our cultural selves of our creatural, animal, and biocentric drives.

Reading, for Maya, is also depersonalizing, but this depersonalization returns her instead to the *collectively human* dimensions she had forsaken, with language, in her attempt to shield herself from the wrath of God the Father. Reading enables her to enter into a human dialogue with Mrs. Flowers, to discover a loving and nurturing intellectual relationship. She loses her *self* but merges with a community of *others*. Bertha Flowers is an ideal other but *not* a mirroring presence: she mediates and guides Maya's entry into a multiplicity of "private lives," which can only enlarge and enrich the girl's point of view, as they become her frames of reference, her lifelines to adulthood. It is worth noting that the literary texts Maya actually mentions correspond to the two secular poles discussed in this chapter, the folk tradition and literary discourse. Some critics read *Beowulf* as a medieval folktale,[30] and *Oliver Twist* is a fictional autobiographical narrative. In this and many other such instances of situational self-reflexivity,[31] the narrative signals to us the frame of reference within which it attempts to situate itself. It thus encodes models of reading appropriate to its messages and intrinsic to its structure, offering to the attentive reader the key paradigms needed for interpretative analysis.

Another such instance of situational self-reflexivity, this one within the religious mode, occurs when Maya starts having "secret crawl[s] through neighborhood churches" (*SS*, 28), in search of a

[29]Friedrich Nietzsche, *Ecce Homo*, from *On the Genealogy of Morals and Ecce Homo* (New York: Vintage Books, 1969), p. 242.

[30]See Daniel R. Barnes, "Folktale Morphology and the Structure of Beowulf," *Speculum* 45 (1970). This critic uses Vladimir Propp's system to argue that point.

[31]See Ross Chambers, *Story and Situation: Narrative Seduction and the Power of Fiction* (Minneapolis: University of Minnesota Press, 1984), pp. 24–28.

way to get back in touch with a heritage and a territory that are gradually eroding under Tosh's white influence. She visits a black fundamentalist Baptist church and the text for the sermon is from the Old Testament: "Dry Bones in the Valley." The preacher is a master of his craft: "He told the story simply at first, weaving a quiet web around us all, binding us into the wonder of faith and the power of God" (31). Hypnotized by his style, she joins in the dancing and singing trances and is "reborn" as she surrenders to the power of the community. The teaching of this particular sermon, as she describes it, is a metaphor for the process of autobiography and anamnesis: "I knew of no teaching more positive than the legend which said that will and faith caused a *dismembered skeleton*, dry on the desert floor, to knit back together and walk" (SS 31; my italics). To re-member and piece together the past in the hope of achieving a degree of self-integration within language which will miraculously redeem her, save her from death and emptiness, indeed give her immortality, is the acknowledged project of writing for Maya. This "legend" of the Old Testament is a powerful way for her to get back in touch with her vernacular tradition after her more "cerebral" excursus into "high" art and literature.

If, living with Tosh, she begins to miss her "religious" tradition, with Make and in his political milieu she will miss "literature." This movement back and forth between religion and literature is dialectical only in appearance, for in both traditions she manages to extract the means of communication, the techniques of storytelling, which help her learn and refine her craft as a writer. She rejects the "white God" of religion but retrieves the cultural heritage of the black church, the sermons and the music, the gospel songs and spirituals, which are so close to the secular blues. When she starts going to church secretly, it is the music that attracts her at first: "The spirituals and gospel songs were sweeter than sugar" (28). This contact with the culture of her slave ancestors keeps her firmly anchored in the reality of her past, putting into perspective the "cerebral exercises and intellectual exchange" (SS 29) that were the basis of her relationship to Tosh. This episode is another allegorical representation within the "autobiographical" text of the history of black people in America. Religious gatherings were forbidden to slaves. Here, Tosh is violently opposed to religion. The slaves would still gather secretly to sing and chant and pray for "freedom" (usually in an afterlife) and to ritualistically glorify death as a release from the ills of this world. The narrator's and Tosh's relationship thus takes on mythic dimensions as it symbolizes an aspect of race (or master-slave) relations during preabolition days. Religion, like literacy, was considered a potentially subversive instrument in the hands of the slaves, and the masters needed to prevent, or severely repress, any hint of resistance or disobedience. Hence the "secret meetings in the woods to praise God ('For where two or three are gathered together in my name, there am I in the midst of them')" as the narrator recalls her great-grandmother, the former slave, teaching her (*SS* 28). Her secret church visits echo and connote that historical past.

Revival services and sermons are a *locus classicus* of black auto-biographical narratives, and the treatment they receive varies according to the degree of alienation the narrator feels toward the evangelism of the black church. Not all black writers share Angelou's belief in the positive elements of black religion. Richard Wright is bitterly opposed to religious rhetoric, believing that it generates hypocrisy, sadism, cruelty, and hatred. Langston Hughes and James Weldon Johnson do not share her emotional response to revivalism. Johnson, for example, has a patronizing and humorous attitude toward the simple faith of southern blacks. Participating in a revival service, he falls asleep, and when someone shakes him, he pretends to be in a trance, and wakes up fully only to recount a "vision" and thus avoid blame.[32] His distance and detachment are in contrast to Maya's surrender to the electrifying atmosphere of the Baptist church. As narrator, she handles the scene with irony and humor; but it is a wry commentary, after the fact, on her capacity for losing herself in the folk process of religious revival, for undergoing an emotional "rebirth."

Structurally, this episode of "rebirth" in the third volume, is a counterpoint to the narrative segment dealing with poetry and Mrs. Flowers in the first volume. Initially, Maya is reborn when she reenters the community of speaking humans via the medium of literature. Here, by contrast, we have a "religious" rebirth in the traditional revival mode: it is in fact a return to her black folk background. She succeeds in avoiding conflict between the various traditions as she adopts from each one the elements that are truly a

[32]James Weldon Johnson, *Along This Way* (New York: Viking Press, 1933), p. 26.

part of "popular" or "vernacular" culture, be it folk tales or folk poems, (fictional) personal narratives, gospels, spirituals, or blues. The experience of rebirth could thus be seen as an exorcism from the self of those "polluting" thoughts and beliefs that lead to the devaluing of the collective wisdom and "mother wit" of her black heritage. With Tosh, the white atheist, it is the dryness of her overly refined life-style which begins to weigh on her: "After watching the multicolored people in church dressed in their gay Sunday finery and praising their Maker with loud voices and sensual movements, Tosh and my house looked very pale. Van Gogh and Klee posters which would please me a day later seemed irrelevant. The scatter rugs, placed so artfully the day before, appeared pretentious" (SS 29). Clearly, "the multicolored people" are so not just because of their "Sunday finery" but because the skin color of "black" people runs the gamut from the "fresh-butter color" of her mother (IK 49) to the "rich black . . . plum" of Mrs. Flowers (78), with all the intermediate variations: the "brown moon" of Momma's face (26), the "dark-chocolate" skin of her best friend, Louise (118): "Butter-colored, honey-brown, lemon- and olive-skinned. Chocolate and plum-blue, peaches-and-cream. Cream. Nutmeg. Cinnamon. I wondered why my people described our colors in terms of *something good to eat* " (GT 14; my italics). In variety and heterogeneity there is a sensual pleasure upon which her talent feeds (much as Augustine tells of "feeding" on God ["fruens te" 4:1]). Marriage to Tosh is a lonely and marginalizing experience, like her year of silence. By contrast, whenever she is integrated in a group of heterogeneous—though marginal—individuals, she feels truly comfortable. It is thus clear that the search for community and audience informs the whole process of narration for Angelou.

The month she spends hiding in a junkyard at the age of sixteen provides the first such experience of real community: a "collage of Negro, Mexican and white" (IK 214) homeless, outcast children become her "family." Liliane K. Arenberg has pointed out that "of signal importance is that these children disprove the racial prejudice—and its concurrent death fantasies—of her earlier experiences."[33] She sleeps in a wrecked car, spends the day scavenging, and learns to survive against the odds. Instead of being acted upon,

[33]Liliane K. Arenberg, "Death as Metaphor of Self in *I Know Why the Caged Bird Sings*," *College Language Association Journal* 20 (1976), 290.

she increasingly gains control by acquiring useful skills: "During the month that I spent in the yard, I learned to drive . . . to curse and to dance" (215). Her brief stay in this small utopia—ironically referred to as Brobdingnag—gives her the self-confidence to accept the perniciousness of the real world while learning to shield herself from it and to use it to her advantage: "Odd that the homeless children, the silt of war frenzy, could initiate me into the brotherhood of man. After hunting down unbroken bottles and selling them with a white girl from Missouri, a Mexican girl from Los Angeles and a Black girl from Oklahoma, I was never again to sense myself so solidly outside the pale of the human race. The lack of criticism evidenced by our ad hoc community influenced me, and set a tone of tolerance for my life" (*IK* 216). This "ad hoc community" of multicolored children teaches her peace. Meanwhile the bulk of the adults are literally and figuratively engaged in war (World War II). Her experience of being unquestioningly accepted changes her completely, "dislodge[s] the familiar insecurity" (216) of displacement and dis-ease which had reached its apex when she was stabbed by Dolores, her father's girlfriend. Textually, she manages to encode a similar variety and diversity because she draws on so many traditions and weaves them into a narrative that integrates as many styles and influences as the "multicolored people" of the church gathering and the junkyard do. We are truly in the realm of *bricolage* here: biological miscegenation, social "junk" or "silt," and textual braiding, or *métissage*, of traditions.

Con Artists and Storytellers

In his discussion of Homer's *Odyssey*, Tzvetan Todorov distinguishes among three properties of speech : speech-as-action, or *parole-action*, speech-as-narrative, or *parole-récit*, and feigned speech, or *parole feinte*. The last, he says, belongs simultaneously to both of the first two categories because it frees the sign from the referent (as in a *récit*, or tale) with the express purpose of performing an act conveying information that can affect reality (as in speech-as-action). Feigned speech, then, is always performative.[34]

[34]Tzvetan Todorov, *Poétique de la prose* (Paris: Seuil, 1971), pp. 66–77, *The Poetics of Prose*, trans. Richard Howard (Ithaca: Cornell University Press, 1977), pp. 56–59. Jonathan Culler has taken Todorov to task for using this particular *linguistic* schema

In talking about the "tactics" and "stratagems" black narrators use to avoid dealing directly with "truth," Angelou stresses the performative aspect of Momma's cautious means of communication. We have seen how she signifies upon this tradition in her use of fictional narrative devices and in her naming, but Angelou also makes use of vernacular traditions that represent a purely constative case of "speech-as-narrative." This is a mode of oral narrative that can be divided into three categories: "poetic" speech (toasts and jokes), ghost stories, and fantasy.

First, the poetry of Maya's maternal uncles. They represent the urban traditions; they like to gossip, tell jokes, and roughhouse. Theirs, however, is a totally gratuitous and playful love of words: "Uncle Tommy . . . strung ordinary sentences together and they came out sounding either like the most profane curses or like comical poetry" (IK 56). The hearer is completely free to adduce his own meaning from Uncle Tommy's droll statements. He is a deft and natural comedian, whose purpose is only to entertain and thereby to reinforce an existing sense of community. The Baxter clan is a tightly knit, highly competitive group in which each individual must pull his own weight and do so with ease and aplomb. They have a high tolerance for variety and difference, so long as this difference does not reflect negatively on their strong sense of family. Here *parole-récit* is a humorous art and discourse, playful pleasure.

Second, the popular oral tradition of ghost stories, which help pass the time on long winter nights. The storytellers usually try "to best each other in telling lurid tales of ghosts and hants, banshees and juju, voodoo and other anti-life stories" (IK 133). Audience and performers share a common fascination for evoking the unknown, for conjuring the eerie. Again, the sense of community is intact. The purpose of these ghost stories is commonly understood: to frighten and entertain, to reinforce rural superstitions or old African beliefs, while the whole group shares sweet potatoes and peanuts slowly

---

as a means of *interpretation* of literary works. See *Structuralist Poetics* (London: Routledge and Kegan Paul, 1975), pp. 108–9. I suggest that Culler ignores the *contextually* problematic nature of exchange and dialogue, as studied by Todorov: cf. p. 75, "Le contenu de l'énoncé est entièrement dicté par le *procès* d'énonciation [the content of what is spoken is entirely dictated by the speech-act]" (p. 62, my italics). Culler then concludes by raising the very issue he has obfuscated in Todorov: "The linguistic model . . . has helped to provide a perspective, but as yet we understand very little about *how* we read" (p. 265; my italics). I will return to Todorov's categories.

roasted under coals or ashes. In an episode of chapter 22 the visitor who comes to spend the stormy evening with them shares their dinner and impersonates his dead wife as he tells a ghoulish tale of her apparitions in the night. Like the parasite who entertains his hosts, he gets nourishment and pays it back with words.[35] Of special interest in the staging of that episode is the intermingling of literature and folklore. Maya and Bailey are keeping warm by the potbellied stove while reading: he is immersed in *Huckleberry Finn* and she is rereading *Jane Eyre*. The arrival of the visitor interrupts that activity but the children remain suspended out of time as the ghost story inserts itself into their consciousness, becoming superimposed on the fantasy worlds of Twain and Brontë, worlds that happen to appeal to the same emotions: fascination with the unknown and escapism.

Third, fantasy, which is Maya's forte. When Momma takes her to a bigoted dentist, Maya imagines a triumphant confrontation between them, her toothache abating as she dreams of her grandmother obliterating the evil Dr. Lincoln. In the embedded story that she recounts to herself to alleviate the pain, the most significant distortion of reality is in the speech patterns of Momma: "Her tongue had thinned and the words rolled off well enunciated. Enunciated and sharp like little claps of thunder" (*IK* 161). She fantasizes that the dentist, on the other hand, stutters, drools, and has a very humble voice. Momma is larger than life and can even "afford to *slip into the vernacular* because she ha[s] such eloquent command of English" (161; my italics). In other words, to use the vernacular is a conscious choice the writer can allow herself after she has shown her ability to articulate her point of view in the "King's English."

In this instance of alienated, imaginary discourse (wishful thinking and feelings of impotence before an all too powerful and degrading social system), the fundamental dis-ease of this marginal character reveals itself. The narrator's conscious remarks about levels of language indicates that mastery of the master's English is the sine qua non of any subversive intent in a fictive utterance. Her fantasy, a counterpoint to the later episode in the dead car junkyard, is like a science fiction tale. It does not claim to have a direct bearing on daily

[35]See Michel Serres, *Le Parasite* (Paris: Grasset, 1980), especially pp. 49–55: "Picaresques et cybernétiques—la nouvelle balance." Also Chambers, *Story and Situation*, pp. 181–204.

reality, yet it satirizes the social structures that generate this alienated discourse, thus providing a powerful comment on reality. Its
message is directed to Maya's initial, original community, the one
that is powerless, and peripheral to the larger social sphere where
Dr. Lincolns gravitate: yet, she implies, her community could wield
mythic force (like Momma) if only it cared to appropriate (the master's) language.

As is becoming clear, the narrator learns many different styles of
human communication from her extended family's tale telling, escapist tales that are antilife (like ghost stories) or triumphant (like her
fantasy world in which villains are dispatched). But escapist tales
involve no risks, and the story is a pleasurable (if sometimes scary)
experience for both narrator and narratee(s). The didactic intent, if it
exists, is of secondary importance. The primary consideration is the
art of entertaining an audience whose presence and feedback are
unproblematic.

But what happens when the storyteller becomes alienated from
this initial community? Language then becomes a means of obtain-
ing what is not willingly given, that is, attention, justice, reparation,
and so on. And indeed it would seem that for Angelou, the process
of writing is a way of articulating those particular alienations and the
demands that ensue. To judge by her use of standard English
(rather than dialectal speech patterns), it would seem that she aims
her book at a primarily "white" audience of urbanized and educated
readers. She does use some slang and colloquialisms, but her grammar is almost always standard, as is her spelling. Discussing her
schooling in San Francisco, she says: "In the classroom we all
learned past participles, but in the streets and in our homes the
Blacks learned to drop s's from plurals and suffixes from past-tense
verbs. We were alert to the gap separating the written word from
the colloquial. *We learned to slide out of one language and into another
without being conscious of the effort*" (IK 191; my italics).

The "written word" is directed toward an audience that may not
have the patience to decode the vernacular. Angelou, the "messenger," thus acts as translator. More important, however, Angelou
self-consciously makes a distinction between written and oral which
implies that mastery of the written language is the prerequisite to
mastery over one's fate. Just as she had realized, with Mrs. Flowers,
that "language is man's way of communicating with his fellow man

and it is language alone which separates him from the lower animals" (*IK* 82), she now asserts that education and the ability to write correctly are tools in the hands of the oppressed, tools that must be honed and sharpened, the better to serve their purpose of communication. Since her stance, as indicated before, is clearly one of *engagement*, she thus assumes a responsibilty which can be fulfilled only if the "written word" is an instrument of social change. It is clear that she sees language as a tool that helps shape destiny. She is interested in its performative as well as its purely sensual aspects.[36] Thus when her brother Bailey becomes estranged from his family and gets into drugs, gangs, and pimping, she notes: "His language had changed. He was forever dropping slangy terms into his sentences like dumplings in a pot" (*IK* 217), whereas he had been apt at manipulating speech patterns: "The double entendres, the two-pronged sentences, slid over his tongue to dart rapier-like into anything that happened to be in the way" (*IK* 76). He could still, when arguing with his mother, be a master of sharp wit: "Bailey looped his language around his tongue and issued it out to Mother in alum drops" (*IK* 219). But when trying to articulate, under stress, his love/hate relationship to ruthless Vivian, who pushes her children out of the nest, Bailey exerts control over his feelings by resorting to careful, almost painful efforts of language: "he chose his words with the precision of a Sunday school teacher" (*IK* 223).

Maya too makes great efforts to please her mother. She drops her southern euphemisms (cf. *IK* 234). She tries to become self-sufficient and worldly and acquires the difficult art of "dexterous lying" (229) in order to obtain what she wants. In one case, she wants a job as streetcar conductor; she wants to be the first black San Francisco "conductorette." As she goes to apply for the job, she must write a résumé: "Sitting at a side table my mind and I wove a cat's ladder of near truths and total lies. I kept my face blank (an old art) and wrote quickly the fable of Marguerite Johnson, aged nineteen, former companion and driver for Mrs. Annie Henderson (a White Lady) in Stamps, Arkansas" (*IK* 229). She does get the job and acquires new status in her mother's eyes. It is hard-earned status, for between

[36]Following Todorov, p. 72, we could then say that she views her narrative as a *parole feinte*, since "la parole feinte est à la fois récit et action [feigned speech is both narrative and action]" (p. 60), at once constative and performative. I will return to this.

Bailey and Vivian, the expert verbal duelists, she is either a neutral third and excluded middle or a mediating confidante in their dialogue of deaf ears. Her normal tendency being to avoid confrontation, she prefers to give up territory and remain silent.[37] As she explains, she does not dare compete with, or interfere in, Vivian's vast capacity to enjoy life and to fly into legendary rages: "Her tongue was sharper than the creases in zoot pants and I knew better than to try to best her. I said nothing" (GT 83).

In order to handle her own family, the narrator learns from a position of weakness how to swerve and to survive. This knowledge prepares her for life in white society, where the safest strategy is to wear masks: "Never let white folks know what you really think. If you're sad, laugh. If you're bleeding inside, dance" (GT 86). This training in adaptive behavior is an apprenticeship in dissimulation, a lesson in how to become a trickster, a manipulator of signs, a con artist and a writer. The trickster is like the fool, the one who draws attention to the king's nakedness and satirizes the accepted norms of a social order. In a pragmatic sense, though, for the satire or social critique to be effective it must be disguised, guileful, or artful, but not so deceitful as to be completely misunderstood, not so deceptive as to make us miss its "point." Of paramount importance, then, is the sense of an audience whose attention must be captured and retained. As a liminal figure, caught between her mother and brother, who are "entangled in the Oedipal skein" (IK 218), the narrator finds her ability to make herself heard severely curtailed. Her new-found sense of self-certainty and community after the junkyard experience collapses on itself as she reenters family life. She cannot share that experience, tell that tale, because her primary audience is indifferent and impatient. Busy Vivian has no time for details and increasingly slick Bailey is orbiting a different planet, no longer the brother she knew: "He may have been glad to see me, but he didn't act much like it. When I tried to tell him of my adventures and misadventures, he responded with a casual indifference which *stilled the tale on my lips*" (IK 217). Having a story to tell and the confidence to do so is not enough. Interaction with a real or virtual hearer is an integral part of the storytelling situation. At the end of

[37]We could see this as an implicit comment on the historical position of black women caught in the conflict between white America (Vivian) and black males (Bailey).

the first volume, the narrator has found her voice, literally (with Mrs. Flowers) and figuratively (she now has a message to transmit). But she has no audience, or more precisely, her audience's indifference forces her into self-imposed silence. This is the familiar position of the spokesperson who feels that s/he is preaching to those who don't want to (can't) hear and who, consequently, either gives up, tries to find alternate means of reaching an audience, or resorts to various violent and confrontational tactics.

Of these alternatives, however, the only one possible for the artist is to seek means of expression which will convey her point of view without provoking blinding fear, disbelief, utter revulsion, and the concurrent tuning out of the audience. Perhaps it was Billie Holiday, the blues singer, who best exemplified that dilemma when she recalled her first rehearsals of the song "Strange Fruit," from Lewis Allan's story of a lynching: "I worked like the devil on it because. I was never sure . . . I could get across to a plush night-club audience the things that it meant to me."[38] When there is no shared experience between singer and audience, the impact of the song can only be weighed hypothetically. Translation of the content into a form of expression that appeals to the subjective desires of the audience and facilitates their entry into the world of the other is hard work for the performer and becomes inseparable from her message.

As singer, dancer, and performer, Maya Angelou has an acute sense of audience interaction. She thus stages her own alienated relationship to her hypothetical reader, knowing full well that the reader must be "conned" into believing that she has a privileged relation to an autobiographical "truth," which the rhetorical features of her style explicitly problematize. This double bind determines her narrative choices of events and metaphors. In the narrative segment that describes her initial attempts at tale telling within the confines of her own indifferent family, we clearly see her giving up. At the other extreme, when she and Bailey come back south to live in the store after the St. Louis episode, the sense of community is unquestioned. All of Stamps would come to the store to be entertained with stories of their trip north, enabling Bailey to sharpen his "silver tongue" at the expense of the naïve country folk. His audience is

---

[38]Billie Holiday, *Lady Sings the Blues,* her autobiography written with William Dufty (New York: Penguin Books, 1984), p. 84. This book and Billie Holiday's mythical real life are implicit intertexts of Angelou's autobiography.

clearly defined and eager to lend its ears, even if he is shown to be considerably alienated from the rural people toward whom he directs his sarcasms. His experience of the urban North has estranged him from this initial community. Congruence between teller and listener need not be perfect if the teller has sufficient firsthand knowledge of the listener's general frame of reference and can tailor his discourse to (partially) fit that frame.

These linguistic skills differ only in degree from those of the successful and affluent gamblers (or numbers men), the real con men, their mother's friends. Foremost among them is Daddy Clidell, who introduces Maya to the colorful characters of the black underground and teaches her the fine art of swindling to keep her from ever becoming "anybody's mark" (IK 187). From Clidell's tales emerges a single pattern: the more stupid the con man acts, the more likely he is to win over his arrogant white "mark." This kind of ingenuity gives the con man hero status in the ghetto, where the ability to turn "the crumbs from his country's table . . . [into] a Lucullan feast" (190) is the most admired of skills. This skill rests on the culture-hero's ability to take control of a situation and assume certain risks while appearing to relinquish all authority. In other words, it involves a carefully planned strategem of deception, feigning, and role playing. We have already seen that the outcome of the rape trial had depended on Maya's ability to do just that: to decode the social system and respond to it in a deceitful way that put her in control. Her lie, or *parole feinte,* brought her to her mother's arms, "her desired destination" (71), while putting her at risk in the eyes of God. For the con artist, the aim is to spin a tale—*parole feinte*—with the express purpose of swindling the mark and profiting by it. The risk involved is in the eyes of the law: the punishment may be prison if the swindler is caught. In both cases, control puts the protagonist at risk with respect to the symbolic (religious or social) order and hence bears tragic or heroic dimensions. To have lied was deeply disturbing for Maya, the child raised in a fundamentalist milieu, and that was the religious tragedy of her success in the courtroom. What she now learns from these smart tricksters is the poetic justice of fighting back with tall tales and becoming wealthy in the bargain. Only then does she see the possibility of becoming the heroine of such triumphant tales.

At the end of her fourth volume, Angelou recounts a tale of Brer Rabbit: how he succeeded in winning his freedom from the angry farmer by pretending to be more afraid of the thorny briar patch than of the farmer's cooking pot. She identifies completely with Brer Rabbit, feeling just as free, standing in the library of the newsroom where she has earned the right to work and write for a living, despite Vusumzi Make's pompous initial objections. She has safeguarded his sense of honor by a ritualistic and complex appeal to his desire for power, control, and authority. In this instance, Maya is the fool and Make, the mark: all previous and implicit racial connotations in the tale of Brer Rabbit undergo a radical transformation. On the level of signifiers, the only remaining element of the tale is that power and control are best defined by an authoritative use of language. Power resides in the narrative figure, Maya, who can best reach out to the other, Make, and articulate *his* desires in terms of *her* needs. This is a technique that the narrative text shows Maya learning from many sources: her oral tradition as well as her newly acquired skills as a dancer and performer. What this suggests in terms of audience interaction is that Angelou's narrator, like Brer Rabbit, often seems to be telling us just what we want to hear, as "unaware persons" deserving only "a part of the truth." Once we understand her "tactics" and "stratagems," however, it becomes clear that for her, writing is a way of claiming her territory from forces that refuse to grant it, a way of telling us "not where she has been, but where she is going." Her technique, then would correspond exactly to what Michel de Certeau has termed "the practice of everyday life": an art of storytelling like the one Homer and the Greeks practiced and the con artists of today continue to perfect. It is a way of operating within a system of power which allows the "weak" to seize victories over the "strong" by employing "tactics" known to the Greeks under the name of *mētis*. It is a form of intelligence and savoir faire, a resourcefulness and an opportunism that is the hallmark of those who will never be the masters of the terrain on which their daily struggles are fought but who develop in practice multiple and polyvalent means of survival that allow them to elude that power system successfully.[39] The double-voiced nature of Angelou's text allows her to oppose an oppressive social system with-

[39]See Michel de Certeau, *The Practice of Everyday Life* (Berkeley: University of California Press, 1984); also Marcel Détienne and Jean Pierre Vernant, *Les Ruses de l'intelligence: La Mētis des Grecs* (Paris: Flammarion, 1974), pp. 3–9, for example, and their discussion of Homer's *Iliad*; also Sarah Kofman, *Comment s'en sortir* (Paris: Gallilée, 1984), p. 36.

out risk of becoming a term within that system, since a part of her message—because it relies on indirect "signifying" practices—will always elude any direct attempt to inscribe it within the general frame of that dominant discourse. This elusiveness bespeaks a form of alienation differing only in degree from Momma's "secretiveness and suspiciousness" and inherent in all survival strategies.

Indeed, in the briar patch Brer Rabbit is free to claim his space in the communal warren, whereas in the library, Angelou relentlessly explores the constantly changing boundaries of alienated human communication. We have the distinct feeling that she would like (us) to believe that her tale is a triumphant one but cannot quite convince herself of it. Hers is a *parole feinte* that mourns the loss of the illusory possibility of pure *parole-récit*, of direct and unmediated communication with interlocutors who share the same referential and mythic world as she does. In other words, she mourns the disappearance of a mirage, the mirage that is Africa for the children of the colonialist diaspora.

As will be seen in the next chapter, the attraction "Africa" as illusory reality exerts on New World blacks is an issue Maryse Condé will face. She raises disturbing questions about the relationship between past realities and present metaphors, and these questions remain unanswered in her narrative. But by denouncing some of the myths that encourage a sterile fixation on imaginary realities, she provides a critical framework that demonstrates the danger of internalizing negative perspectives on self and other, on language and communication.

5

Happiness Deferred:
Maryse Condé's *Heremakhonon*
and the Failure of Enunciation

Wilt thou tell a monstrous lie, being but half a fish, and
half a monster?

Shakespeare, *The Tempest*

I am an ambiguous animal, half a fish and half a bird.
A new style of bat. A false sister. A false foreigner.

Heremakhonon

Africa has been a powerful magnet and a source of inspiration for
several of the the major writers of the French West Indies—those of
Martinique and Guadeloupe especially. Maryse Condé is no excep-
tion to the rule, and her recent series, *Ségou*, was a resounding
success. In it, she creates a vast historical saga and goes back to the
eighteenth-century splendors and miseries of a West African king-
dom. But in her first novel, *Heremakhonon*, her narrator and negative
alter ego Véronica confronts a myth, the myth of Africa as welcom-
ing mother. In measuring the myth against the depressing realities
of contemporary neocolonialist Africa, Véronica discovers its short-
comings: "Africa" turns out to be a fantasy and a will-o'-the-wisp,
which continues to elude her grasp after a disappointing three
months' stay: she fails to open up to its cultural realities, to learn its
languages; she remains caught up in the grammar of her own
alienations.

Véronica comes to this unnamed West African country in search
of roots and ancestors: "Who am I? We have said it over and over
again. I'm a down-and-out traveller looking for her identity"(89).[1]
Her quest is a misguided attempt to be reborn, "to emerge again
from [her] mother's womb"(166), to re-create a different past, and to
be reconciled with herself. She wants to envisage a different personal history, a new genealogy that has not been marred by slavery and

[1]Maryse Condé, *Heremakhonon*, trans. Richard Philcox (Washington, D.C.: Three
Continents Press, 1982). I shall also refer to the French edition (Paris: UGE 10/18,
1976). All references will be given in the text.

the Middle Passage, by her bourgeois parents' blind need to mimic European standards and to idolize French culture. To fall in love with "Africa"—"cristalliser l'amour qu'à travers elle je cherche à me porter [to crystallize the love I am seeking for myself through her]" (261/146)—would be a way for her to rediscover and retrieve that aspect of herself which she cannot love, because it has been erased or devalued, thanks to colonial patterns of hatred and domination. The narcissism of her quest is made abundantly clear: by means of identification with an idealized maternal symbolic system the narrator attempts to gain mastery over her past traumas. But her voyage only proves to be an aimless detour that brings her back to her point of departure, Paris, where she had been living in exile for the previous nine years.

Heremakhonon is thus the autopsy, the post-mortem, of Véronica's illusions, of the myths typified by a certain image of Africa as maternal figure, as enveloping womb where a return to plenitude becomes possible at last. The novel is Condé's somewhat hermetic and allegorical treatment of the problem of exiled Antilleans, who, for lack of political self-determination in their own islands (which are still French "départements d'outre-mer"), cannot imagine empowering structures of meaning grounded in the cultural realities of this "poussière d'îles" (131), and thus become nomads.[2] Véronica is dimly aware of this problem, but as a figure for the Antillean peoples' lack of political purposiveness, she is a passive individual who cannot act upon her own limited understanding of the situation: "If I wanted to come to terms with myself, i.e. with them, i.e. with us, I ought to return home" (71). Yet return and reconciliation are not possible, for she is still too much a product of that restrictive environment to be able to cope with its demeaning aspects: just as the black bourgeoisie of her parents' generation mimics Europe, she falls victim to another—the same—mirage created by her desire for the (African) other.

In his remarkable theoretical text on the political and cultural dy-

---

[2]This "sprinkling of island specks" (my trans.). This phrase is attributed to General Charles de Gaulle, during a trip to the French islands of the West Indies: he meant to imply that between Europe and America lie nothing but a few specks of land, hardly to be taken into serious consideration in policy decisions. See, e.g., Edouard Glissant, *Le Discours antillais* (Paris: Seuil, 1981), epigraph page, *Caribbean Discourse*, trans. J. Michael Dash, forthcoming from the University Press of Virginia in 1989.

namics of the Antilles, *Le Discours antillais*, Edouard Glissant has argued that in the New World populations forcibly exiled through the slave trade, who continue to undergo economic exploitation, have been unable to take possession of their social and material environment because of a duplicitous form of domination by the "Other." Such cultural domination involves a hidden process of assimilation of great magnitude, an urge to mimic the "Other" which is a form of insidious violence. Furthermore, he argues, this domination tends to favor models of resistance which are universalizing and self-defeating because they follow the same pattern of mimetic illusion while displacing those patterns onto a "One" that is but a mirror image of the "Other." As a strictly oppositional category, the "One" leaves no room for difference and diversity, for the elaboration of new cultural forms more resistant to assimilation:

> Domination (favored by dispersion and transplantation) produces the worst kind of change [le pire des avatars], which is that it provides, on its own, models of resistance to the stranglehold it has imposed, thus short-circuiting resistance while making it possible. . . .
> The first impulse of a transplanted population, which is not sure of maintaining in the new surroundings the old order of values, is that of Reversion [le Retour]. Reversion is the obsession with the One, with a single origin: being must not undergo change [il ne faut pas changer l'être]. To revert is to consecrate permanence, to negate contact [consacrer. . . la non-relation].

It is through this obsession with being ("l'être") as a stable category, and the concurrent essentialist, Manichean notions of race and origin, says Glissant, that the lure and seduction of the "Other" can become effective. For the Antilleans, the situation is most acute because "the community has tried to exorcise the impossibility of Return by what I call the practice of Diversion [le Détour]."[3] Glissant sees Antilleans as being particularly prone to a collective and unconscious attempt to deny or negate the realities of domination because they have not squarely confronted the legacy of slavery and because they possess a dangerous semblance of democratic self-determination which co-opts all serious efforts of emancipation.

[3]Glissant, pp. 29, 30, 32. I have altered J. Michael Dash's translation whenever I found it necessary to emphasize a particular nuance not fully rendered in his English version. Here, I have modified the quotation from p. 30.

"Return"—real or metaphoric—to an authentic past was always impossible for the slaves and their descendants because connections to the mother country had been abruptly and artificially severed; it therefore became a psychic necessity to retrieve and conserve shreds of history through oblique and duplicitous means—a practice with which Afro-Americans are quite familiar, as was discussed in the previous two chapters on Hurston and Angelou. These duplicitous tactics can constitute, in Glissant's terminology, a practice of the *détour* or diversion, which may end up, unfortunately, in a mythifying enterprise grounded in denial—the overriding situation in the Antilles. Some of the most insidious and traumatic consequences of the slave trade, Glissant adds, can be obscured and disguised by this denial, which leads the Antillean to pursue solutions involving a mystical return to an imaginary place, to "France" or "Africa" (as the case may be), a return that is but a detour leading to a dead end. What is needed instead, Glissant points out, is a painstaking effort aimed at reinserting the self into the concrete realities of Caribbean diversity ("le Divers") with its de facto relationships of creolization, *métissage* and cross-cultural fertilizations (or *transculturación*, as Nancy Morejón, the Cuban poet, has explained it).[4]

In that respect, Glissant is theorizing about a practice that is already quite familiar to readers of Hurston's corpus. Hurston' search for a symbolic geography brings her back again and again to those parts of the New World where descendants of slaves have been forced to create new cultural forms. Such forms are resistant to domination precisely because they exist in a realm outside of, or marginal to, obviously oppositional practices. Hurston's genius is to have recognized the importance of delineating the concrete realities of what Glissant would later call "le Divers." Her search for maternal connections thus bypasses a simplistic focus on an imaginary "Africa." Rather, we might say that she attempts to unveil present connections to an occluded history, fully aware of the transformations that cultures undergo through time and transplantations. Hers is not an impulse to "return" but a determined effort to articulate those transformations within the marginal realms where they occur. For Hurston, to unveil and re-member the mother's face is, by the same token, to refuse to have it be frozen in an imaginary dimen-

[4]See Nancy Morejón, *Nacion y mestizaje en Nicholás Guillén* (Havana: Unión, 1982), p. 19. I refer to this work in my introduction.

sion—like Véronica Mercier's "Africa"—where time stands still and myths contribute to the paralysis of future generations.

By contrast, Véronica Mercier epitomizes this paralysis: hers is a pathological desire for the African other and with all its lethal consequences. Since this desire is metonymically displaced onto the protagonist Ibrahima Sory, he figures as the locus of her most profound alienation. Because he corresponds to the authentically mythical idea of the "nègre avec aîeux [nigger with ancestors]" (311/175), as she has imagined it, he functions as a symbolic screen that prevents her from decoding the nature of his brand of tyranny. In her relationship with him, she is made into an object, and knows it: "But there's a secret unhealthy voluptuousness in being treated like an object" (89). She acquires a tremendous *vis inertiae* that stops her from taking sides in the very real conflicts of the people and the students and from acting upon the obvious connections between their situation of exploitation and her own.

Again, Glissant plainly states the question : "Diversion is not a systematic refusal to see . . . Rather we would say that it is formed, like a habit, from an interweaving of negative forces which go unchallenged. . . . Diversion is the ultimate resort of a population whose domination by an Other is concealed: they then must search *elsewhere* for the principle of domination." And we might add that in the case of Véronica this *"elsewhere* . . . may be internal."[5] Véronica is not totally blind to the nexus of forces that paralyze her. Indeed, hers is not a refusal to "see" but an inability to act, because the "elsewhere" as she has internalized it is constitutive of her subjectivity and finds in the external world its own reinforcement. Ibrahima Sory buttresses the myth precisely because he represents an interesting inversion of that myth: whereas the idealized and sexualized image of "Africa-as-Mother" is the common archetype used by male writers of the diaspora (Aimé Césaire, for example, in his *Notebook of a Return to the Native Land* makes extensive use of such female imagery), here it is on a male character that desire for the absent "other" is displaced and crystallized.[6]

[5]Glissant, p. 32.
[6]As Jonathan Ngaté has shown, Condé—like Césaire—uses the myth of a "maternal" Africa, except that Condé implicitly refers to Africa as "step-mother." See Ngaté, "Maryse Condé and Africa: The Making of a Recalcitrant Daughter?", *A Current Bibliography on African Affairs*, 19 (1986–87), 5–20. My point, however, is that it is a *male* character who represents the myth for Véronica.

As a figure of the Lacanian Imaginary, the protagonist Ibrahima Sory cannot fall under the scrutiny of Véronica's gaze: in him are bound up complex unconscious processes in which the split between Real and Symbolic is confirmed and binary Manichean positions prevail.[7] Véronica can recognize and assume the negativity of her situation, the "interweaving of negative forces" about which Glissant is so perceptive, but this simple fact prevents her from having to deal with alternative solutions, decisive resolutions. Ibrahima Sory reinforces Véronica's delusions and obsessions by obscuring the "real," that is the struggle embodied by Saliou, his political double, who dies for his convictions and whose murder eventually galvanizes the narrator into cutting short her "detour" through Africa on her way to "finding herself." In the final analysis, that is how Sory—and "Africa"—function in the text: as a catalyst and a mediator who can ultimately reveal the Real by obscuring it. It is because of Sory's opacity that Véronica ends up realizing how completely desultory it is for her to appropriate him as symbolic object of desire, as signifier for "Africa." To make the myth her own, that is, to make it "Real," she would have to place herself outside the fundamentally Western posture she retains, something she cannot do, because she clearly cannot be free of her upbringing—and neither can Sory.

Although the ending does not constitute a positive resolution of conflicting ideologies, it does offer the suggestion that the impasse of mimetic identifications has been recognized and attempts at transcending it initiated. This knowledge, and Véronica's dawning awareness of the dead end she has reached spell the beginning of wisdom for her and, it is hoped, for other Antillean émigrés as well. The narrative illustrates the urgent need to bring to the forefront of Antillean consciousness—by this "practice of Diversion" or this detour through the realm of symbolic identifications—the imaginary realities of political disenfranchisement and its attendant existential "angoisse." But the narrative raises those very questions that it cannot answer directly, because it can offer neither visionary constructions nor blueprints for the future, remaining as it does in the realm of a reality its author feels powerless to transform. On that point

[7]For a lucid explanation of the Lacanian classification, see Anthony Wilden, *System and Structure: Essays in Communication and Exchange* (London: Tavistock, 1980), pp. 247–77 especially (Appendix by Gerald Hall).

Condé has made her position quite clear : "The role of literature is to provoke thought and reflexion, to articulate the existential anguish which burdens people."[8] In other words literature can invite and provoke reflection, not directly influence change in the world. Its function is to disturb and disrupt : "inquiéter."[9]

Heremakhonon succeeds well at perturbing its readers. Critics and reviewers alike have generally noted the disturbing elements of the book, its negativistic posturing, but not the means by which this disquieting effect is produced. In this chapter, I would like to analyze the way in which meaning is produced in *Heremakhonon:* how does the unfolding of the story reveal the inner workings of the protagonist's mind and translate the anxiey that inhabits Véronica? What are the devices that allow the text to manifest those inner conflicts? Are there particular structures that allow Condé's fundamentally political message to be transmitted without didacticism? To answer these questions, I shall look briefly at the textual strategies and rhetorical features that reinforce patterns of passivity and disjunction. These strategies usually consist in a skillful manipulation of the traditional techniques of interior monologue and in strict control over the flow of narrative time, which mimics and reproduces psychological *durée,* or lived time.

Exemplary Passivity

Published in 1976, *Heremakhonon* was Maryse Condé's first novel, although she was already known for her critical essays and her plays. So controversial is the novel that it has been out of print for several years, although an English translation is available. It is a first-person narrative, but as the author has strongly stated, not *stricto sensu* an autobiography: "The use of the first person was simply a writer's device."[10] Although Véronica's family clearly resembles Condé's own, and the events with which the heroine is confronted parallel those Condé had to witness during her first stay in

[8]Marie-Clotilde Jacquey and Monique Hugon, "L'Afrique, un continent difficile: Entretien avec Maryse Condé," *Notre Librairie* 74 (April–June 1984), 21–25 (25), hereinafter *NL.* All translations are mine.

[9]Condé quoted in Jonathan Ngaté, p. 7.

[10]"Interview de Maryse Condé" by Ina Césaire in Maryse Condé, *La Parole des femmes: Essai sur des romancières des Antilles de langue française* (Paris: L'Harmattan, 1979), p. 124, my translation.

Guinea in 1960, the book is the story of an "anti-moi,"[11] an ambiguous persona whose search for identity and origins is characterized by a rebellious form of sexual libertinage. Her pride over having read Laclos's *Liaisons dangereuses* at an early age, over her precocious curiousity about sexual matters, reveals her ironic reliance on common stereotypes of early sexualization of nonwhite women. Having received a classical French education in Guadeloupe and Paris, she refers in her text to Pascal, Laclos, Spinoza, Rousseau, Hugo, Flaubert, Stendhal, Zola, Bergson, and Proust. These writers constitute the formal model of philosophical and literary expression for Véronica, and it is within a very specific stylistic and narrative tradition that we can situate her story of those three months in Africa, of her *éducation sentimentale* in the manner of Frédéric Moreau or Julien Sorel.

In her unsuccessful attempt to re-create herself and to find the personal happiness she naïvely longs for, Véronica represents a version of the formal paradigm of the nineteenth century hero of Bildungsromane. Transplanting a European project of self-fulfillment and self-gratification onto African soil, though, she is bound to fail, for in Africa, as her lover implies, the self cannot be conceived outside of a community that determines its options and legitimates its choices: "There's no room here for little personal problems, sentimentality, whims" (78). The obsession with private childhood experiences, scrutinized to derive psychologizing interpretations of a person's state of mind, as well as the concurrent need to display one's inner landscape, "the outbursts at first sight, the exhibitionism, the tears, the whole arsenal of pathos" (93), are sarcastically denounced as a symptom of decadent individualism. The confessional mode always gets aborted in the text: it is either directed at the wrong narratee (e.g., 7) or cut short by Sory's indifference (36, 52)— a predicament strangely similar to the one faced by Maya Angelou's narrator when she returns "home" after her utopian adventures in the junkyard and is forced into self-imposed silence by her family's indifference.

For Véronica, however, the absence of a "natural" audience (that is, of Guadeloupeans aware of her alienation and conscious of being caught in a similar predicament) is compounded by the fact that she

[11]Ibid., p. 125.

and Sory do not even share a common language, let alone a common grammar of the "self." The canonical trajectory of the autobiographical heroine from blindness to insight is nonetheless followed here: Véronica reaches a new form of knowledge, if only a negative one, still based in a Nietzschean form of anarchic and negative *ressentiment*. But she goes *through* this stage of negative mediation, this being a necessary and unavoidable step in the history of her *conscience malheureuse*, following Sartre's famous analysis in "Orphée Noir."[12] The narrative is divided into three parts, and there is a clear progression from interior monologue to more description and commentary in the final part. But this progression is literally forced upon Véronica. In particular, the focus on external events becomes determined by her arrest (137–39) and by the students' rebellion. As she says, "For the first time I'm afraid" (150). External political factors are the real determinants of Véronica's discovery, not introspection and reflection.

The narrative thus provides implicit answers to the questions it asks: it privileges action over reflection and self-analysis in the movement from blindness to insight. But the narrator's failure to act upon the insights she gleans point to a passivity and a lack of will symptomatic of her colonial background and ambiguous situation. She represents the impasse of exile for the colonized self and the difficulty of finding a viable position within the cultural constellations of the "other," be that "other" French or African, because for either she will remain "A false sister. A false foreigner"(137). Véronica's "history" of childhood traumas ("I still have a complex from my awkward days of childhood" [24]), reenacts on a personal level the collective cultural difficulties of a people, and it is possible to read her attempts at "confession" as an allegory of the historical conditions that have determined the "in-between" state of New World blacks: "Years of being downgraded in comparison with my two sisters" (24), the sisters being seen as the "perfect" bourgeois siblings of this "degenerate" and rebellious offspring. Marginalized by these sisters (whom I am tempted to read as personifications of Europe and Africa, not culturally or symbolically, of course, but because of the unproblematic assurance they exhibit, because of

---

[12]See Jean-Paul Spartre, "Orphée Noir," Preface to Léopold S. Senghor, *Anthologie de la nouvelle poésie nègre et malgache de langue française* (Paris: Presses Universitaires de France, 1948).

their self-righteousness and their lack of self-doubt), Véronica is the stereotypical *métis*, the one who embodies the maledictions of miscegenation: the boundary crosser. She is the third term, the excluded middle and the voice of the Antillean double bind.

Frantz Fanon has lucidly delineated the historical contradictions that contributed to this polarized weltanschauung of the people of the French Antilles. In an essay included in the collection *Toward the African Revolution*, Fanon writes:

Until 1939 the West Indian lived, thought, dreamed . . . , composed poems, wrote novels exactly as a white man would have done. . . . Before Césaire, West Indian literature was a literature of Europeans. The West Indian identified himself with the white man, adopted a white man's attitude, "was a white man."

After the West Indian was obliged, under the pressure of European racists, to abandon positions which were essentially fragile, because they were absurd, because they were incorrect, because they were alienating, a new generation came into being. The West Indian of 1945 is a Negro. . . .

Then, with his eyes on Africa, the West Indian was to hail it. He discovered himself to be the transplanted son of slaves; he felt the vibration of Africa in the very depth of his body and aspired only to one thing: to plunge into the great "black hole" [le grand "trou noir"]. It thus seems that the West Indian, after the great white error, is now living in the great black mirage [le grand mirage noir].[13]

Condé's "anti-moi," her negative alter ego echoes Fanon's analysis when she exclaims: "Ce que j'imaginais? Qu'est-ce que j'imaginais? . . . En fin de compte, je n'imaginais rien. Un grand trou noir. *The Dark Continent* [What I imagined? What did I imagine?. . . Actually, I never imagined anything. A great black hole. The Dark Continent]"(106/56). Véronica strikingly illustrates Fanon's critique of the double alienation of the intellectual who cannot embrace his or her own geopolitical and historical situation and gets caught in a hopeless dualism. Her derisive attempts to explain, "I opened my mouth to explain. Explain" (20), aim at justifying an unjustifiable position, the position of absolute negation and of bad conscience.

[13]Frantz Fanon, *Toward the African Revolution* (New York: Grove Press, 1967), pp. 26–27, *Pour la révolution africaine* (Paris: Maspéro, 1964), pp. 35–36.

She engages in a picaresque search for a *different* past, for a "before" (12), for a beginning ("But where did it all begin?" [6]) which existed prior to contact with the Europeans. But she is still wrestling with her own internalized stereotypes about the cultural commonplaces of "the great black mirage." Yet, by making the myth available for parody, the narrator derides her search and thus implicitly deconstructs her own motives, her romantic delusions.

As a disillusioned post-negritude "intellectuelle de gauche [left-wing intellectual]" (22/9) who refuses to let herself be taken in by a purely sentimental need to fill in the gaps in her family's history, Véronica retains an ironic stance on her search for origins, but her distancing attitude is soon revealed to be the sign of an inability to commit herself to political *engagement*. Despite her attempts to free herself from the contradictory ideologies of her family, she is still a colonized individual who mirrors the antinomies of her culture as well as the oppositional politics of those she befriends in Africa. Indeed Maryse Condé would say in her interview with Ina Césaire that "Véronica is just a mirror which reflects both sides," echoing Stendhal's famous dictum in *The Red and The Black*: "A novel is a mirror carried along a high road. At one moment it reflects to your vision the azure skies, at another the mire of the puddles at your feet."[14]

The narrator's private failure to reach a satisfying conclusion at the end of her stay also bespeaks the historical political failure of the people of this newly independent African nation to progress toward revolution and popular power. During Véronica's stay there as a *coopérante* (or French technical assistant) with assigned duties as a philosophy instructor—an aberrant situation, since she is there to teach Western philosophy within the framework of the educational system exported by France—the regime becomes increasingly authoritarian, severely repressing opposition, imprisoning students and dissidents. Although Véronica is caught in the middle of this political struggle (Ibrahima Sory is the strongman responsible for putting down the rebellion, whereas her friends at the institute—Saliou and Birame III—are under fire for opposing the regime), her vain and presumptuous attempt to remain neutral proves self-serv-

---

[14]Condé, *La Parole des femmes*, p. 128; Stendhal, *The Red and the Black*, trans. C. K. Scott Moncrieff (New York: Modern Library: 1953), pp. 446–47.

ing and ultimately self-defeating: she soon loses her already tenuous self-respect and having reached bottom, decides to run away, back to Paris, to a future that offers, ironically, a very dim possibility of renewal: "Spring? Yes, it's Spring in Paris" (174).

This return to Paris repeats an earlier flight from Guadeloupe after her first unhappy and secret love affair at age seventeen. The three months' hiatus in Africa, which corresponds exactly to the narrative time of the story, thus figures as an abortive attempt to break out of an illusory cycle of juvenile rebellion and contestation, of pseudo-sexual "liberation," which only indentures her to another form of patriarchy, the one practiced by her Moslem lover, who mocks her "identity crisis":

> —Pourquoi êtes-vous venue en Afrique?
> Ah, tout de même! . . . Attention à ne pas le rebuter en dégoisant en bloc tous mes problèmes! Depuis le temps que l'envie de me confesser me démange! Essayons d'être désinvolte.
> J'en avais marre. Je vivais à Paris avec un Blanc.
> —Avec un Blanc!
> Le ton est nettement choqué. Oui, oui. Laisse-moi continuer. Tu comprends, je voulais fuir mon milieu familial, le marabout man-dingue, ma mère, *la négro bourgeoisie qui m'a faite, avec à la bouche, ses discours glorificateurs de la Race, et au coeur, sa conviction terrifiée de son infériorité.* Et puis j'en suis peu à peu venue à penser que cette forme de fuite n'était pas valable, qu'elle cachait tout autre chose. Car enfin j'aurais pu fuir en sens inverse. Combler la distance qu'ils avaient créée. Me réenraciner. Tu comprends?
> —En somme, vous avez un problème d'identité? [99–100; my italics].

> ["Why did you come to Africa?"
> Ah, at last. . . Be careful not to discourage him by pouring out all my problems in one go. It's been some time since I've been dying to make a confession. Let's try and be relaxed.
> I was fed up. I was living in Paris. With a white man.
> "With a white man?"
> Really quite shocked. Yes, yes. Let me go on. I wanted to escape from the family, the mandingo marabout, my mother, *the black bour-geoisie that made me, with its talk of glorifying the Race and its terrified conviction of its inferiority.* And then gradually I came round to thinking that this form of escape was not valid, that it was hiding something

else. I could have escaped in the other direction. Make up for the distance they had lost. Put down roots within myself. Do you understand?

"In other words, you have an identity problem?" (52)].

The critique of confessional modes of introspection such as autobiography and psychoanalysis is evident throughout. The tension between Véronica (who yearns for soul-baring displays of emotion) and Sory (whose opacity paradoxically seems to be that of a perfectly transparent, uncomplicated, and forthright character lacking any interior life precisely because *his* frame of reference does not intersect with Véronica's) are especially revealing. In this passage the impossibility of genuine dialogue between the two protagonists is made amply clear; they talk past each other rather than to one another. In fact, direct speech is Sory's alone. Véronica's answers, and what she thinks to herself *in petto*, are rendered in direct free thought ("Yes, yes. Let me go on") so that we never know exactly what she actually says to Sory. This device seems to set Véronica's discourse within a frame of reference so alien to Sory's own that whatever she may say will not be heard by him. Her language is literally not the African's: Véronica has not made the effort to learn any local languages and can only communicate in French, hence the symbolic disjunctions that operate on the level of communication and exchange.

The use of the pronouns *vous* ("Pourquoi êtes-vous venue en Afrique?") and *tu* (Tu comprends, je voulais fuir . . .") reinforces their failure of intimacy, their inability to relate on an equal level. Furthermore, Véronica's use of the familiar form connotes the French colonialists' demeaning usage of the *tu* in their interaction with African natives and thus produces an uncanny sense of discomfort and disease at the pronominal shift. But on the other hand, Sory's *vous* reduces the woman to just another partner to whom respect is due but with whom intimacy is superfluous. Exchange and dialogue are stalled and foreclosed.

Véronica never speaks directly, for she is spoken *by* the discourse of the "négro bourgeoisie," the patriarchal other. Like them, she suffers from an inferiority complex, from a disjunction between what can be said ("avec à la bouche") and what is felt ("et au coeur"), indeed between what must be said and what can't be believed.

Véronica does not have a language she can call her own since she cannot subscribe to any of the voices that possess her. Attempting to relate to Sory as an imaginary "other," she fails to establish communication because patriarchal structures short-circuit any possibility of a different syntax as well : "Me réenraciner [Put down roots]" is a meaningless phrase for Sory, who has never known exile and belongs to an ancient landed aristocracy. The phrase, sarcastic though it may be, can only expose the sentimentality of a speaker who pretends to "take root" outside of the common local languages, nurtured by the very soil of Africa.

As she progresses toward greater awareness of her state of complete ignorance, Véronica recognizes that she does not have "the key to the characters"(88), that Oumou Hawa's "code of behavior is completely beyond [her]" (159), whereas the point of view of the more Westernized characters, that of Ramatoulaye, for example, who has furnished her house with antique French furniture, "a le mérite de la clarté [has the merit of being clear]" (284/159). She thus comes to accept the opacity and silence of Sory as inevitable: "I accept his silence because there is nothing to say. To be more exact, I've understood there is nothing we can say that doesn't end up dividing us. And the only form of dialogue is the one that satisfies him, whereas I consider it inadequate, even despicable in my Westernized infantilism" (157). Unresponsiveness and impenetrability become metaphors that subtend the shaky ground of their relationship, since there is literally nothing they can say that doesn't end up dividing them.

Indeed, the polyglot doctor Yehogul, a foreigner like Véronica but one who speaks all five of the main languages of the country, tells her insistently: "Learn the languages! It's not difficult" (87). The key to the discovery of the other is to learn to speak his/her language and not to allow oneself to be passively spoken by the language of the master code, French, which will necessarily color her perceptions of reality and deform her vision: "I shall never know the truth. . . . the prisms of my desires and dreams would have distorted the reality. It's a fact there's no such thing as reality. The facts are made of Venetian glass" (94). The title of the novel, *Heremakhonon*, ironically underscores this fact while criticizing Véronica's search: in Malinké, *here* means "happiness" and *makhonon*, "to wait for."[15] It implies a colonized passivity coupled with the Western fallacy that life is a search for "happiness" rather than a struggle for survival and emancipation.

Heremakhonon is also the "Welcome House," the name of the compound where Ibrahima Sory and his extended family live and where Véronica spends many hours either waiting for him or happily tucked in bed with him, indifferent to the world outside with its disturbing poverty and repressive politics: "En somme ce qu'il me faut pour voir la vie presque en rose, c'est *a good fuck* [What I need to see life through rose-colored glasses is a good fuck]" (222/125). In *Heremakhonon* she is passively content to obliterate the outside world, to gratify her sensuality and satisfy her physical needs. She is in love not with the man himself but with his past, and she hopes to be magically restored to a lost form of plenitude: "I now realize why he fascinates me. He hasn't been branded" (37); "Through him I shall at last be proud to be what I am" (42). But the "idea" of Africa, "that of an Africa, of a black world that Europe did not reduce to a caricature of itself" (77) is an impossible dream because material political realities forestall any such construction of a totalizing entity named "Africa." What do exist are only concrete situations in which class distinctions and problems of oppression take on the universal appearance of a master-slave dialectic. But to recognize the dilemma, to be lucid about her compromising situation, is not enough to empower Véronica to act upon her insights: "It's not the first time, but perhaps never as clearly, I realize my place is not here. At least what I came to do is absurd. Yet I know I won't move. Held back by a hope I know is thwarted from the start" (100). This is precisely the double bind of the nomad, whose journey is nourished by the hope of returning to an imaginary origin while knowing full well that her pursuit is bound to remain unsatisfied.

Heremakhonon is thus an indictment of the sentimentalism of many New World blacks—"neurotics from the Diaspora"(52)—who come to Africa in a selfish search for personal fulfilment, remaining safely uninvolved in the revolutionary struggles of the local populations. The narrative draws out the social and political implications of Véronica's private and deeply personal conflicts. While attempting to

[15]Condé's own explanation in the interview with Ina Césaire, in *La Parole des femmes*, p. 129.

face those conflicts, the narrator remains nonetheless strangely unable to summon up the will to become a truly free agent, one who can accept and thus overcome the determinants of her situation. At the end, she "knows" what is to be done but cannot commit herself to it. As Condé puts it, "She has learned some lessons from her stay but she has not understood her situation as completely as she could have" (*NL* 24).

A Transparent Mind

This lack of agency and focus is reinforced by a narrative technique that makes systematic use of free direct and indirect discourse, giving the reader unmediated access to the narrator's mind. Past and present voices are telescoped into one another in a confusing array of internalized points of view which seem to divide and tear at Véronica's consciousness, making it difficult to determine exactly when the voices are shifting and when their superposition spells a deadening conflict between different cultures, different moral and political codes.

Dorrit Cohn, in *Transparent Minds*, talks about the "singular power possessed by the novelist: creator of beings whose inner lives he can reveal at will," and she invokes the "unreal transparencies" to which the novel has accustomed us.[16] To be able to enter into the thought processes of a narrator or a character is a feature of narrative which we have come to take for granted. Condé's technique in *Heremakhonon* is to take this representational power to an extreme of psychological realism that conveys the polyphonic nature of all mental processes and the paralyzing effect that this multiplication of social voices can have when the mind experiences them as a "transmission de mots d'ordre [transmittal of a set of orders]," as Gilles Deleuze and Félix Guattari put it, but more specifically here as schizophrenic "mots d'ordre" that contain conflicting messages and ideologies.[17]

The most striking features of *Heremakhonon* are this multiplication of points of view within Véronica's interior monologue and the com-

---

[16]Dorrit Cohn, *Transparent Minds: Narrative Modes for Presenting Consciousness* (Princeton: Princeton University Press, 1978), pp. 4, 3.

[17]Gilles Deleuze and Félix Guattari, *Mille plateaux* (Paris: Minuit, 1980), p. 100, my translation.

plete absence of Véronica's own voice in direct quoted speech: she is never engaged in direct conversation with any other character. We enter into her consciousness, and like her, we experience a whole array of voices, simultaneously or in sequence, as they emerge from the past or are expressed by other protagonists in the present. This technique creates an uncanny sense of distance and disengagement, a feeling that she is simultaneously living in two worlds, her consciousness shifting gears, as it were, in response to the direct stimulation of past and present voices, which carry on in a totally disassociative manner, feeding her nothing but cliches and making her unable to decode the reality of Africa as she sees it around her every day: "Play-acting? Sincere? . . . I look around me, but *I can't read a thing on these faces*" (46; my italics). Her perceptions are always filtered by the ideology on which she has been brought up, and which she tries to shake off, but which continues to plague her. The opening paragraphs of the book illustrate this phenomenon well:

> Franchement *on* pourrait croire que j'obéis à la mode. L'Afrique se fait beaucoup depuis peu. *On* écrit des masses à son sujet, des Européens et d'autres. *On* voit s'ouvrir des centres d'Artisanat Rive gauche. Des blondes se teignent les lèvres au henné et on achète des piments et des okras rue Mouffetard. *Or c'est faux.* Sept heures dans ce DC 10, à la gauche d'un Africain rageant de ne pouvoir engager la conversation, derrière un couple de Français tout ce qu'il y a de plus moyens. Mais enfin, pourquoi? A présent tout se brouille et l'entreprise paraît absurde.
>
> Je les imagine. Ma mère soupirant. Mon père tordant ses lèvres minces. (Tous les nègres n'ont pas les lèvres "éversées.")
> —Une folle! Une tête brûlée! Avec l'intelligence qu'elle a, elle ne fait que des conneries.
> Une connerie? Peut-être que, pour une fois, il a raison.
> —Raison du voyage? [11; my italics]

[Honestly! *You*'d think I'm going because it is the in thing to do. Africa is very much the thing to do lately. Europeans and a good many others are writing volumes on the subject. Arts and crafts centers are opening all over the Left Bank. Blondes are dying their lips with henna and running to the open market on the rue Mouffetard for their peppers and okra.

Well, I'm not! Seven hours in a DC-10. On my left, an African desperately trying to make small talk. Behind me, a French couple as average as they come. Why am I doing this? At the moment, everything is a mess, and this whole idea seems absurd. I can see them now. My mother, sighing as usual. My father pinching his thin lips. (Not all blacks have protruding lips.)

"She's insane! So headstrong! All those brains and nothing but foolish ideas."

Foolish? Maybe he's right for once.

"Purpose of the visit?" (3; my italics)]

The impersonal pronoun *on* marks the common place knowledge of the moment, the Eurocentered reality that surrounds Véronica. She must deal with it, even if only to situate herself in opposition to its discourse. That is when the sudden shift occurs, without transition, from free indirect speech, attributed to an indistinct *on*, to a statement made in/by Véronica's oppositional consciousness : "Or c'est faux." This swift, irregular movement of the prose, with abrupt and sudden juxtaposition of sentences, produces discontinuity. Since there is no obvious transition from the clichés, the *ouï-dire*, to the "direct free thought" of the narrating instance, it is the reader who is left with the task of filling in the gaps, of effecting the perspectival shifts.[18] In other words, the reader is forced to participate actively in the production of meaning, while the narrator is in the more passive position of having to submit to the meaning produced by the voices that speak through her. The text thus simultaneously coerces the reader into active decoding, while representing a transparently passive narrator. By ruling out reader identification with the narrator, the text stages its own "interweaving of negative forces," revealing its oppositional ideology.

Whereas Véronica's abortive attempts at "confession," discussed

---

[18]Seymour Chatman, *Story and Discourse: Narrative Structure in Fiction and Film* (Ithaca: Cornell University Press, 1978), p. 182. See also John T. Booker, "*Style Direct Libre:* The Case of Stendhal," *Standford French Review* 9 (1985), 137–51. Booker prefers the term "free direct discourse" to "direct free thought" (which I borrow from Chatman) when describing the "*relatively brief* representation of a character's thoughts, which, if carried to any length, would be called free interior monologue" (141). I follow Booker's analysis of Stendhal's style in *The Red and the Black,* which is a definite intertext of *Heremakhonon.* In *Heremakhonon,* however, the representation of the character's thoughts are *consistently* made through this device of "direct free thought," hence my preference for that terminology, which is itself a subcategory of the free, untagged, interior monologue or "narrated monologue" as defined by Dorrit Cohn (chap. 3) and Booker (141 n. 10).

earlier, resulted in a failure of communication and could thus be said to function as an antimodel for the specular relationship necessary to produce understanding between implied author and implied reader, here, by contrast, the narrated monologue or direct free thought requires sustained reader involvement in order for it to be decoded as an instance of conflictual weltanschauung. The text requires active participation from its "ideal" reader, one who would be ready—unlike Ibrahima Sory—to engage the narrator on her own terms. Such a reader would have to be able to recognize Véronica's oppositional stance and remain alert to the frequent shifts in conceptual or ideological perspective. A careless reader, on the other hand, would quickly confuse the level of *ouï-dire*—the alienating internalized viewpoint of French "others"—with the beliefs the narrator wants to communicate as her own.[19] Unlike Augustine and Marie Cardinal, for example, who provide us with embedded figures of their own ideal readers and thus suggest to us ways in which we might identify with that type of reader (the one I called X in the *Confessions* and the narrator's husband in *The Words To Say It*), Condé systematically abolishes any possibility of identification. All the protagonists of the novel are caught up in their own different worlds, none of which overlap. Véronica's isolation is thus compounded by a narrative technique that forces the reader to admit his/her own antithetic situation before a text so adverse to relying on mimetic principles to establish any conceivable parallel between narrator and narratee.

The mimetic illusion of *durée* thus reproduces on a textual level the alternatively mimetic and oppositional stances of the narrator, short-circuiting any possibility of a more authentic vision set outside of this binary framework. Despite the use of a narrating "I" with which we would normally have the tendency to sympathize, we remain nonetheless voyeurs before a transparent mind in which, to quote Glissant, the "secretive and multiple manifestations of Diversity" are represented but then thoroughly negated.[20] We are never seduced into an intimate relationship with the narrator. Possibilities of closeness or complicity are neutralized by irony, detachment, and a singular lack of purposive enunciation: we are kept at a distance,

[19] As Oruno Lara does at times in his review. See *Présence Africaine* 98 (2d quarter 1976), 253–56.
[20] Glissant, p. 12.

never trusted. The scrambled interior monologue has a jarring and confusing effect, but it is through this simple narrative device that the split nature of Véronica's subjectivity is revealed. We are the addressees of her failed confession, cast in a role homologous to that of those textual narratees who are but strangers and chance encounters (cf. the blond woman on the subway platform and the bald man in the bar, p. 7). Our active participation is demanded, yet subverted by distancing irony and sarcasm. The narrator undermines the tragedy of her situation by turning herself into an object of derision.[21]

The scene in the DC 10, in limbo, in transit between point of departure and point of arrival, contains all the major elements of the novel in embryo: the narrator stages herself. She is sitting next to an African and behind a French couple. Her mind is filled first with cliches, then with the memory of her parents' disapproving faces and voices: "Une folle! Une tête brûlée." Suddenly the present interferes in the shape of an immigration officer: "Raison du voyage?" His words provoke a dreamlike free association: "Une connerie? Peut-être que, pour une fois, il a raison." Although the sentence (which refers to her father's opinion of her) comes, for the reader, before the officer's question, it is clear that it is the question that triggered the actual wording of her thoughts in her daydream, just as sometimes we may awake from a dream only to realize that environmental stimuli had provided a particular sound around which unconscious images could crystallize.

Véronica's subjectivity is determined to a large extent by her obsession with the past, even when she briefly focuses on the events of the present. The future, however, is remarkably absent from her speculations, or it figures in a negative way. When she entertains

---

[21]As Fanon clearly outlines in *Toward the African Revolution*, "One must be accustomed to what is called the spirit of Martinique in order to grasp the meaning of what is said. . . . It is true that in the West Indies irony is a mechanism of defense against neurosis. . . . A study of irony in the West Indies is crucial for the sociology of this region. Aggressiveness there is almost always cushioned by irony" (19). It is thus not hard to see why irony is the dominant feature of *Heremakhonon:* negativity and failure function as antimodels of the forms of emancipation which might be available to a protagonist once her "mechanisms of defense against neurosis" have been stripped bare of their layers of irony. Because of their identical political dependence on France, I feel justified in extending Fanon's remarks about Martinicans to the people of Guadeloupe as well.

the moot possibility of returning home to Guadeloupe, she can only imagine an unpleasant confrontation with disapproving parents; the notion that such a return might be spurred by the desire for positive involvement in the local struggle for independence never enters her mind. She cannot even imagine such an emancipating gesture. Like other heroines of recent Antillean literature—such as Myriam Warner-Vieyra's Juletane and Simone Schwarz-Bart's Télumée—Véronica sees herself as impotent, barren, and sterile : "In any case, I'll never have a child. Only little bastards" (20); "What would have happened if I had been pregnant? . . . Thank goodness my womb was already sterile" (55). She is a failed daughter and a unlikely mother, and her connections to the past and to the future are thus metaphorically severed, leaving her in limbo, in a "no-man's land" (29) where long-term choices have become pointless. She has internalized the scientific racist discourse about infertile hybrids and mulattoes which the author implicitly parodies here.

Heremakhonon is, first of all, this narrative representation of barrenness and failure. The failure is one of enunciation, and it marks a failure of political agency on the individual and collective levels for the colonized subjects of history whose lives are lived on the periphery of events beyond their control. Maryse Condé gives us a glimpse into the mind of an Antillean woman whose lack of commitment, dedication, and direction is symptomatic of a broader cultural problem, one which may not be solved for quite some time, since its resolution would imply the adoption and successful implementation of a different political economy in the French West Indies. After showing the abortive process of revolution in Africa, *Heremakhonon* ends on a pessimistic note; it has become even harder for Véronica to envisage new structures of meaning which would empower her to adopt a discourse directed toward the future, to imagine new and purposive forms of political self-invention.

Her inability to take sides, to "choose between the past and the present" (161), to renounce this sterile stance of impartiality and objectivity which paralyzes her, is a narrative device that allows Condé to explore nondidactically the numbing predicament of many Antillean intellectuals, who are culturally "French" and affectively "African" and thus ignore the possibility of becoming what they already are—Caribbeans, geographically situated in a cluster of islands with ties to each other which should be reinforced, because, as

Condé has said, "beyond our differences in terms of socio-cultural organizations, we want to believe in the unity of the 'Caribbean world.'"[22]

Condé has always refused to be duped by the idealist project of previous generations of Antilleans—represented here by Véronica's parents and the "negro bourgeoisie"—with their unproblematic focus on a notion of "cultural identity" which bypasses the often unconscious political realities of life in Guadeloupe. She feels that the generations who searched "elsewhere" for self-legitimation, looking either to France, which continues to impose its system of education on the children of the islands, or to Africa, whose history is radically different from that of the New World (since its citizens have never suffered from the prolonged effects of the Middle Passage and of slavery), are indeed mystified and deluded. She has forcefully criticized this kind of cultural alienation, arguing that as long as Guadeloupe and Martinique remain political dependencies of France, it will be impossible even to talk about "cultural identity" because there are no existing economic and political infrastructures through which local and indigeneous cultural responses can be articulated. It is only after political independence is achieved and a federation of Caribbean states is created that Antilleans—Martinicans and Guadeloupeans—will be able to begin to effect changes on the symbolic level, to think and act in terms of their own geopolitical situatedness:

It may be necessary to recall briefly some of the historical background of these two Francophone islands. Because Martinique and Guadeloupe are very small, the phenomenon of Maroon slaves could not develop the way it did in larger islands such as Jamaica where a real form of oppositional power had already taken shape in the eighteenth century. Furthermore, the relatively small number of slaves and the diversity of their origins forbade the preservation of African religions such as Voodoo in Haiti or *santería* in Cuba. What is left [in the French Antilles] is a group of practices known as "le quimbois." Later, the French school system, which was put in place as soon as slavery was abolished, completed the work of depersonalization of the black populations and can claim some spectacular results.

[In the Antilles], the colonial problem was not that of the importation

[22]Condé, *La Parole des femmes*, p. 5.

of a foreign culture and of its imposition onto a national reality which it slowly attempted to destroy—as is the case in most colonized countries. Rather, the problem lay in the difficulty inherent in the attempt to construct, from the incongruous and dissimilar elements that coexist in such a general climate of aggression, harmonious cultural forms. Until now, the conditions under which the Antillean personality has been allowed to develop are largely the consequence of this situation. There remains a vast horizon which the Antilleans of tomorrow will have to discover.[23]

The difficulties involved in the creation of a quilted "state" made up of the heterogeneous pieces of the colonial past is a question to which I shall return in detail in my discussion of Marie-Thérèse Humbert and the island of Mauritius. Condé's concerns are quite similar, but unlike Humbert, who writes after independence has been achieved, Condé can only paint a negative picture of the status quo in Guadeloupe, leaving it to the reader to draw the appropriate conclusions concerning the homologous relationships that inevitably exist among literary agency, textual production, and political emancipation. Because she believes that Antilleans will continue to find themselves in an impasse so long as they do not succeed in shaking off the complicated structures of domination that rob them of self-determination, her portrayal of Véronica is a dramatic enactment of the debilitating myths that fossilize the colonized self. Véronica's efforts to reject and transcend those myths end in failure because she remains unable to imagine empowering and enabling countermyths. Having absorbed all the racist myths about miscegenation and *métissage*, Véronica becomes the living symbol of sterility and barrenness. She cannot legitimate her own existence, let alone envisage a genuine future for her own country. As a negative model of hybridization, she represents everything that nineteenth century science subsumed under the word *mulatta*. It is thus quite clear why Maryse Condé calls her an *anti-moi*: as a fictional character, Véronica is the parodic embodiment of racist beliefs, the negative pole around which all such beliefs have condensed. She can therefore be used as a useful contrast to the ideas of abundance

[23]Maryse Condé, "Propos sur l'identité culturelle," in *Négritude: Traditions et développement*, ed. Guy Michaud (Paris: Complexe/Presses Universitaires de France, 1978), pp. 82–84, my translation.

and creativity which Condé, Glissant, and Morejón associate elsewhere with the concepts of *antillanité* and *mestizaje*.

Maryse Condé herself has now returned to live in Guadeloupe after almost thirty years of exile, and she is involved in the nonviolent political struggle for the independence of the island. She has also written a children's book on local history, which is now used in the primary school system.[24]

In the chapters that follow, I will attempt to show ways in which the impasses of exile and nomadism have also been overcome by two female subjects who succeeded in creating positive and visionary narratives of the self. Marie Cardinal and Marie-Thérèse Humbert will first have to deconstruct the patriarchal notions of selfhood and of national or cultural identity, as well as the representational practice that subtends their own discourses. By suggesting that utopian images of the future can empower us to act in the present *and* to reinterpret our past, they celebrate the relational patterns Glissant posits as the necessary first steps toward a positive "pratique de *métissage*." [25] These writers will thus show us different and mutually complementary allegories of emancipation, inspired by the colonial histories of Algeria and Mauritius.

[24]As she explained during a recent talk given at Pomona College on April 8, 1988. She emphasized the need for Afro-Caribbeans to respect diversity among all the Antilleans, stating quite categorically that it is "because we are so diverse that we can be united. If we are not allowed to be diverse, we'll never be united." She is active within the nonviolent UPLG party, the Popular Union for the Liberation of Guadeloupe.

[25]Glissant, p. 462.

6

Privileged Difference and the Possibility of Emancipation: *The Words to Say It* and *A l'autre bout de moi*

Miranda: But how is it,
That this lives in thy mind? What seest thou else
In the dark backward and abysm of time?
　　　　　　　　　Shakespeare, *The Tempest*

Mais je rêve, j'utopographe, je sais.
　　　　　　　　　Annie Leclerc, *Parole de femme*

Marie Cardinal and Marie-Thérèse Humbert are contemporary Francophone women writers. They were both born and raised in colonial environments and saw their respective countries go through a process of social and political emancipation which had profound and lasting effects on their private lives. Along with decolonization came the realization that their lives as women had been transformed in ways quite different from those of men. They set out to express this new awareness and to articulate the historical dimensions of their personal conflicts. Cardinal is a *pied-noir*, or Algerian-born Frenchwoman, who now lives and works mostly in Montreal, Canada, whereas Humbert is a Mauritian who lives in the Berry, a province of central France made famous by the novels of George Sand. Both Humbert and Cardinal present us with new ways of reading the heroine's text, new ways they clearly perceive as emancipatory. Claiming a cultural background that reaches far beyond the confines of France's *hexagone*, both authors return to their colonial roots to find sources of creativity and to denounce the grounds of colonial exploitation. Finding themselves at the confluence of different cultures, they sort out their loyalties and affiliations on a personal as well as social and political level and their predicament is analogous to that of any woman writer who tries to come to terms with her own sexual difference in a male-dominated society. They draw heavily on their personal colonial experience but publish their works as *romans*, first-person narratives of young women who are determined to make sense of their past and to inscribe themselves within and against the cultures that subtend that experience. They take us, their readers, on a journey of personal discovery where the silent other of sex, language, and culture is allowed to emerge and is given a voice. This process of discovery thus becomes the source of rebirth and reconciliation, the mode of healing of the narrating self.

Both Cardinal's and Humbert's tales center on the debilitating sexual and racial stereotypes of their colonial past and the degree to which their narrators have internalized them. Indoctrinated into a blind acceptance of these values (which at the time seem the only possible course for survival), the protagonists become progressively unable to cope with "reality" as presented and depicted in the master narratives of colonization.[1] They are thus alienated from something at once internal and external to the self. It is at that precise moment of disjunction between inner and outer or past and present reality that the narrative text articulates a dialogue between two instances of the self, the "I" and the "she," the "I" of the here and now, who reconstructs the absent, past "she," the emancipation of the "I" being triggered and actualized by the voice of the "she" taking shape on the page. These two instances of the self figuratively alternate roles as narrator and narratee in the context of different narrative segments.[2] The interaction between the narrator's self-image and her interlocutors—the reconstructed "she" as well as the various other protagonists of the story in their role as virtual narratees—gives dynamism to the unfolding of the narrative and elicits a particular response from the reader. What the narrator focuses on and what she omits to represent simultaneously set her narrative in motion and create certain expectations. As Wolfgang Iser puts it: "Effect and response arise from a dialectical relationship between showing and concealing—in other words, from the difference between what is said and what is meant."[3] The *topos* created by this interaction is the privileged textual space where initially un-

---

[1] I use this term in the sense of Jean-François Lyotard's *grand récits* in *La Condition postmoderne: Rapport sur le savoir* (Paris: Minuit, 1979).

[2] For a comprehensive approach to narratology, or general theory of narrative, see Seymour Chatman, *Story and Discourse: Narrative Structure in Fiction and Film* (Ithaca: Cornell University Press, 1978).

[3] Wolfgang Iser, *The Act of Reading: A Theory of Esthetic Response* (Baltimore: Johns Hopkins University Press, 1978), p. 45.

questioned assumptions about self and other, sex and language, belief and culture can be examined in a dramatic mode: this is where autobiography acquires a meaning and a function not unlike those of fiction with its mythmaking and myth-deflating power. The truth value of a discourse about a hypothetical self is no longer at issue; what matters is the empowering potentiality of this discourse when it aspires to emancipate its subject from the forces that constrain her. Self-writing is thus a strategic move that opens up a space of possibility where the subject of history and the agent of discourse can engage in dialogue with each other. New modes of interaction between the personal and the political are created, and metaphors of abortion and rebirth are given narrative significance within the larger social and historical spheres in which these women's lives unfold.

The Words to Say It and *A l'autre bout de moi* have many formal and thematic similarities and offer a critique of colonialism from two different class perspectives.[4] Cardinal's narrator belongs to the French landowning bourgeoisie whose stance toward the Algerian Arabs was benevolent paternalism laced with Catholic missionary zeal; in Humbert's novel, the narrator's family lives on the margins of the rich white settlers' world, which scorns them because their imperfect pedigree ("some Hindu great-grandmother who was all but forgotten since we carefully avoided talking about her" [28]) is not offset by any redeeming financial success. Despite this important class distinction, the childhoods of the protagonists benefit from a similar cultural diversity (a mothering of sorts by the natural environment and the nonwhites who are part of their daily life, in the absence of a truly nurturing biological mother, in the presence of a flamboyant and indifferent father). Both protagonists come to identify with the non-European, Third World elements of their "alien" cultures, learning to accept the privileged difference of *métissage* and to recognize the value of cultural hybridizations. For Humbert's heroine, this acceptance also becomes a telling trajectory back to her

[4]Marie Cardinal, *Les Mots pour le dire* (Paris: Grasset et Fasquelle, 1975); *The Words to Say It*, trans. Pat Goodheart (Cambridge, Mass.: VanVactor and Goodheart, 1984); Marie-Thérèse Humbert, *A l'autre bout de moi* (Paris: Stock, 1979). All further references will be given in the text. All translations of Humbert's novel are mine; a possible rendering of the title in English might be "At the other extremity of myself" or "Through the mirror of my self."

"sang-mêlé" origins, after a murderous confrontation with subjectivity in the guise of her twin sister, the mirror image, the "monstre" who steals her illusory individuality.

Motherland, (M)other Tongue

The structure of *The Words to Say It* parallels Cardinal's experience of Freudian psychoanalysis. Having reached a point of dislocation and dis-ease after resettling in Paris with her family, she decides to enter analysis. The combined influence of her church and class, along with the traumas of a difficult relationship with her rejecting mother have made her completely "aliénée," "folle" (insane or alienated—mad). After years of analysis, she succeeds in unlocking the source of the pain, and the process of writing becomes the process of rebirth : "I must think back to find again the forgotten woman, more than forgotten, disintegrated. . . . She and I. I am she. . . . I protect her; she lavishes freedom and invention on me. . . . I have . . . to split myself in two" (8). This is the most complete and radical sort of rebirth: "self-engendering as a verbal body,"[5] the discovery of language and its infinite possibilities, the realization, the surfacing of an enormous creative potential: "I and the words were both on the surface and clearly visible" (239); "words were sheaths, they all contained living matter" (239; trans. mod.). Not so much the story of an analysis as an investigation of the analogies between the dialogical analytic process and the healing, self-directed exchange that allows the unmasking of the woman, the novel belies all attempts at labeling it as a social document about psychoanalysis.[6] It enacts a coherent staging of that practice, but, in so doing, subverts it.

[5]Rodolphe Gasché, "Self-Engendering as a Verbal Body," *MLN* 93 (May 1978), 677–94. This is a study of Antonin Artaud, relevant for two reasons: madness, language, and writing are central to Cardinal's understanding of her access to the status of subject of discourse; furthermore, the plague, Freud, Marseilles (Artaud's birthplace), and Algiers would figure as the scenes of *dédoublement* for both writers: the plague being at once a *fléau*, like Cardinal's hemorrhaging, and psychoanalysis, as Freud once put it. Upon arrival in the United States, he said that he was bringing "the plague" to America.

[6]See in particular Bruno Bettelheim's Preface and Afterword to the English translation by Pat Goodheart; Marilyn Yalom, *Maternity, Mortality, and the Literature of Madness* (University Park: Pennsylvania State University Press, 1985); Elaine A. Martin, "Mothers, Madness and the Middle Class in *The Bell Jar* and *Les Mots pour le dire*,"

At the beginning of the novel, the narrator is emotionally comatose, chemically tranquilized, silent, obedient, and submissive; her body, however, is hysterically alive, constantly generating more blood, more fibroid tissue, anarchically feminine. She *is* her fibromatous uterus, and when her surgeon decides to cure her physical symptoms—the constant hemorrhaging—by the "aggressive" method of hysterectomy, she knows that this would be a mutilation, an amputation of the madwoman who is a part of her and with whom she must learn to live: "I began to accept [the insane one], to love her even" (10). She escapes into the dark office of the analyst, where, for the next seven years, she will come at regular intervals to lie on the couch "curled up like a fetus in the womb"; she feels herself to be a "huge embryo pregnant with myself" (12, 13; trans. mod.). The imagery she uses to describe the location of that office is particularly suited to the birthing metaphor: it is an island of surprising calm and tranquility in the midst of Paris, at the end of a narrow cul-de-sac,"une ruelle en impasse" (7), just as her life is lived in an impasse, in limbo, while she undergoes analysis. She is only enduring until she can be strong enough to survive without the protection of the womblike room with its mirroring presence of the "little dark-skinned man" (2) who never judges and will remain impersonal and masked till the end of the book. In this he is the opposite of the tall, dynamic surgeon who wears white and examines his patient in a glaringly lit room with a ceiling "white as a lie" (7).

How are we to understand this contrast between the surgeon and the analyst? Clearly, the surgeon stands for a patriarchal society intent on annihilating the disturbing signs of a feminine difference flowing out of control. But in the textual context of the narrative situation, he is also an antimodel for the critic, whereas the analyst figures as ideal other. The analyst's silent, invisible (she cannot see him from the couch), but very attentive presence casts him in the role of a midwife who helps the narrator pregnant with her effaced self. The text constructs him as an ideal listener-reader, one without preconceived and Procrustean notions of literary or autobiographical canon. It is in this implicit contrast between the two doctors that

French-American Review 5 (Spring 1981), 24–47; and the following reviews: Diane McWhorter, "Recovering from Insanity," *New York Times Book Review*, Jan. 1, 1984, p. 15; and Fernande Schulmann, "Marie Cardinal: *Les Mots pour le dire*," *Esprit* 452 (Dec. 1975), 942–43.

the narrative signals itself as a communicative act and provides us with the model of reading most appropriate to the "point" it is trying to make.[7] This is a model, needless to say, that would neither amputate the meaning of the text nor fit it into a preexisting theoretical framework: here, the text figures as the female body of the writer and the critic, as the midwife of its meaning. What is being advocated is a female reappropriation of the best form of ancient Socratic *maieusis*, not surprising for a feminist author who was trained as professor of philosophy. The metaphor "physician of the soul" is, of course, well known to readers of Augustine's *Confessions* ("medice meus intime" [10:3]),[8] where God, the transcendental addressee, is the model of Augustine's ideal reader, the one who can help the narrator transcend his own corporeality so that his soul may be reborn. In a reversal of this mind/body dichotomy and of the traditional quest of spiritual autobiographers for a transcendent self, Cardinal aims (in a Nietzschean manner) at rediscovering the body in its female specificity as the source of her own discursive practice.

The specular relationship created between writer and reader (or critic) in the analytical situation suggests that for the writer as well there is an antimodel of creativity; her inability to write without constant reference to a rigid code and pious reverence for the great masters stifles her completely:

That's what writing was for me: to put correctly into words, in accordance with the strict rules of grammar, references and information that had been given to me. In this area improvement consisted in expanding vocabulary in so far as it was possible, and learning Grevisse almost by heart. I was attached to this book, whose old-fashioned title, *Good Usage*, seemed to me to guarantee the seriousness and suitability of my passion for it. In the same way I loved saying that I read *Les Petites Filles modèles* when I was little. In Grevisse, there are many doors open to freedom and fantasy, many good-natured winks, like little signs of collusion, meant for those who do not wish to be confirmed in the orthodoxy of a dead language and a tightly corseted grammar. I felt that these evasions were, nevertheless, not for me, but were reserved for writers. I had too much respect, even veneration, for books to

[7]Cf. Ross Chambers, *Story and Situation: Narrative Seduction and the Power of Fiction* (Minneapolis: University of Minnesota Press, 1984), pp. 3–15.

[8]Augustine, *Confessions*, Loeb Classical Library edition (Cambridge: Harvard University Press, 1977).

imagine that I could write one. . . . Writing itself seemed to be an important act of which I was unworthy. [215–16; trans. mod.]

Such a thorough internalization of the repressive rules of the symbolic order puts the writer in the role of a surgeon operating a ruthless censorship on her own text, asphyxiating any free play of subjectivity.[9] It is not surprising that when she does start finding her own "mots pour le dire," she hides herself to write and then hides her notebooks under her mattress, as though this transgression of the symbolic order can only be effective if it is not subjected to the judging eye of the literary law—a law to which the very title of the book refers ironically, since it connotes Boileau's seventeenth-century *Art poétique:* "Ce qui se conçoit bien s'énonce clairement / Et les mots pour le dire viennent aisément [What one truly understands clearly articulates itself, and the words to say it come easily]."

This eye is also the one that she sees in her hallucination (chap. 8) and which terrorizes her: it is the eye behind the camera of her father, who had attempted to photograph her as a toddler while she was urinating on the ground. This experience, lived by the child as a violation of her secret desires, unleashed a formidable anger against this peeping father: "I strike him with all my strength. . . . I want to kill him !" (152). Her hatred is then promptly repressed by the shame she is made to feel for her violent impulses: "You mustn't hit mama, you mustn't hit papa! It's very wicked, it's shameful! Punished, crazy! Very ugly, very naughty, crazy!" (152, trans. mod.). Once the "eye" of the hallucination is exorcised, she can begin to deal with her fear of being "a genuine monster" (165). This is the combined fear, as Barbara Johnson puts it, of "effecting the death of [her] own parents" and of being creatively different, free and successful.[10] To overcome this fear, which paralyses her writing, she has to learn to let the words flow freely, without regard for gram-

[9]The rules are the *règles*, the female menstrual cycle, which "may provide a near perfect metaphor for Cardinal's dialectic . . . of subversion and conformity," according to Carolyn A. Durham in her excellent study of another of Cardinal's works: "Feminism and Formalism: Dialectical Structures in Marie Cardinal's *Une Vie pour deux*," *Tulsa Studies in Women's Literature* 4 (Spring 1985), 83–99.

[10]See Barbara Johnson, "My Monster/My Self," *Diacritics* 12 (Summer 1982), 9. In this review of Mary Shelley's *Frankenstein*, Nancy Friday's *My Mother/My Self*, and Dorothy Dinnerstein's *Mermaid and the Minotaur*, Johnson suggests that these "three books deploy a *theory* of autobiography as monstrosity" (10).

matical rules or objective reality: the flow of words must mimic the anarchic flow of blood and eventually replace it. Describing her apprenticeship at self-portrayal, she explains: "With pencil and paper, I let my mind wander. Not like on the couch in the cul-de-sac. The divagations in the notebooks were made up of the elements of my life which were arranged according to my fancy: going where I pleased, living out moments I had only imagined. *I was not in the yoke of truth, as in analysis.* I was conscious of being more free than I had ever been" (215; my italics).

The distinction between the analysis and the book we are reading is clearly established. Later on, allowing her husband to read her manuscript, she confesses with some trepidation: "I should have stopped to consider that I was writing, that I was telling a story if only to the paper [que je racontais une histoire à du papier (266)]; I should have spoken about it to the doctor" (226). The freedom to write, and to write secretly, is yet another transgression, a transgression of the rules of psychoanalytic practice. But the risk she takes of being judged by Jean-Pierre, her husband, the *agrégé de grammaire,* is not a gratuitous one: the book exists in a homologous relationship to her analytic discourse, and just as analysis has changed her perception of herself, so reading her text will change Jean-Pierre's perception of his wife : "How you've changed. You intimidate me. Who are you?" (228). The invitation to read/know her anew is thus an invitation to love again after the long estrangement caused by her "illness." Sharing in the power of language to redefine reality, to name the woman who had become effaced under her social role as wife and mother, "model young wife and mother, worthy of my own mother" (219), Jean-Pierre now sees the new/old face of the narrator, the one that conveys a harmonious relationship to Mediterranean nature, where the sea, the sand, the sun, the sky are one continuous whole, interacting in their difference to allow the free play of meaning. The female is again the equal partner of the male, who needs her to assume her difference so he can become capable of a genuine act of love, an act of loving/reading. The staging of Jean-Pierre as the receptive reader par excellence can be interpreted as *mise en abyme* of the reading process and of its effect as it is encoded in the narrative structure.[11] The power to be read on her

[11]See Lucien Dällenbach, *Le Récit spéculaire* (Paris: Seuil, 1977); and also Chambers, pp. 18–49.

own terms is thus inseparable, for the female writer, from a genuine "suspension of disbelief" on the part of her audience, whereas her right to be a narrator is acquired through an arduous effort at self-emancipation from the laws of preexisting and distorting master discourses (such as the literary tradition and psychoanalytic practice).

Not surprisingly, this newfound freedom results from her understanding and acceptance of the specificity of her female experience, a specificity that stretches her beyond the personal to the political and historical context of Algeria. Along with the discovery of what it means to be a woman and a victim, comes the realization that her victimization as daughter coexisted with her mother's inability to assume and legitimize her own lack of sexual and maternal love and to face her fear of sexual difference. Hence the mother's complicity with the repressive, paternalistic colonial order despite her qualities of intelligence, sensuality, and integrity (cf. chap. 16). Although the narrator rejects her as mother, she can see the woman and relate to her as victim. Like Algeria during the war of independence, the mother's agony is the scene of a civil war between conflicting ideologies. Rather than reexamine all the values she lives by, the mother prefers to let herself go completely, to give in to the profound distress that had inhabited her psyche all along. She loses all self-respect, is drunk and incontinent, and subsequently dies. Her daughter finds her "on the floor. She had been dead for ten or twelve hours already. She was curled up in a ball. Rigor mortis had fixed horror on her face and body. . . . She grimaced terribly in pain and in fear . . . her features tortured by all the amputations to which she had submitted" (289). It is the mother who is now the monster, the fetuslike creature whose posture mirrors her unsuccessful attempts at abortion of the fetus-daughter; that daughter, now safely beyond her nefarious influence, can at last say "I love you" (292) and make her peace with the past.

It is during a visit to her mother's grave that the narrator is able to recall with poetic tenderness the moments of genuine joy that she had experienced when walking on the beach or gazing at the stars with her mother. Looking for the shells washed ashore by the waves, looking at the stars in the warmth of the Mediterranean night, together, they had been "in contact with the cosmos" (202). Her mother knew the names of all the shells—"the mother-of-pearl shells, cowries, pointed sea snails, ear shells and the pink razor clam shells" (291)—and of all the stars—"the shepherd's star . . . the Big Dipper . . . the Charioteer . . . the Little Dipper . . . Vega . . . the Milky Way" (202; trans. mod.). This naming of the universe is her most precious maternal legacy and the daughter is able to insert herself, her book, her words into that universe. The daughter thereby erases the narrative of hatred and unsuccessful abortion which her mother had divulged to her when she was twelve. They were standing on a sidewalk of Algiers, "the same sidewalk on which later would run the blood of enmity" (132). The recounting of these secrets had been the mother's *saloperie* (131), her villainy (105) to her daughter. This information about the girl's gestation (that prehistoric time of her life) thwarts her feminine development. She does not start menstruating before the age of twenty. The doubly archaic revelation (reproduction as a "female problem" and excavation of her prediscursive past), is lived by the narrator as the murder of her femininity.

Indeed, language can kill (as we saw in Angelou's narrative), and a story can be what Peter Brooks calls "un acte d'agression."[12] To counter this mortal effect, another story, more powerful in its enabling, nurturing, or life-affirming characteristics, is needed. Such are the tales and legends that the old Algerian woman, Daïba, tells to the children on the farm while feeding them "pastry dripping with honey" (98) and unleavened bread. Hers are mythic tales with a powerful, positive, imaginary content, "sudden flights on winged horses prancing all the way to Allah's Paradise . . . adventures of black giants who shook mountains, fountains springing up in the desert, and genies inside bottles" (98). These days on the farm were magic: contact with an archaic civilization, games with the Arab children, freedom from French reason and religion. The richness and diversity of these early experiences give the girl a strength to draw from when she is forced to leave Algeria and to cope with the psychic wounds that her mother and the war inflicted upon her.

Talking to her dead mother in the cemetery, she recalls trips to another cemetery in Algeria, where her dead sister lies and where her mother used to take her. Inconsolable over the loss of that "exceptional" child, the absent daughter who can never be replaced,

[12]Peter Brooks, "Constructions psychanalytiques et narratives," *Poétique* 61 (Feb. 1985), 64.

the mother remained indifferent to the living child: that loss is the original cause of the mother's profound and murderous contempt for the second daughter. The death of the mother then frees this daughter who can simultaneously terminate her analysis and end her narrative. Writing *is* symbolic matricide. But unlike Augustine, whose embodied self metaphorically dies with his mother at the end of his narrative, only to be reborn as pure spirit, Cardinal's narrator experiences a physical liberation, a healing of the body. For her, writing is the act of self-emancipation which allows the daughter to reach autonomy, despite her painful bleeding, much as Algeria won independence through its own bloodbath.

The novel contains two parallel chapters (6 and 16), which describe the Algerian tragedy and the mother's demise in much the same terms: "French Algeria lived out its agony" (87) and "During this last year of my analysis, my mother was living through her final agony" (270); " While lacerated Algeria showed her infected wounds in the full light of day, I revived a country of love and tenderness where the earth smelled of jasmine and fried food" (88) and "On the contrary, she [the mother] didn't give a damn, she exhibited herself as if she took pleasure in exposing her wounds" (280). Colonialism, like sexism, is degrading and abject. It is their combined forces that kill "the mother and the motherland"[13] and give the narrator the opportunity to discover what femininity really means in that context. The role of women is to be mothers of future soldiers, who will fight wars and perpetuate inequality and injustice. The way out of that impasse is a heightened political awareness of the complicated structures of domination that amputate freedom and self-determination from people and countries:

It is only now that I understand that I had never really read a newspaper or listened to the news. I'd looked upon the Algerian war as a sentimental matter, a sad story of a family worthy of the Greeks. And why was that? Because I had no role to play in the society where I was born and had gone crazy. No role, that is, other than to produce sons to carry on wars and found governments, and daughters who, in their turn, would produce sons. Thirty-seven years of absolute submission.

[13]See Marguerite Le Clézio, "Mother and Motherland: The Daughter's Quest for Origins," *Stanford French Review* 5 (Winter 1981), 381–89. This is a study of Marie Cardinal and Jeanne Hyvrard.

Thirty-seven years of accepting the inequality and the injustice, without flinching, without even being aware of it! [264]

Even something as private as childbearing takes on enormous social and political significance when understood against the larger framework of a country engaged in war and needing soldiers who are willing to die for its colonialist ideology. The narrator thus realizes that her so-called illness is none other than her progressive inability to cope with this oppressive "reality," constructed by the dominant ideology and imposed on its victims, whose voices are silenced by violence. This violence may be obvious, as in war, or it may be surreptitiously performed by various modes of linguistic and cultural oppression which deploy an image of the female body as instrument of reproduction under the control of the producers of culture.

For Cardinal, the only way to break out of that cycle of war and exploitation is to start sharing in the power of man to make decisions that affect all of our lives, in other words, to become an active participant in society, to produce culture instead of remaining a passive term within a given system of exchange. In fact, as Cardinal asserts, it is precisely because of her feelings of impotence in affairs of the state that she is overwhelmed by her first major attack of anxiety, by the "Thing" that is going to drive her crazy: "It seems to me that the Thing took root in me permanently when I understood that we were about to assassinate Algeria. For Algeria was my real mother" (88). The Algerian war was engineered by politicians whose personal involvement in it was minimal. By contrast, the narrator, her mother, and the people of Algeria have everything at stake, are caught in the political storms of history, in events over which they have no control. Only political self-awareness can bring about change. Cardinal views psychoanalysis as a means to a "prise de conscience," or higher awareness of the existing links between psychological *repression* and political *oppression*. When her narrative is viewed from that angle, Algeria becomes the central character of the novel, the alter ego of the narrator, whose main physical symptom of hysteria is the constant menstrual bleeding, the hemorrhaging, which cannot be stopped until she succeeds in emancipating herself from the cultural straightjackets that prevent her from living freely and imaginatively as a writer.

Indeed, as the title of the novel implies, the narrator is struggling to find her *own* words to say it, to verbalize the contradictions of her historical situation, not just to say those words to the analyst who mediates her attempts here but to tell a story that will reach an audience and carry larger social implications. The process of psychoanalytic dialogue thus has a double function in the text : (1) to show the woman's access to language, to the repressed (m)other tongue buried under the cultural and patriarchal myths of selfhood, to liberate the power of words when they are appropriated by a female subject who assumes her difference triumphantly; and (2) by comparing the analyst/analysand dyad to the writer/critic dyad, to implicitly formulate a feminist aesthetics of reading which would allow the text to speak to the reader without risk of being amputated by the imposition of a preexisting theoretical framework, a preconceived notion of feminine discourse. There is a constant interplay between the "story" and the psychoanalytic "discourse," each shedding light on, while subverting, the other. Similarly, the colonial history of Algeria and the private life of the narrator are shown to be so closely intertwined that any attempt to understand her "madness" outside of the sociopolitical structures that generated and amplified the illness is indeed bound to be a reductionist exercise.

For example, the "sick" woman is "cured" thanks to her progressive awareness of the past. She succeeds in unearthing her childhood experiences and emotions, focusing more and more on the patriarchal system that is at the source of the repressive mechanism of her unconscious. In other words, she understands repression to be a consequence of oppression: oppression of children by parents, of the body by culture, of the colony by the *métropole*. It is this oppression that causes the hysteria of war, the conflicts of colonialism and schizophrenia. In the narrator as individual this conflict causes the hemorrhaging (of the body), which her surgeon wants to cure with the "aggressive" method of hysterectomy (i.e., culture), much as France tries to cure the ills of colonialism by imposing a political order that results in war and torture, in the escalating violence of archaic conflicts:

> Bathtub tortures, electrodes, open-handed blows, fists in the face, kicks in the belly and the balls, cigarettes put out on nipples and pricks . . . it was the shameful agony of French Algeria. The degradation of everything was in the blood of civil war which ran into the

gutters and overflowed onto the sidewalks, following the geometric patterns in the cement of civilization. The end was accompanied by the age-old ways in which Arabs settled accounts: bodies disemboweled, genitals cut off, fetuses hung up, throats slashed. [88, trans. mod.]

"The blood of civil war"—Algeria's body is bleeding from the conflicts created by "civilization," which imposes this "geometrical" path or framework on its destiny. This is exactly the point where the question of motherhood and motherland are raised in all their complexity and ambiguity. For it is the daughter, the narrator as daughter who bleeds. Yet the cause of this bleeding, as we saw, is inextricably tied to the traumas of the unsavory revelation which the biological mother inflicted upon the girl. The mother was about to get divorced and did not want to have to carry to term a pregnancy that could only make it more difficult for her to cope with the aftermath of divorce. The "saloperie" (131), this scandalous act of the mother, takes place outside, on the sidewalk, like the wartime murders to which it is metaphorically linked: "We were on a downtown street, a street full of noise and passersby. What I saw, for my head was lowered while she spoke, were the cement squares of the sidewalk, and, on the surface of the squares, the residue of the city: dust, spittle, cigarette butts and excrement. The same sidewalk on which later would run the blood of enmity. And, twenty years later, the same sidewalk on which I would be afraid of falling, driven into a corner with death, by the Thing" (132). The narrator conflates this tale telling with an experience of mutilation and amputation carried out by the mother on the daughter: "If I could have known the harm she'd do me, if instead of having no more than a premonition, I'd been able to imagine the incurable and ghastly wound she was going to inflict on me, I'd have sent forth a howling. . . . I'd have shrieked even to death, thus never having to hear the words she was about to inflict on me like so many mutilating swords" (135, trans. mod.).

Read allegorically, this episode prefigures the violence of war and its attendant mutilations and monstrosities. France wants to abort its colonial progeny, the *pieds-noirs* being a burden and an embarrassment. The mother, like the *métropole*, kills and mutilates with language that tortures. The mother's situation is not unproblematic, though, for as we have seen, she dies of an agony as abject as the war was. And she dies in France, having left *her* motherland, the farm in Algeria. The displacement among Algeria, the mother, and the narrator points to a suicidal gesture on the part of the mother when she discloses her secrets to her daughter: for to hurt the child is to hurt herself in her child. To be sure, the imagery used to describe her dead body is that of fetal pain, as I indicated. The agony of the mother, the bleeding of the daughter, the torturing of Algeria—all collapse into one and the same image: that of pain inflicted on the female body of woman and the geographical body of Algeria by the discourses of patriarchy and colonialism. And it is worth noting briefly that in the familial configuration, the biological father is French, not *pied-noir* like the mother: he represents the arbitrary fatherland, the *patrie* to which the narrator will be exiled for a time, banished to an inhospitable place where her feelings of dis-ease and dis-location culminate in madness. The conflation of maternal body and country of origin is brilliantly accomplished in this novel, and all the ambivalence of the daughter toward her painful historical heritage is played out in subtle and illuminating ways. By showing the inescapable links between agency and historicity, Cardinal broadens our understanding of the processes that leave their mark on human subjectivity. By denouncing war and torture as part of the same social machines that inscribe their despotic laws on the body, the author suggests that the internalization of these laws is a subtle form of torture that guarantees inequality. The mother's murderous language, written on the body, is an unforgettable kind of memory, a bleeding wound.

I would like to return briefly to the textual level of the narrative to underline how such a feminist aesthetic of reading would work in practice. As a critic, I can decide to focus on specific aspects of a textual corpus and thus bracket—eliminate or negate—those elements that cannot be integrated into my own theoretical framework. I would then be acting like the surgeon who blithely "cures" feminine hysteria by doing hysterectomies. Cardinal's strongly allegorical context implies that this is exactly the problem when "theory" ignores history and geography, that it tends to privilege certain factors at the expense of others, thus perhaps reducing a complex work to the dimensions of an "autobiographical testimony" on psychoanalysis. Indeed, in the Preface and Afterword to the English translation, Bruno Bettelheim, talks about the Freudian aspects of the novel without once mentioning Algeria, let alone noticing that it is a central character of the story. Thus the political dimension of the story is lost, obscured, and obfuscated in a strangely ironic way by a psychoanalyst who is deaf to the discourse of the (m)other tongue, which cries to be heard under the apparent simplicity of the "auto-biographical" text. But perhaps the translator too is at fault here: for the last chapter of the French version is severed from the English version. It is a very short chapter consisting in one single line: "Quelques jours plus tard, c'était Mai 68 [A few days later it was May 68]." This historical marker concludes the novel on a distinctly optimistic and utopian note, pointing to the revolutionary potential of psychoanalysis when it favors political emancipation.[14]

The status and function of psychoanalysis in Cardinal's novel are thus highly political: they trace the path to social consciousness. That path is a nomadic or "crooked" one, unlike the geometrically ordered patterns of civilization, which impose meaning by repressing what they cannot accommodate. The path of madness and controlled hysteria (Nietzsche's "die schiefe Bahn")[15] is the "crooked" way: it transgresses the dominant social codes through which we become self-aware as a body politic. This transgression favors a new dawn of awareness for the individual and the collectivity, addressing the collective delusions of a community and giving voice to its "political unconscious." By unmasking the genealogies of social power and the inscriptions of political law on the body, psychoanalysis provides the tools needed to dismantle those structures of domination, and that is what the representation of the "talking cure" really aims at here.[16]

Métissage, Emancipation, and Female Textuality

The year 1968 was also an important one in the history of Mauritius. It marked the island's independence from Britain, its

[14]May 1968 marked a turning point in contemporary French social and cultural history: with the student revolt and the workers' strike which paralyzed the nation, intellectuals entertained high hopes for a different political future.

[15]Friedrich Nietzsche, *Ecce Homo*, in *Sämtliche Werke* (Stuttgart: A. Kröner, 1964), 8:390.

[16]As Gilles Deleuze and Félix Guattari have forcefully shown in *Anti-Oedipus* (Minneapolis: University of Minnesota Press, 1983). I will be discussing Nietzschean and Deleuzian approaches to history, culture, and politics in my last chapter on Marie-Thérèse Humbert.

access to the rank of country. Independence was achieved with little bloodshed, because none of the diverse ethnic groups of the island could really claim original ownership of the place. The island was known to Arab sailors since the Middle Ages, but it had no native population. The first Europeans to discover it were the Portuguese, in 1510, and they named it Ilha do Cirne (Island of the Swan: they thought the indigeneous dodo birds were a kind of swan). They left and were followed by the Dutch, who remained on the island from 1598 till 1710. The Dutch named the island Mauritius in honor of Prince Mauritius of Nassau, but their settlement was never prosperous and they abandoned it after having ruthlessly exploited the forests of ebony trees and exterminated the dodo bird. They also brought in slaves from Africa and Madagascar, a number of whom became Maroons. Between 1710 and 1715, these free men and women were the virtual masters of the island. But the French took over in 1715, renaming the island Isle de France, and it became a prosperous colony. A century of French rule has left an indelible mark and, to this day, the lingua franca of the island is a French creole dialect. In 1814, the Treaty of Paris ceded the island to the British, who renamed it Mauritius. The conditions of this cession stipulated that the language, religion, and customs of the Francophone population be safeguarded, and they were. The island is now peopled with the descendants of the French settlers and the black slaves, the Indian indentured laborers who came to work the sugarcane fields after slavery was abolished in 1835, the Chinese and Muslim shopkeepers, and a sizable population of *métis*, whose status varies greatly depending on the relative darkness of their skin and the size of their fortune.

Located in the Indian Ocean, far from any continent, Mauritius was nonetheless visited, and written about, by famous men: Bernardin de Saint-Pierre, Darwin, Baudelaire, Conrad, Mark Twain, and Gandhi, to name but a few. V. S. Naipaul called it "the overcrowded barracoon" in an essay of that name: Mauritius has a population of over a million in a geographical area of 720 square miles.[17] Although quite isolated, it has become a paradise retreat and an ideal vacation spot for the international jet set. The luxury hotels they frequent provide employment to some, but most of all, they help perpetuate the myths and fantasies the people of the island entertain about

[17]V. S. Naipaul, *The Overcrowded Barracoon* (New York: Penguin Books, 1976).

themselves and about the rest of the world—that the island is a privileged place attractive to the rich and the famous, that the rest of the world is somehow well represented in the foreigners who do come there.

That is the geopolitical reality of Mauritius, the background to keep in mind when reading *A l'autre bout de moi*. Marie-Thérèse Humbert's novel is the story of Mauritian *métis*, these "apatrides de la race [racially homeless people]" (22), the coloreds or mixed-bloods, whose marginality is partly the result of their own inability to assume their nonwhite heritage because they have internalized the ideals of the racist colonial society. Twin sisters, Anne and Nadège, live in a house on the outskirts of the vast colonial domains of the white bourgeoisie and a short distance away from the Hindu quarter. This "house on the margins, on the limits, without ties and without parentage" (17) is a metaphor for their racial and cultural contexts. Coming of age in the 1950s, the decade preceding independence, the sisters are set on a collision course, for they choose to be loyal to different traditions. Nadège gleefully accepts her *métissage*. She is chameleonlike, adventurous, imaginative, interested in Hindu culture and religion as well as popular superstitions; she is a free spirit, at once the Ariel and the Caliban of this "enchant'd isle," full of humor, impossible to define, and constantly changing. She is the favored daughter of the family and she has an affair with a young Indian politician. For both reasons, she incurs the wrath of Anne, the controlled, reasonable, calculating one, whose rigid need for respectability includes the romantic hope of a bourgeois marriage, like those of the heroines of the romances she reads. These hopes are thwarted by Nadège's pregnancy, for in Anne's world of almost-white-but-not-quite, any wrong step can be the first on the road back to complete ostracism by the whites. When Nadège proudly announces her condition, Anne's murderous hatred is unleashed. She tells Nadège why she had always resented her, she shouts her contempt and her fury, disclosing her own profound distress. In an act of love for Anne, Nadège decides to obtain an (illegal) abortion, and dies hemorrhaging. Her death and the police investigations that follow rob Anne of her pretensions to a purely Western style of life, revealing the "air d'étrangeté" (398), the uncanniness, the *Unheimlichkeit,*, of her very own home and country. At the end, the impossible fusion with her twin is realized in

Anne's appropriation of Nadège's place as the lover of the Indian, Aunauth Gopaul.

Anne's autobiographical narrative is an attempt to return Nadège's love, Nadège's loving offer to "immolate" her (pro)creation. It engages Anne, the narrator, in a dialogue with Nadège and with the repressed (sister) in herself. She can begin to tell her/their story after she has allowed Nadège's voice to emerge: "But the voice which used to be Nadège's is mine now; I know it, I am certain of it" (12). The narrative is framed by a Prologue, which situates Anne and Aunauth as exiles in Paris, where they are studying at the Sorbonne. This seemingly self-imposed exile creates sufficient distance from the recent past to reveal Anne's narrative impulse, the Archimedean fulcrum[18] she needed to lift the veil of silence on that past and on her country. The present reality of Paris now silences her too: it is lived as a jarring hiatus from the past, and her impulse to write is a defensive one, spurred on by the desire to re-create that past and reintegrate it into a new present, to shout "Mauritius (Nadège) exists!" to people who have never paid any attention to it, been indifferent to its fate. Like her island, she feels "abolie [negated]" (12) by the ignorance of others, especially since France is a spiritual motherland for the Francophones of Mauritius. Her situation as Mauritian in Paris thus triggers the memory—enacts the repetition—of an earlier trauma: her parents' inability to see her as different from Nadège. She still resents their mother's legacy of shame, hatred, bitterness, and silence: "Mother-Silence, Mother-Gloom, our marine silence" (43). And now in France, she also resents the sea of ignorance in which Mauritius floats. Like her parents' indifference, the ignorance of the *métropole* makes her feel painfully nonexistent.

Anne the protagonist can become Anne the narrator only after she has decided to return to her privileged "place of origin" and let the island tell itself through the voices of its inhabitants—all of whom have their own different stories, "life/lines," to tell her, in direct or indirect discourses of which, as we shall see later, she is both the

[18]I purposely use this image as Myra Jehlen has in "Archimedes and the Paradox of Feminist Criticism," reprinted in *The Signs Reader: Women Gender and Scholarship* (Chicago: University of Chicago Press, 1983), in order to propose that exile and marginality are perhaps the necessary preconditions for "our seeing the old world from a genuinely new perspective" (94).

narratee and relayer. In this return to the "origins," Anne is like Augustine's narrator in the *Confessions*, who is finally whole after he has reached his resting place in God, who can then speak through him and whose words are translated textually by the weaving of scriptural verses into the narrative. Anne's autobiographical gesture implicitly resembles the Augustinian project but covertly aims at subverting it: the narrative is divided into thirteen parts (like the *Confessions*), and as it unfolds, Anne confesses her "sins" to her sister. These are the sins of Western metaphysics: to wish desperately to *be* a unique individual, "être à tout prix [to be at any cost]" (419), and to capture one essential truth about oneself—whereas life is flux, theater, dream. Striving to occult in her the elements of a different race, her Hindu ancestry, and the qualities embodied by Nadège, she is a victim of the Western obsession with being, an obsession that shows nothing but contempt for its unassimilable opposites. Nadège, who is remarkably free of this totalizing goal, is self-assured in her difference. She has no distance, no duality: inner and outer are the same for her. Her life is lived in harmony with the passing of time, the mysteries of life. "Strangely intimate with the earth's profane mysteries and long seasonal gestations, with the winds' and the clouds' infinite wanderings " (312), she projects a persona that needs no mirror to reassure itself of its own existence:

> Nadège never cared about being. . . . Never, but never, did she try to see herself elsewhere than in *the eyes of others*. She would amuse herself with these fortuitous mirrors as a child would with the changing colors of a prism, perpetually enjoying her ability to create new shades, becoming by turns intrigued, charmed, shocked, or seduced by these external reflections, and thus deviating constantly from herself. There is nothing less imaginative and less true than a mirror! she used to declare contemptuously. But while she played, I would contemplate with despair my own dull shadow, lusterless compared to the shimmer of her multiple reflections; my wretched face, never quite mine because it was always too similar or too different from hers. [419; my italics]

Nadège is interested in Christian mysticism as well as Hindu rites. She participates every year in the Hindu festival of lights, the *Divali*, adorning their house with a small brass lantern, and the Hindu gods with colorful flowers. She is like a joyful Zarathustra, she does not need origins. Her very name also connotes nirvana, emptiness, nothingness: *nada*, Nadège. Anne, on the other hand, cannot surrender to polysemy and experiences it as a threat to her ego. She is always narcissistically searching for approval in the form of a reflection that would give her substance, ground her firmly somewhere "Where is the place where I should live?" (122) she asks. But the reflection she finds always turns out to be illusory and elusive: "When I look in the mirror, it is you I see, you who need no mirror, you who *are* without a mirror. The image of myself that I try to capture deceives me, escapes me; it's you who are there in the mirror, only the expression of the eyes differs and the reflection that I see, my own image, looks like a bad photograph" (121).

The place where she can and should live, of course, is on the page, in the book that embodies these tensions in its own narrative structure, combining the self-portraits of all the characters, these *others* who are Nadège's mirrors, her infinite dispersion. The words "my own image looks like a bad photograph" connote the scriptural phrase "per speculum in aenigmate" (I Cor. 13:12), which Augustine repeatedly uses to signify his state of imperfection, to be reversed when he reaches the "intellectual heaven." In book 12, chapter 13 of the *Confessions*, Augustine articulates his project of self-knowledge as the search for completeness and perfection. Augustine the sinner is now converted and the book is a reflection of the man as a creature in the image of God, ready to enter "the intellectual heaven, where the intellect is privileged to know all at once, not in part only, not as if it were looking at a confused reflection in a mirror [non in aenigmate, non per speculum] , but as a whole, clearly, face to face [facie ad faciem]."[19]

Humbert's text never makes explicit reference to Augustine's *Confessions*, as it does to Shakespeare's *Tempest*, for example, but it embodies in its structure an undeniable reflection of that *architexte* of Western autobiographical discourse, while reversing its messages: it points to a negative view of mirroring, in the Western sense, as usurpation, occultation of difference. As Roland Barthes has said: "In the West, the mirror is an essentially narcissistic object: man conceives a mirror only in order to look at himself in it; but in the Orient, apparently, the mirror is empty; it is the symbol of the very

[19]Augustine, *Confessions*, trans. R. S. Pine-Coffin (New York: Penguin Books, 1979), p. 289. The Latin is from the Loeb Classical Library edition.

emptiness of symbols . . . : the mirror intercepts only other mirrors, and this infinite reflection is emptiness itself."[20]

It is in chapter 12 of *A l'autre bout de moi,* during the police interrogation, that Anne recalls (privately, not publicly) her confrontation with Nadège: "I had slapped her face with all my strength and rage. She took another step with her arms spread out. Then she slowly lowered them, as if in a daze. And before me, there was only her strangely distorted face, like a mask. No, I felt no pity, but once again this hideous joy, so keen that it seemed closer to pain than to pleasure; *before this unexpressive mask, at last, I had a face!* (427; my italics). Anne's insults literally deface Nadège, steal her face, effecting her death as surely as the botched abortion will on the following day. It is not just the abortionist who is on trial; Anne too must account—on the page, by writing—for her inability to tolerate Nadège's polysemic difference and for her secret desire to assimilate it. She recalls how, during their altercation, Nadège had fallen down in the sand and had lain there, curled in a fetal position; she, Anne, had shouted "Fetus! Hideous fetus! Die!" (428), aiming the insult at her sister but thereby amputating herself, depriviliging otherness as radically *other* in order to co-opt it, to abort it.

I would like to suggest that what is implied (and at stake) here is the immolation of the *métis,* the *créole,* as symbol, product and (pro)creation of Western colonialism, on the altars of Western belief in the One and the Same, in a humanism that subsumes all heterogeneity. Anne the narrator sees herself as the product of this indoctrination, which damaged her self-image. In that, her predicament is analogous to that of all individuals who have internalized their society's negative view or ignorance of their specificity. This includes women in any patriarchal system, and women writers in particular, as they face the dilemmas inherent in recapturing what has been effaced or diminished. Anne's journey back to the past aims at deconstructing that indoctrination, peeling off the layers of a damaging belief in the importance of origins and rootedness.

Her journey, then, is that of her island itself at the time of its political independence from Britain. Its multiracial society was faced with the burdens of two centuries of colonization first by the French,

---

[20]Roland Barthes, *Empire of Signs,* trans. Richard Howard (New York: Wang and Hill, 1982), pp. 78–79. *Architexte* is Gérard Genette's term. See his *Introduction à l'architexte* (Paris: Seuil, 1979).

then by the English, whereas its survival had been ensured by the labor of the Indian and black populations who were not natives either. All these diverse ethnic groups had to devise a mode of pacific coexistence that would allow the free play of influences and exchanges among different cultures. The issue, therefore, was not to define the national identity of the island (since it did not have any) but to use this geographical space, this *topos*, this "house without ties and without parentage" (17) as the place where a mosaic of forms, styles, and languages could interact and survive.

Viewed from that angle, the political problematic of the island becomes the personal problematic of the woman writer. She has no specifically female tradition to build on; to survive, she must quilt together from the pieces of her legacy a viable whole—viable in that it calls for the use of a multiplicity of elements that can allow the writer to assume the past (the literary tradition) as past and therefore to reintegrate it into a radically different present,[21] making it the implicit or explicit intertext of her text, adding that past to the texture of her voice so she may begin to transform and reinterpret history—as Hurston, Angelou, and Cardinal all do in their own intensely personal ways. This method would point to a notion of the female text as *mé-tissage*, that is, the weaving of different strands of raw material and threads of various colors into one piece of fabric; female textuality as *métissage*. It would emancipate the writer from any internal or external coercion to use any one literary style or form, freeing her to enlarge, redefine, or explode the canons of our discursive practices.

Humbert's text encodes heterogeneity through this use of intertextual references to various generic and ideological models or anti-models—to Augustine and Shakespeare, but also to Corneille, Racine, Baudelaire, Nietzsche, Conrad, Faulkner, Sylvia Plath, Michel Tournier, and others. Intratextually, she encodes it by giving her text over to a polyphonic chorus of voices who relate their own stories to us by means of her narrative. The purpose of these stories is twofold: to give a voice to the silenced ones of history and to allow Anne to become the heroine of her own tale by choosing a script for the way she will live her life from the various life stories that are

---

[21]I am paraphrasing Brooks's discussion of transference (p. 65) in Balzac's *Le Colonel Chabert*.

recounted to her. Her situation as listener and interpreter of these stories is homologous to ours before her text, suggesting that she encodes certain models of reading appropriate to her own discourse. Without going into a detailed analysis of the many instances of situational self-reflexivity that would illustrate my point here, I would like to focus on two embedded stories ("narrational embedding") of abandonment, which Anne retells in order to deal with and break away from that age-old script of female passivity.[22] They are the stories of Sassita, the young Indian maid, and of her own mother. Both are quiet, submissive, "dead to desire as well as to revolt" (352), as Nadège will become when she too is all but abandoned by her lover, who wants to protect his political image.

Sassita was married at the age of fourteen to a fifty-six-year-old man who promptly repudiated her on their wedding night because the bedsheets had failed to become stained with blood. Dumbfounded at her ill luck and at the man's obstinate attempts to draw blood, she had rejoined her family and resigned herself to their daylong beatings as punishment for tarnishing the family's honor. She fatalistically accepted the guilt imposed on her by external circumstances. Listening to her story, Anne is filled with shame at the troubling unfairness of life and at the fatalism of the Indian woman.

The mother's story is disclosed when the sisters discover her diary after her death; they learn how disappointed she had been at their birth because they were "of a golden terracotta color" (130), not pink and blond and safely beyond their nonwhite ancestry. Also, her fear of sex and her disappointment in her husband's infidelities added to the debilitation of her young daughters. The discovery of their mother's secrets further accentuates the sisters' alienation from each other: Anne is progressively absorbed by her hopes to live a normal/respectable life, whereas Nadège gives free rein to her "blaze of vital energy" (120).

These pictures of effaced, obliterated femininity are the only paradigms or frames of reference Anne and Nadège have, their only lifelines to the status of female persons. In a reversal typical of the deployment and resolution of Humbert's narrative text, it is Nadège who is abandoned when her father threatens her lover with a political scandal (Nadège is still a minor at the time of her affair). She

[22]Chambers, pp. 18–49 especially (33).

resigns herself to her fate as Sassita had, becoming a "tragic heroine," whereas Anne learns to dissimulate, to swerve, and to survive,
thus gradually distancing herself from her role as "romantic heroine," deviating from the traditional script and thereby freeing herself
to say her own lines on her own stage, the island, to which she
decides to return.[23]

When her father reveals to her his view of married life, Anne
writes: "I think that the most embarrassing thing for me was not just
the content of these confidences, but the mere fact of listening. The
habit of silence is a hard one to give up, and I sensed all too clearly
that this kind of thing was never meant to be a one-way street.
Wasn't I too committing myself to speak in turn, to emerge from the
opportune shadow where I stood?" (134). Paradoxically, then, these
(negative) stories do have a positive effect, for they will contribute to
Anne's impulse to break the code of silence that had been the mother's legacy to her daughters. Listening to "confidences" (reading
autobiographical novels) propels the hearer into a dialogical encounter: one that can only empower her to speak, to write.

But being empowered to write is but the beginning. The female
subject must now learn to create new images and to engage in a
dialogue with the more familiar ones of literary history. And her
new images have to be vivid enough to superimpose themselves on
the old myths they mean to transform and sublate. My final chapter
will analyze just how Humbert succeeds in accomplishing such a
transformation of the *topos* of utopia.

[23]This decision to return after having first left for Paris is set in implicit contrast to
the move planned by her Uncle André: he decides to emigrate to South Africa with
his family, thus getting an official seal of approval that he safely "passes" for one of
pure European descent, since there is indeed "no whiter white than the South African
white man" (cf. p. 449).

7

Anamnesis and Utopia:
Self-Portrait of the Web Maker
in *A l'autre bout de moi*

Must I still seek the last happiness on blessed isles and far
away between forgotten seas? But all is the same, nothing
is worthwhile, no seeking avails, nor are there any
blessed isles any more.
                          Nietzsche, *Thus Spoke Zarathustra*

For it is man who creates for himself the image of woman,
and woman forms herself according to this image.
                          Nietzsche, *The Gay Science*

From Plato's Atlantis to Michel Tournier's Speranza, islands have
been a *topos*, a rhetorical device used by writers to create a fictional
environment, to inspire a visionary or romantic imagination. Since
Thomas More's *Utopia* (1516) the myth of an idyllic place where a
new vision can take shape and a new order develop has often been
linked to the idea of islands: the *ou-topia* being that nonexistent *topos*,
the perfect (*eu-topia*) island. Writers as diverse as Shakespeare,
Swift, Defoe, Rousseau, Bernardin de Saint-Pierre, Samuel Butler,
George Sand, and Aldous Huxley have used the concept for satirical
as well as mythical purposes.

For Bernardin de Saint-Pierre, the inspiration stemmed from the
discovery of a real island and subsequent travel there: *Paul et Vir-
ginie* takes place in Mauritius. George Sand's *Indiana*, on the other
hand, was inspired by the journals of her Berrichon friend, Jules
Néraud, who had traveled extensively to the French islands of the
Indian Ocean, Madagascar, Mauritius, and Réunion (then known as
Ile Bourbon, the setting of *Indiana*). Real or fictional, islands have
been the objects of many mythologies, creations of the romances
and fantasies of the (mostly male) European literary imagination
since the time of Plato.

It is in this sense that islands are like women: their realities are
masked behind the social and political constructs of history, the
tales and legends of the first explorers and their contemporaries.

The mythologizing of islands took on new dimensions with the Renaissance seafaring explorations, which marked the beginning of the European colonial era. The island colonies were visited, settled, and traded like pawns in the game of colonialist expansion. After wars the colonial powers fought among themselves and treaties they signed with each other, the islands were finally abandoned. The many name changes of the colonies amply testify to the plurality of their political affiliations, becoming a kind of palimpsest of their multiple identities. Today, the masking continues even more thoroughly with the advent of mass tourism. Colorful travel brochures about "tropical paradises" are the staple of our winter dreams in snowbound Paris or New York. The Club Med myth of "sun-sex-sand"[1] is alive and well in Guadeloupe, Martinique, Mauritius, Réunion, or Tahiti. One of the slogans the Club Mediterranée has used to advertise itself, "the antidote to civilization," is a phrase which would certainly have amused Nietzsche, who claims in Beyond Good and Evil that "tropical man" is indeed the antidote to "moral" or "temperate," that is, "civilized" man.[2]

For Nietzsche, tropical man is "natural" man, but not in the sense of Rousseau's "bon sauvage," who represents a return to the original goodness of innate morality. Nietzsche's tropical man is sheer vitality and power: he is the one who can transcend morality, in order to live beyond or on the margins of the democratic, liberal society, which is but the triumph of "herd-animalization."[3] This tropical man, according to Nietzsche, has been fundamentally misunderstood by the mediocre and the moralists: they see in him only the projection of their own inner state of morbidity, a product of Judeo-Christian beliefs and attitudes.[4] The moralists are those, like the timid and the weak, who have been subjected to the influence of culture, the violent dressage of the mind, which constitutes the "disease" of civilization. For the prophet Zarathustra, who cele-

[1]The phrase is from an article of the periodical L'Express, reprinted in L'Express: Ainsi va la France, texts selected by Ross Steele and Jacqueline Gaillard (Lincolnwood, Ill: National Textbook, 1984), p. 90.

[2]Friedrich Nietzsche, Beyond Good and Evil, trans. Walter Kaufmann (New York: Vintage Books, 1966), ¶197, pp. 108–9.

[3]Friedrich Nietzsche, Twilight of the Idols, in The Portable Nietzsche, trans. Walter Kaufmann (New York: Viking Press, 1967), ¶38, p. 541. Hereafter cited as TPN.

[4]Nietzsche, Beyond Good and Evil, ¶197, pp. 108–9; Nietzsche, The Antichrist, 15, in The Portable Nietzsche, p. 581.

brates laughter and wanders among islands, these moralists are the "good," are "pharisees" who must be overcome by the creators of new values. In his search for new values, Zarathustra visits his "blessed isles," which include the "isle of tombs" where he looks back on his past and on the "murdered" visions of his youth, and the "isle of fire," a volcanic island where he expounds on the earth's "skin diseases," "man" and the "fire hound."[5]

Nietzschean Self-Portraiture

Using Nietzsche's insights into the repressive influence of Western culture and adopting many of his metaphors, Marie-Thérèse Humbert proceeds in her first book, *A l'autre bout de moi*, to deconstruct the utopias of Western imagination, its mythologies about tropical islands and about women. Born and raised in Mauritius (which is a tropical, volcanic island), she writes about her youth, her past, and her country. To do so is necessarily to confront images both of women and of islands and to unmask the realities behind centuries of rhetoric. Her work exposes the debilitating myths that obscure the unpleasant facts of life in any colonial environment with its rigidly defined social roles. As we shall see, she proposes a demystification of those myths while attempting to create another kind of utopia: one in which the island is no longer a construct, a spectacle, and an object of male imagination, but becomes the paradigm for a polysemic female subject who speaks up and discloses the conflicts and contradictions of her historical situation. Her work seems to answer—*avant la lettre*— the questions formulated by Alice Jardine in *Gynesis*. Jardine concludes by asking: "Are there not ways in which feminism, as concept and practice, might be productively redefined in light of the new conceptual paths cleared by the texts of modernity? Do those paths not offer new directions with which women can link up with other minorities within and against the dominant Western conceptual systems?"[6] In a footnote to that passage, Jardine adds: "I use the word "minorities" here in the Deleu-

[5]*Thus Spoke Zarathustra*, pt. 3, in *The Portable Nietzsche*, pp. 324, 223 (The Tomb Song: "And only where there are tombs are there resurrections"), p. 242. Hereafter cited as Z.

[6]*Gynesis: Configurations of Women and Modernity* (Ithaca: Cornell University Press, 1985), p. 258.

zian sense—i.e., those who are fighting for their survival under the majority rule of the Western-white-male-heterosexual-adult." As a creole woman writer and professor of French literature, Humbert stands at the intersections of those dominant conceptual systems with the "real world" problems of colonialism, racism, and sexism. As I shall make clear through Deleuzian and Derridian readings of Nietzsche, her autobiographical narrative dramatizes the process of becoming "woman" and "maternal," that is, the process of becoming a *writer*.

Published in 1979 as a novel, *A l'autre bout de moi* is a first-person narrative and a kind of schizophrenic self-portrait, the story of a *dédoublement*. Its main protagonists, the twin sisters Anne and Nadège Morin, figure as a two-faced, Janus-like, incarnation of the author herself. Like Janus, the Roman god of gates, Humbert's narrator—and, by extension, her island—stands at the crossroads with one face looking to the East and the other to the West. The narrative is Humbert's story as well as the story of Mauritius and its diverse ethnic groups. It ends with a utopian vision of Anne, the Catholic, *métis* narrator, and her Indian lover-to-be, Aunauth Gopaul, as the mixed-race couple who might perhaps harmonize East and West and live beyond the racial prejudices of the island: "If I were to have children, and I hoped to, they would be able to come back here. . . . they could daydream while gazing at both Angel Gabriel and Vishnu, who would continue smiling at each other in this paradise of glass."[7]

Anne is referring here to the Chinese shopkeeper's store window, a recurring *topos* of the narrative. Thematically, it is a matrix for the major metaphors of the text. With its bric-a-brac of incongruous objects, the shop is a magical place for the twin sisters and a haven of cultural diversity: "There, statues of the Virgin stand side by side with benevolent fat Buddhas. Sometimes even Civa stretches out his multiple arms, as if trying out the poses best suited to his dignity; or Vishnu, asleep on his snake, gets ready to turn into one of his incredible avatars, while Saint George, armor-plated in his coat of mail, crushes a dragon whose forked red tongue lashes fire. Such marvels for children not favored by fortune! (62).

---

[7]Marie-Thérèse Humbert, *A l'autre bout de moi* (Paris: Stock, 1979), p. 462, hereafter cited in the text. All translations are mine.

Christian and Oriental symbols tolerantly coexist in this "para-dise" that knows no hierarchies. It is the narrator's metaphor for a unique but idealized microcosm, the multicultural society of Mauritius, a paradoxical country that manages to survive the politi-cal storms of history by combining opposite tendencies and allowing them to thrive, while finding for itself "a strange foundation sup-ported by contrary winds" (370). Such a view is part reality, part mythmaking, the kind of utopian vision that can inspire a sense of positive belonging to the inhabitants of that microcosm, since, as Robert Sayre expresses it, "utopia, in a nonmystical, secular society, has almost the status of religion—the one source of the myths of the ends of life."[8]

The narrative incorporates the personal history, the self-portraits of the various protagonists: the members of Anne's *métis* family, the Morins; Lydia, the abortionist; Mme Marget, the dutiful bigot; the Indians, Sassita and Aunauth Gopaul; the white boy friend, Pierre; and the French Marxist doctor, Paul Roux, whose utopian political theorizing is the ferment, the catalyst, that eventually enables Anne to imagine a different future. The embedded self-portraits of these characters are narrated directly or indirectly in Anne's text. By al-lowing their heterogeneous discourses to take center stage, the au-thor encodes diversity within the narrative text, giving the reader an inside and very private view of those who are normally ignored or silenced by official, public history. Each of the characters is placed in the position of (unreliable) narrator whose perspective on the others proves limited and incomplete. But when brought together in the narrative, these points of view provide "a series of very short vignet-tes, all of them meaningful, yet incongrous" (239), a multifaceted picture of reality in that microcosm.

Ostensibly, Anne writes and re-creates past events in an attempt both to understand her sociocultural situation, as mediated by the chorus of voices emerging in her memory, and to examine her choices for the future. Consequently, her recollections are insepar-able from an ultimate visionary dimension, for, as Sayre says, "there is no new image of the future without a corresponding new image of the individual, including [her] image of [her] past."[9] In this case, the

---

[8]Robert F. Sayre, "Autobiography and Images of Utopia," *Salmagundi* 19 (Spring 1972), 19.
[9]Ibid., p. 20.

individual's image of her past is by no means static. It is a series of kaleidoscopic vignettes, which are allowed to interface and interact. Put another way, the narrator's past is "a locus of cross-references, . . . differential perceptions:" it is a relational construct derived from "a given element['s] . . . *difference* from other elements, and ultimately from an implicit comparison of it with its own opposite."[10] This quotation from Fredric Jameson, who thus summarizes the concept of binary oppositions as used in the structuralist method, aptly describes Humbert's technique: her text incorporates the use of a series of contrasting elements; aspects of one culture echo those of another, and characters tend to be paired off as mirror images, opposites of each other (the twin sisters, the mother and Sassita, Paul Roux and Aunauth Gopaul, the father, Philippe, and his brother André, and so on). Furthermore, these pairs exist in homologous, but polyvalent relationships with each other. It is from the interaction of these doubles and the new pairs they generate (Anne and her mother, Nadège and Sassita, Anne and André, Nadège and Philippe, Anne and Paul, Nadège and Aunauth) that a changing but progressively conclusive picture of the past can begin to emerge.

Ironically, this book is also the story of a road not taken, a choice not made, a dream unfulfilled: in point of actual fact the author lives in France, was married to a Frenchman active in local politics, and has five (French) children. When she planned to return to Mauritius, hoping to collaborate on the movie version of her book, threats were made against her life, and the movie project seems to have been abandoned. It is not safe to expose the illusions of a small tropical nation. "Tropical man," to return to Nietzsche's phrase, can be just as self-righteous as "civilized man" in his efforts to hold on to his mythologies.

On one level, the novel is a romantic melodrama, worthy of any nineteenth-century Bildungsroman, with a "romantic" heroine, Anne, and a "tragic" one, Nadège. In that theme of the twins, of the doppelgänger, is also a direct allusion to Michel Tournier's *Météores*, which was published a few years earlier, in 1975. But hidden, dissimulated under that surface structure as traditional narrative, is a complex self-portrait that undermines the very notion of "heroine" and that conforms in all points to Michel Beaujour's rhetorical analy-

[10]Fredric Jameson, "Metacommentary," *PMLA* 86 (Jan. 1971), 14.

sis of that genre in *Miroirs d'encre*.[11] Instead of reading the novel as another avatar of nineteenth-century realism in a colonial frame, we can therefore situate it in another tradition, that of a tropological "écriture inachevée [unfinished writing]," the tradition of self-portraiture which Beaujour traces from Montaigne to Roland Barthes by way of Bacon, Nietzsche, Michel Leiris, and others. But we can go a step farther than Beaujour. In his analysis, only a nonlinear, fragmented text qualifies as "self-portrait." Here, however, we have both a linear narrative and a fragmented self-portrait, which enter into dialogue with each other, engaging in what Abdelkebir Khatibi, the Moroccan philosopher, calls an "entretien en abyme."[12] This elusive dialogue, which is extremely hard to elucidate, constructs the narrative in the very gap, the very space where it has deconstructed the identity of the female *heroines* while reconstructing that identity as female *writer* or self-portraitist (in other words, we are moving from woman as tragic or romantic heroine to woman as writing subject and agent of discourse).

Indeed, the names of the heroines, Anne and Nadège, when pronounced together, quickly, and with the vernacular creole accent of the island, phonetically sound like "anamnèse": Anne-Nadège or [anadɛ3] becomes "ananèse" or [ananɛz] since one of the main characteristics of creole pronounciation is to soften all consonants and to change the alveolar fricatives into dentals, that is, the [3] sound into a [z] sound. Anne thus literally figures as "the one who returns" (*ana-*) and Nadège, as her "memory" (*-mnesis*), or previous self. This book would then figure as Humbert's journey back to her native island and to her previous selves, as embodied by Anne and Nadège. We thus have a perfect illustration of what Derrida says in *Glas:* "The dialectic of language, of the tongue [*langue*], is dialectophagy;" and "A text 'exists,' resists, consists, represses, lets itself be read or written only if it is worked (over) by the illegibility of a proper name."[13] Here, the "proper names" of the heroines point to the very lack of "proper name" and identity for the *métis* woman

[11]Michel Beaujour, *Miroirs d'encre* (Paris: Seuil, 1980).

[12]Abdelkebir Khatibi, "Bilinguisme et littérature," *Maghreb pluriel* (Paris: Denoël, 1983), p. 179.

[13]Jacques Derrida, *Glas,* trans. John P. Leavey, Jr. and Richard Rand (Lincoln: Nebraska University Press, 1986), pp. 9 and 33.

writer who must live, and attempt to create her self-portrait in the interval between patriarchal cultures and colonial heritages.

It may be useful to recall again Memmi's and Fanon's pronouncements about the generalized cultural amnesia of colonized peoples. By contrast, we have in this narrative an anamnesis in all the senses of the term (which clearly relates Humbert's view of history to Zora Neale Hurston's, as discussed in Chapter 3). Let me explain this by turning briefly to etymology: the word *anamnesis* is from the Greek *ana-*, "back again" or "up," *-mneme*, " memory," and the suffix *-sis*, "process": the process of re-membering. This word has a variety of meanings depending on the context. Webster's definitions include the following: in Platonism, it is the recollection of the Ideas the soul had known in a previous existence; in psychiatry, it is a case history as recounted by the patient; and in Catholic liturgy, it is a prayer in the Eucharistic service recalling the Passion, Resurrection, and Ascension of Christ. All these meanings are useful to the understanding of Humbert's text, which elaborates a complicated and polysemic set of implicit correspondences between the Platonic meaning and the Hindu notion of metempsychosis, or reincarnation; between Christ's immolation and Nadège's fate; and between the Nietzschean/Freudian/Lacanian notions of *Aufhebung* and the construction of the narrative.[14] Once we understand how the word *anamnesis* can be derived from the creole vernacular, we can use it as model for reading and interpreting the text. The vernacular paradigm becomes, to use Chambers's term again, an instance of "situational self-reflexivity" through which the text encodes its own theory of reading, its own way of producing meaning.[15] In other words, Humbert's text contains *en abyme* its own mode of interpretation, and it is the vernacular paradigm that can help us generate that interpretation. We can now draw from the text those Nietzschean

[14]For a discussion of the concept of *Aufhebung* in Hegel and Nietzsche, see Walter Kaufmann, *Nietzsche: Philosopher, Psychologist, Antichrist* (Cleveland: Meridian Books, 1956), pp. 204–6, and his translator's note, in Friedrich Nietzsche, *On the Genealogy of Morals* (New York: Vintage Books, 1969), p. 73. For a discussion of the concept in Hegel, Freud, and Lacan, see Anthony Wilden, "Lacan and the Discourse of the Other," in Jacques Lacan, *Speech and Language in Psychoanalysis* (Baltimore: Johns Hopkins University Press, 1968), pp. 195, 279, 285, 286.

[15]Ross Chambers, *Story and Situation: Narrative Seduction and the Power of Fiction* (Minneapolis: University of Minnesota Press, 1984).

elements that emphasize its dual generic status. In what follows, I want to show how the textual layers allow for this double reading.

Becoming "Woman" and "Maternal"

The Prologue, which frames the narrative, corresponds to the here and now of the narration—the exile in Paris—and is echoed, in the body of the text, by two other such temporal instances where the past and the present are telescoped into each other: Anne interrupts the thread of the story to reflect on her reasons for writing and on the experience that triggered her narrative impulse. She lived that Parisian exile as a numbing episode: "The Sorbonne where I used to listen to those grave men full of the same learned words as Paul Roux, . . . with the same serious look, this gaze which renders you anonymous and insignificant. I liked that gaze because it stripped me of my very name" (316). The episode is a salutary one, however, since it proved to be the motivation she needed to face the past: "In the labyrinth where I was lost, I stubbornly tried to look for the thread that would take me back to the old country of my childhood" (313). To re-create the past is a defensive need, an attempt to give depth and dimension to her childhood world negated by the present reality of Paris. Anne-Ariadne, having abandoned her island, finds herself writing in order to bring both her island and her dead sister, her "second departed self" back to life, recalling "real life, the one which awaits me, . . . very far away from Paris, from the subway which I take like a zombie, from the Latin Quarter where I am just another foreigner" (316).[16] It is this decentering experience of absence and fragmentation which generates her narrative discourse. Words are needed to thematize "this overflowing past, bubbling over like a flooded river" (315), and to elaborate the discursive universe where the narrator can begin to confront and overcome the past. (This Heraclitean image of the "river" strongly connotes the sheer energy of rememoration as well as the fluctuating perspectives of memory, the relativism of individual or cultural standpoints, as represented in the book.)

The phenomenon of depersonalization, absence, and loss experi-

[16]The phrase "second departed self" is Nietzsche's in *The Gay Science* (New York: Vintage Books, 1974), pt. 2, ¶60, p. 123.

enced by Anne in Paris is, according to Michel Beaujour's rhetoric of the self-portrait, the symptom that defines and inaugurates that literary "genre": "The inaugurating experience of the self-portraitist is one of emptiness and absence."[17] We have seen that *A l'autre bout de moi* exhibits the characteristic traits of that "genre" while maintaining, on a superficial level, the appearance of a traditional, linear narrative. The narrative thread allows Anne to find her way in the maze of memory. But her efforts at self-portrayal lead her to reconstruct the whole cultural world that *was* hers, and yet was not *hers*, because she could never belong to it: being a *métisse* puts her in a marginal situation with respect to all the ethnic groups represented in her text. The exile in Paris brings home (so to speak) the dilemma inherent in her condition of *métisse*. It cruelly confirms her feelings of ambiguity and instability, her existence condemned to the periphery, to limbo. Her discursive effort of memory, therefore, does not aim to reestablish a lost "identity." Instead, it is a rhetorical device used to create a series of paradigms homologous to that "departed self": Anne, Nadège, Mauritius, the Chinese shop and the verbal corpus of the book are isotopic and can be substituted for one another. This system of correspondences and analogies is, to quote Beaujour, the organizing principle of the "autoportrait:" The self-portrait "tries to constitute its own coherence through a system of recalls, repetitions, superimpositions or correspondences among substitutable and homologous units". That is why the verbal constructions that mimic and simulate the processes of memory are a matrix for structures, figures, and *topoi* by means of which the writer recalls, stages, and transcends the past and her own individuality: "The writing process . . . produces the mimesis of a . . . kind of anamnesis which could be called 'metempsychosis': at any rate, this is a type of memory both very archaic and very modern by which the events of an individual life are eclipsed by the recollection of an entire culture, thus creating a paradoxical form of self-effacement" (this process being that of *Aufhebung* itself). It is therefore not surprising, Beaujour goes on, that one of the "figures" that most frequently structures meaning in the "autoportrait" is that of Christ at the moment of his death. We saw that that was indeed the case with Augustine who identifies, in the ninth book of his *Confessions*,

[17]Beaujour, p. 9.

with the figure of Christ resuscitated. Such is also the case with Nietzsche's *Ecce Homo*, which highlights "the relation between the self-portrait and the Incarnation and the Resurrection," and which contains "in [its] center a microcosm of the literary corpus of [its] author."[18]

In Anne's narrative, the process of *écriture* enacts the narrator's "paradoxical form of self-effacement," first by creating the paradigmatic chain of substitutions between Anne, Nadège, the island, and the book. Then the death of Nadège casts her in the role of a female Antichrist, immolated because of her sister's (her island's) intolerance, sacrificed to the narrow Christian values of the white society to which Anne was striving to belong. Finally, after her death, Nadège is resurrected in the person of Anne: a substitution occurs, Anne undergoes a metamorphosis. She is compelled to assume Nadège's place as Aunauth's lover and to espouse Nadège's point of view on the illusory nature of her own Apollonian or Western quest for a stable ground to subjectivity.

A l'autre bout de moi, unlike *Ecce Homo* for Nietzsche, is a first book. But it, too, contains a "microcosm" in its center. I would even argue that the novel is really the island's self-portrait, not just Anne's, since the book re-creates textually a panorama of life in preindependence Mauritius. The island, like the female autograph of the story, writes itself into literary history, inscribing its mosaic of points of view and its fragments of diverse cultures into the existing corpus of traditional writings about islands. The island thus manages to insert itself into an ancient genre of writing (the object of which it had been), adopting the same rhetorical devices and sign systems, but using those to articulate a different vision, to invent new kinds of subjectivities.

The relationship between Anne and Nadège, between the two faces of Janus as textual persona of the author, is a complex one. The two sisters initially choose to adhere to two different traditions, both of which are an integral part of themselves, since they are *sang-mêlé*, mixed-bloods, whose nonwhite ancestry is a heavy liability in a colonial society that keeps a meticulous count of every element in each person's pedigree. Nadège, the face that looks to the East, overcomes that which in her colonial culture, in herself, contributes

[18]Ibid., pp. 9, 26, 320.

to labeling *métissage* almost a "skin disease." Anne, on the other hand, must be cruel to the point of murder toward her sister (or the sister in herself), because she prefers to be the face that looks to the West, to her European heritage, and would rather mask, obscure, and deny all traces of her Hindu ancestry.

In Nietzschean terms, then, Nadège is the Dionysian principle, stifled by the Apollonian strivings of Anne, only to recur in Anne, once she has succeeded in overcoming her denials of the Dionysian, in healing her divided consciousness. It is the process of writing which allows her to confront and reject the Apollonian as symbol of the Western will to power over others. Writing is the thread, "le fil," which lets her explore the labyrinth of the past and transforms her into the legendary Ariadne. The couple she forms with her sister Nadège is the counterpart of Nietzsche's "divine couple," Dionysus-Ariadne, in which Dionysus figures as the labyrinth.[19] Nadège(-Dionysus) is Anne's labyrinth, her unconscious, and Anne(-Ariadne)'s journey takes her beyond a narcissistic Western belief in the importance of a stable individuality. In achieving fusion with her opposite, she reaches a state of self-dispossession: this is not, however, her synthetic recuperation of dialectical oppositions, merely her absorption into an infinitely fragmented universe, like the labyrinth itself and like the island that is hers.

The deployment of the narrative takes Anne back to the chaotic events of the past as she attempts to gather all the elements of her fragmented consciousness. Retracing her way through the familiar sites of her childhood (including an abandoned cemetery behind her home), she adopts the rhetorical devices of a ritual journey, "so that," as Beaujour states about another self-portrait, the book is also "an attempt to remember and piece together the subject all along an initiatory path."[20] The starting point of that journey is her family's house, haunted by the presence of her mother's blank, obliterated femininity. That house is linked to her other "home," the "boutique-chinois [Chinese shop],"[21] her favorite shelter, the "abri accueillant

[19]See Nietzsche's poem "Ariadne's Lament" in "Dionysus Dithyrambs," *The Portable Nietzsche*, p. 345: Be clever, Ariadne! / You have small ears, you have my ears: / Put a clever word into them! / Must one not first hate each other if one is to love each other? / I am your labyrinth."

[20]Beaujour, p. 283.

[21]In the creole dialect of the island, adjectives very rarely take the mark of the feminine.

[enchanting refuge]" (97), whose unusual stock of incongruous objects from all over the world fascinates her:

> On y trouvait tout: du moins tout ce que mes désirs d'enfant pouvaient imaginer, chaussures made in China, statues de saints ou de Bouddha, cahiers-crayons-gommes-compas, pièges à souris et mort-aux-rats, bâtons de santal-porcelaine de Chine, fil à broder-papier mousseline, tue-mouches et attrape-nigauds, pâte d'amande et protège-flamme, am stram gram et colegram en ai-je oublié? Oui, ces sacs de farine par exemple, tout gonflés d'odeurs d'amidon, ces âcres boules de tamarin vous fixant comme des yeux noirs sans pupille, ce poisson salé raidi contre le mur dans le mystère de l'arrière-boutique; et dans cette anti-chambre du paradis, le Chinois ne cessait de sourire, demandez seule-ment, demandez et vous recevrez, que n'avait-il pas? il opinait du chef, il servait, servait, ça me confondait d'admiration et de reconnaissance. [16]

> [One could find everything there: at any rate all that my childhood desires could imagine, shoes made in China, statues of saints or of Buddha, notebooks-pencils-erasers-compasses, mousetraps and rat poison, sandalwood sticks and Chinese porcelains, embroidery thread and tissue-paper, fly-swatters and booby traps, almond paste and fire screens, eenie-meenie-minie-moe, have I forgotten anything? Yes, those flour sacks, for example, full of the smell of starch, those acrid balls of tamarind, which stare at you like pupilless black eyes, that stiff salt fish against the wall of the mysterious backroom of the store; and in this vestibule of paradise, the Chinese storekeeper would never stop smiling, ask, you only have to ask, ask and you will receive, what didn't he have? he would nod, serve, and serve, and I would be con-founded with admiration and gratefulness.]

That store is a vestibular place, the antichamber of a kind of paradise that is a source of uneasy fascination. There, all seems possible and everything obtainable. The anarchic style of this descriptive para-graph is paradigmatic of the dis-orderly principles under which the store functions. This microcosm of heterogeneity, like the island itself, is the very matrix of the narrative, the cocoon out of which the author spins her yarn, using her "fil à broder" to elaborate "attrape-nigauds," or fictional traps, which, like spider webs, must catch the reader, seduce and fill him/her with wonder and gratefulness, "d'admiration et de reconnaissance," provide him/her with all the links to the multiple traditions that are represented in the text.

The store is also a maternal imago, a protective shelter, like Momma's general store in Angelou's narrative. It is the source of happiness and wonder and an emblematic *topos*, at once mother and motherland, "a second home where reality is embellished by magic" (63). It conveys heat and protection like a womb: "I remain inside the shell of the store" (164), says Anne, and she often falls asleep on the sun-warmed floor. When it comes time to wake up and leave, she suffers an excruciating separation: "It was terribly painful to get up. All my muscles would snap, as though Mother were giving birth to me anew, and to be born was exquisitely painful" (166). Expelled from the womb as from paradise, Anne feels banished, exiled to an inhospitable land. The pain of exile and marginality, the torture of separation from the original source of happiness and well-being: the predicament of the narrator, like that of Adam and Eve or Cain and Abel, is the founding experience of the human condition.

But her paradise is by no means a stable and unchanging resting place, an immutable center in the flux of life. On this island, subjected almost yearly to tropical hurricanes, the store is a seductive shelter but an ephemeral one. It is destroyed and must be rebuilt after the passage of the storm: "at the crossroads . . . the store's disemboweled [éventrée] carcass stood erect" (461).[22] On a closer look, though, it is only partially destroyed: "Some light shone through the shutters of the backroom of the store [l'arrière boutique] which remained miraculously intact" (461). What evades destruction from the elements, that mysterious "arrière boutique," is like the unconscious core of memory, the source of language and discourse, the clue (or coil) that allows the writer to spin her web of images and metaphors.[23] The core of the imago is untouched. Dismembered, "éventrée," though it is, it will soon manage to reestablish its network, its system of economic exchange throughout the neighborhood : "In a year or two, by dint of patience, economy, and hard work, the store would have reestablished itself, spreading out the ramifications of its economic rule throughout the neighborhood" (461). It is quite clear that nothing remains stable in this microcosm. Only a network of relationships can allow for survival.

[22]Compare this passage to page 64–68: at the beginning of the narrative, the store seems to be invincible, indestructible. It is the process of writing itself which seems to contribute to the slow and gradual erosion of that stability.

[23]It is well worth noting here that Montaigne used to call his memory or inner self his "arrière boutique."

This network, or web, is emblematic of the very process of *écriture*, which creates a similar system of ramifications among various temporal instances, diverse cultures, and a set of locations and characters that mirror each other textually. The store is the maternal womb as well as the matrix of discourse, which generates the metaphors and the symbolic correspondences between the linguistic body of the text and the narrating self or her alter ego, her family, her race(s), her culture(s), and her homeland.

Another recurring metaphor is the road, "the beautiful, smooth road—so beautiful with its blue macadam, always so warm, so smooth under the feet, just like milk! " (97), which has a maternal, nurturing connotation. The road is at once umbilical cord and narrative thread. It takes Anne to the various locations or *topoi* of her childhood, each of which is of significant importance in the anamnesis, much as the Way of the Cross takes Catholic faithful through the same steps as Christ during his Passion. Here, the road, "cool and hot asphalt . . . sea-asphalt, asphalt-sea" [mer-asphalte, asphalte-mer]" (161) is both marine and maternal (*mer/mère*). It winds its way through the cane fields to the Hindu quarter, alongside the mosque, the spacious colonial domains of the whites, and on to Aunauth Gopaul's house. The road connects all the idiosyncratic and heterogeneous elements of this fragmented society; it is at once comforting and threatening, because Anne cannot accept a plurality of identities as readily as her sister does: "too blue, too smooth, this road is like milk! poisoned milk!" (268). The carefree and self-assured ease with which Nadège negotiates all the apparent contradictions of her cultural background, moving in and out of Hindu or Catholic subcultures, is at once attractive and repulsive to Anne: "Trying to catch up with her on the roads, I would lose my breath, and she would mischieviously pretend to escape" (313–14).

At other times, Nadège is the pursuer, the one chasing Anne, who escapes and retreats into the protective shell of the store: "On the road Nadège follows me, the shadow is getting longer behind me and I feel Nadège in the air, invisible presence or absence . . . quickly, the store, the smell of its spices, the comings and goings of its customers" (160). As she tries to keep up with Nadège's games, Anne is gradually, reluctantly, pulled in the opposite direction from that she considers her own: "Again the road, that road as smooth as milk, that river which used to carry me off, pulling me against my will like a countercurrent, pushing me as it had pushed Nadège, hauling me gasping toward this house which I found surprisingly close, the house of Aunauth Gopaul, the forbidden Indian" (332). Here the road is a river ("fleuve"); it is the unconscious impulse to remember and verbalize the repressed, which is pure energy. As a model of artistic creativity, it is the Dionysian metamorphosis or ecstasis outside of oneself which strips Anne of her individuation, returns her to the chaos of memory out of which she constructs meaning, for as Nietzsche says, "one must still have chaos in oneself to be able to give birth to a dancing star."[24]

The same road brings to their house the outsider, the stranger whose role as a catalyst is important to the development of the narrative. He is Paul Roux, the French doctor, who has been sent to the island by the World Health Organization to conduct a study for the United Nations. His naïve, European, Marxist views (what Anne's father terms his "idéalisme fumeux" [245]), are developed in long conversations with Nadège. They open new horizons for her, preparing the way for her interest in the Indian politician. At first, Nadège listens to him intently, totally absorbed in his speeches, "even during those moments when I [Anne] happened to think that the Frenchman was talking nonsense, was foundering in the most ludicrous utopia," (244) says her more "reasonable" sister. Paul's clear, organized, and coherent scenarios for a better tomorrow seem too logical and simplistic. Something of the complexity of Anne's life is missing in those discourses that tend to organize experience into neat categories, although the ideas interest the narrator: "And yet, during the two months he spent with us, I studied him with more passion, more lucidity than I had ever studied anyone" (239). His presence "fait fonction de révélateur" (239), triggers the actions and reactions that reveal characters: "So it was in fact the others, the others who captivated my eye perpetually; each one was playing a complex part in front of him, continually changing masks, as if performing an unreal and fantastic ballet" (239). As he gets closely involved in the life of the Morin family, it becomes clear that Paul Roux would be "a good catch" for Nadège and he does attempt to propose marriage, offering to take her back to his native mountains, in the Vosges region. In an ironic way, he corresponds to Zarathus-

[24]Nietzsche, Z, Prologue, 5, p. 129.

tra: he comes down from his mountain, visits an island, and preaches a new gospel. But he turns out to be "une proie empoisonnée [a poisoned prey]" (239), a kind of pharmakon, caught as he is in a web of complex social relationships between Anne, Pierre, Nadège, Aunauth, and the father. He proves unable to understand the necessity for dissimulation and camouflage as a survival strategy for the *métis* of the island: "Paul Roux the censor disapproved of all secrets" (288). His intransigence is that of a moralist who wants to herald a new era of social justice but whose limited Western perspective can only betray the heterogeneity of Mauritius and its complicated social structures.

His role as interpreter of the social text of Mauritius corresponds to a possible critical approach to the narrative text itself, an approach that is rejected as too narrow. He is a well-intentioned but somewhat limited critic, blinded by his rigidly ideological and utopian biases. He is grounded in a world that cannot intersect with that of the author/narrator. His social theories are thus encoded as an anti-model of the plurality of interpretations generated and demanded by the narrative text.

His clarity of thought is antithetical to the ambiguous situation of the Morins. His narrowly utopian vision does not take into consideration the specificity of the Morins' experience as *métis* islanders, which rests on a duplicitous relation to the white world, since it is assumed by all, including the *métis*, that acceptance into that world is their primary goal, and a bourgeois marriage the means by which the coloreds eventually succeed in "passing" for white. Hence their effort to hide all traces of nonwhite "blood" that might mar a family's past. Nadège, who refuses to adopt such hypocrisy, cannot, therefore, accept the double bind of marriage to the European, Paul, and turns instead to his Indian counterpart, Aunauth Gopaul.

Anne's utopian vision, on the other hand, is the belief that she can cover up the family's painful secrets, its past and present scandals (the father's drinking). She compares her efforts to the slow and painstaking work of darning:

Qu'elle [Nadège] me laisse là, en paix, et à moi seule, patiemment, comme Sassita quand elle ravaudait les socquettes, je rattraperais maille par maille les trous qui béaient dans notre vie, j'effacerais le scandale, je tisserais une nouvelle toile solide, étanche, immaculée. [125]

[If only she [Nadège] could leave me alone, in peace, I would patiently work all by myself, like Sassita when she was darning socks, and mend stitch by stitch all the gaping holes of our lives, I would erase the scandal, I would weave a new cloth, strong, impermeable, immaculate.]

This reference to darning ("ravaudait") is another metaphor for her narrative technique. It borrows from the maid's feminine *ouvrage*, her needlework, to retrieve and gather together the many threads of experience in an effort to attone for the gaping holes in the family's history.[25] Implicit in this quotation is a reference to Lacan's "béance ambiguë," the hole, the unmendable Freudian gap or lack in the fabric which orders the subject's consciousness. This hole, according to Freud, can never be filled out: only patched over by the delusions that the same subject constructs in order to cope with the external world.[26] In Lacanian terms, the delusions are the scaffolding of words which the subject erects over the "Real" in order to obscure it.

Initially, then, Anne's effort to efface the past by weaving a new "toile . . . immaculée" is a delusion that the past can be ignored and shrouded in a dishonest purity, an "immaculate perception" as Nietzsche would say.[27] Her mother had done just that, shrouding herself in bitterness and silence. The paradoxical wish of the narrator, though, is more like the utopian wish for a "blank page" or a "white canvas," a life story that would not need to be told, a narrative that would not exist because her life had been happy and uneventful ("les gens heureux n'ont pas d'histoire [happy people(s) have no history]").

But the past is scandalous and painful, and Anne's state of total disarray in exile demands its only antidote: writing. Writing helps mend the original holes created by her family's refusal to address *métissage*, to accept ambiguity. But the impulse to write, to speak up, perhaps creates new delusions, other utopias: Anne's dream of raising mixed-blood children who can return to the "paradise of glass"

[25]This process is the same as that of *mé-tissage*, the view of female textuality as heterogeneous "tissage" as I discuss it in Chapter 6.

[26]Jacques Lacan, *Ecrits* (Paris: Seuil, 1966) p. 248. The *patch* is a Freudian term used in the paper "Neurosis and Psychosis," Sigmund Freud, *Standard Edition*, 19:151. See the discussion in Wilden, p. 98 n. 23.

[27]Nietzsche, Z II, On Immaculate Perception: "Behind a god's mask you hide from yourselves, in your 'purity,'" p. 235.

of the Chinese shop conforms to what Beaujour calls "the phantasm of a blissful city" which is but a scaffolding of words, a skeleton on which to construct new images.[28] The hurricane has destroyed ("éventré") the store, the maternal imago around which the whole book is structured, but what remains intact in that "arrière boutique" is the wall on which hang visions of death: "ce poisson salé raidi," and the ghostlike "sacs de farine" with the "boules de tamarin vous fixant comme des yeux sans pupilles" (16). These recall the ghost of the biological mother, and the "sépulcres blanchis [whited sepulchers]" (272), the pharisees and the bigots who judge and determine the Morins' social standing and their reputation. The book, therefore, while it attempts to re-create those "vanished places, disrupted harmonies," as Beaujour calls them, undermines and erodes its utopian project, which becomes identified in the filigree of the text with a death wish.[29]

For example, the narrative ends on hopeful (musical) notes: Anne arrives at the house of Aunauth where she comes to take Nadège's place. Her mother, father, and sister are all dead. In her suitcase is a record: Rachmaninoff's Symphony No. 2. On one level, this record is an important romantic vehicle: it is a gift to Anne from Pierre; Nadège borrows it secretly to share with Aunauth. They first make love while listening to it. This music, "full of passion and violence," plays a decisive part in opening Nadège's eyes to the folly of a "marriage of reason" (424) with the French doctor. Finally, as the last sentence of the book implies, it is the background for Anne and Aunauth's first romantic encounter: "He then walked toward the record player and, after putting the record on the turntable, he guided the needle to the edge of the symphony" (463).

Here, as in Nietzsche, music is the privileged art. It touches the whole gamut of human emotions, affirming diversity and multiplicity, lifting barriers and harmonizing opposites. It symbolizes a Dionysian resurrection for Anne, a self-dispossession as she is transformed into Nadège, whose whole life was like a symphony: "Her life was lived the way one plays a symphony; she had an absolute need for the continual concordance of inside and outside; passions, people, nature, words, everything had to be in unison,

[28]Beaujour, p. 22.
[29]Ibid.

with no wrong notes" (420). This harmony is Nadège's aim in life, but it is paradoxical: a Dionysian symphony that is not stifled by an Apollonian will to order or an imposed and artificial arrangement. This state of creative tension is what Anne seeks as a writer, and this characterization of Nadège is also an apt description of the novel.[30] That is why I would like to suggest that accompanying the Symphony No. 2 is, in fact, an implicit reference to Rachmaninoff's symphonic poem known as the *Isle of the Dead*. This pair of symphonies covertly echo and reflect the whole binary structure of the novel while implying that such a system of signs grounded in the traditional dichotomies of Western metaphysics is a vehicle of death: Nadège has an abortion and dies; by contrast, Sassita, who listens to Indian music on the local radio, reaches autonomy and decides to remarry and adopt an orphaned baby.[31]

In an emblematic episode of chapter 6 we are plunged into the general atmosphere of death and decay which surrounds the Morin family. In this grotesquely funny scene, Nadège stages a masquerade for the purpose of disconcerting Paul Roux, whose humanitarian harangues are getting on her nerves. She involves her father and Anne in the masquerade, during which Anne herself adopts a "masque" (247), which conveniently exempts her from her role as "native informant" vis-à-vis the French doctor: "Paul Roux was unable to read anything on my face." As the father ironically exclaims: "We pay too much attention to the living around here, and not enough to the dead," they all march to the abandoned backyard cemetery where (with the energy of despair) Nadège endeavors to

[30]The novel seen as verbal mausoleum for Nadège, as her "tombeau mallarméen," which exists, like the book, around an empty center. See Beaujour, pp. 230–32.

[31]In "*A l'autre bout de moi* de Marie-Thérèse Humbert et la littérature mauricienne" (in a publication of the Centre d'Etudes Francophones, Université de Paris XIII, *Itinéraires et contacts de cultures* [Paris: L'Harmattan, 1982], 2:113–39), Jean-Louis Joubert writes: "The record is a very concrete object, a thing. . . . Its jacket is described with precision . . . ; the typography of the title is reproduced in the shape of a design . . . which magnifies the word 'SYMPHONY' printed in capital letters. (The reader who is interested in musicology might note the oddity of this 'Symphony No. 2 for piano and orchestra by Rachmaninoff.' Bizarre!)" (p. 122, my translation). Indeed, what I would like to suggest here is that Humbert does invite her reader to wonder about the significations of this record as a "magical object" (Joubert, p. 123), and my interpretation leads me to believe that the referent of "Symphonie No. 2" is none other than 'The Isle of the Dead' and that, as a privileged sign in this novel, the record simply refers to another sign and not to external reality.

scrub the old tombstones and moss-covered crosses. This comedy takes place in a putrid physical environment and under the affect-less, petrifying, and petrified gaze of Paul: "In the stifling air, the smell of ripe mangoes rotting on the ground mingled unpleasantly with that of chicken droppings in the coops. This combination gave off a rank scent of fermentation which made you gasp. The French-man had followed us without uttering a word, he was standing back slightly, his face as expressionless as those of tourists who stare at Hindus in a trance during processions, too impressed to even dare show any kind of emotion" (248).

The native woman puts on a gruesome spectacle for the benefit of the "tourist," Paul, who is in the uncomfortable position of observer and voyeur of the "macabre customs of Francophone Creoles" (249); it is but an exaggeration of the role he had adopted to begin with, launching himself into grand analyses of the political and social context of their lives. As an antimodel for the critic, therefore, he is constructed as deficient, not just because of his narrow political perspective but also because of his inability to show emotion or affect before the (textual) events he witnesses. His pretense of objec-tivity is a fallacy: it is the wisdom and the neutrality of death.

On the other hand, Nadège's gift of theater, her ability to mock is the mark of an unconventional wisdom. Her nihilism, her "will . . . to dominate herself, . . . to subdue herself" (369), as Aunauth says, is a protective device, a dissimulating strategy against the hypocrisy of colonial society and the intolerable scrutiny of Paul (cf. 286–87). Impertinence personified, she illustrates well one of Nietzsche's in-sights about the dilemmas of women: "Young women try hard to appear superficial and thoughtless. The most refined simulate a kind of impertinence."[32]

Nadège is the "spirit full of gay sarcasm" in more ways than one. She adopts masks, changes roles, and dresses in a plurality of selves, thus avoiding, temporarily, the death-dealing blows of cul-ture and civilization. It is her mother, in her passive, yet bitter acceptance of the tenets of nineteenth-century European culture (and its pseudoscientific, racist beliefs in heredity), who figures as the main agent of death and *ressentiment*. Her rigid need to instill respectability in her daughters is described as an absurd effort to

[32]Nietzsche, *The Gay Science*, 2:7, p. 128

hide—to kill—the "subhuman" in the *métis*: "This tanned skin [cet épiderme hâlé], everyone around us confirmed the idea that that was something of the animal in us [quelque chose de la bête en nous], something filthy, which pricked up its ears [quelque chose d'immonde, qui pointait l'oreille] and which had to be hidden from sight. Behave yourself, Nadège, behave yourself, Anne! Come on, dressed like this, you could be mistaken for some little Indian girls! When Mother had said this, she had said it all" (39).

"Cet épiderme hâlé" is one of numerous references to the skin as symptom of a disease, as cultural sign of decadence. As indicated earlier, this metaphor of the skin is used by Zarathustra in "On Great Events" (Z, part 2): "The earth . . . has a skin, and this skin has diseases. One of these diseases, for example, is called 'man.' " In Anne's narrative, it is "quelque chose d'immonde" in the make up of the *métis* women which shows up as "hâle," as the outward sign of cultural sickness and bestiality, as these are defined by the mother, who has thoroughly internalized the racist colonial ideology.

But Nadège's unconventional behavior allows her—unlike Anne—to take in stride the social stigmas attached to the color of her skin and to refrain from following the "herd" of complacent and passive *métis*. Her strength is her insolence, as illustrated in this incident which occurs during an English lesson at school:

Exercise no. 1. Cross out the wrong words. *What colour are your eyes? Blue-grey-green-brown or dark?* . . . *What colour is your skin? Yellow-white-brown or black?* In Mauritius, the correct answer was *yellow* or *brown,* rarely white. . .

But seven-year-old Nadège used to protest. My skin is neither white nor yellow, neither black nor brown. How is it then? The school-mistress, a colored woman herself, would say: Nadège Morin, always trying to be sassy! Put down *My skin is golden,* that'll be all right. But it was not all right. Nadège would snicker and write *My skin is dirty.* Nadège would be punished. Punished because of her skin: that afternoon, after hearing what happened, Mother would take sides with the mistress. [28; words in italics are in English in the text]

Nadège is able to subvert rigid social codes by laughing away the foolishness of society, whose power is doubly represented here by the school system and by the English language, the language of the master: Mauritius is under British rule at the time. The school-mistress, like the mother, is a slave to the system and can only perpetuate its demeaning aspects, despite a tentative effort to give a positive connotation ("golden") to the idea of color. But this "foreign" language and the reality it creates must be learned early: it impresses upon the colored children their nonbeing, their absence from representation within that symbolic order. Since there is no unambiguous term for what they are, it means that they have no existence in that realm of language, or that they can only be defined negatively by what they are not: not white, not black.[33]

Thus indoctrinated, Anne plays the game by the rules, in order to survive. She is like the ape, the "foaming fool," who unwittingly parodies Zarathustra's style;[34] like a number of *métis* who desperately try to imitate the whites' wealthy and glamorous standards ("our people tried to ape their life style" [39]), Anne is anxious to be accepted by white society. That is why she secretly dates Pierre, who cannot quite bring himself to be open and public about their romance. As a result, Anne feels most ashamed of her skin : "I was hurting in my skin, I had shame in my skin, I was fed up with the pain and the shame, I was holding in my anger, I was being patient" (291). As for Pierre, with a measure of bad faith (or bad conscience), he tries to explain to her that he, too, feels oppressed by the conventions of his bourgeois milieu but that "you cannot take off your white skin and put it down on the furniture, like a discarded piece of clothing" (175). He cannot escape the determinations of his social and cultural milieu any more than he can escape the color of his skin. But he feels pity for her and his spineless goodwill casts him in the role of a "good" and "weak" Christian who cannot oppose the moral establishment of his time. He is a pharisee and a "despiser of the body,"[35] whose respect for Anne's virtue inescapably turns into

[33]The "races" these adjectives refer to are fallacies, creations of nineteenth-century racist "scientific" discourse, as I discuss it in my introduction, and as Stephen J. Gould has amply shown. See especially *The Mismeasure of Man* (New York: Norton, 1981) and *Ontogeny and Phylogeny* (Cambridge: Belknap Press of Harvard University Press, 1977). We have inherited these categories which still mold our thinking in many ways.

[34]Nietzsche Z, pt. 3, On Passing By, p. 287. I owe an important debt to Margot Norris's discussion of mimesis and camouflage in "Darwin, Nietzsche, Kafka and the Problems of Mimesis," *MLN* 95 (Dec. 1980), 1232–53. It provided insights that allowed me to see patterns in Humbert's work which relate directly to those problems.

[35]Cf. Nietzsche, Z, pt. 3, On Old and New Tablets, 26, p. 324–25; pt. 1, On the Despisers of the Body: "I want to speak to the despisers of the body. It is their respect that begets their contempt," p. 147.

contempt when his calculated and timid lovemaking proves a poor match for Anne's disappearing caution : "In playing this little game, we gradually learned to despise each other" (299).

This textual string of "skin" metaphors points to a critique of the "civilizing" influence of culture over nature. Like the skin on the body, culture is a shroud that veils the instincts or the bestiality ("quelque chose de la bête en nous") of that body, repressing them, banishing them to the unconscious. The scission or split that accompanies this dichotomy between nature and culture, the instincts and consciousness, constitutes what Nietzsche calls the "*internalization of man*," the instincts for freedom (or will to power) being turned inward and becoming the origins of "bad conscience."[36] The question of culture is central to Nietzsche's understanding of the repression of the body, as it will be for Freud in *Civilization and Its Discontents*, and Eric Blondel has shown that for Nietzsche, "life is fundamentally a sickness. . . As the metaphor of the repressed body and as Dionysus dismembered, culture is nothing other than the obverse of [instinctual, natural, or adaptive] morality."[37] Nietzsche's anger focuses specifically on the Judeo-Christian bedrock of Western civilization and is evident in all his writings, but especially in *The Antichrist*: "To become *perfect*, he was advised to draw in his senses, turtle fashion, to cease all intercourse with earthly things, to shed his mortal shroud: then his essence would remain, the 'pure spirit.' . . . Here too we have reconsidered. . . . The "pure spirit" is pure stupidity: if we abstract the nervous system and the senses—the "mortal shroud"—*then we miscalculate*—that is all!"[38]

This "mortal shroud", like the epidermal surface of the skin and the life of the body, is what culture represses in order to make room for the "pure spirit," the "soul" or "ego,"[39] which Nietzsche equates with the "sickness" or "disease" of cultural conditioning. This sickness, however, is "*pregnant with a future . . .* as if man were not a

[36]Friedrich Nietzsche, *On the Genealogy of Morals*, pt. 2, ¶16, in *On the Genealogy of Morals and Ecce Homo* (New York: Vintage Books, 1969), pp. 84–87.

[37]Eric Blondel, "Nietzsche: Life as Metaphor," translated from the French and reprinted in *The New Nietzsche: Contemporary Styles of Interpretation,* ed. David B. Allison (Cambridge: MIT Press, 1985), p. 165. I have added the words in brackets to clarify Blondel's point. He is refering to *The Antichrist*, 15, in which Nietzsche discusses "fictitious morality and religion . . . the very formula for decadence" and opposes those to "nature" and "reality" (*TPN*, p. 581–82).

[38]Nietzsche, *The Antichrist*, 14, p. 581.

[39]Ibid., 15, p. 581.

goal, but only a way, an episode, a bridge, a great promise."[40] If man is only an episode and a promise, then it is through his capacity for change and rebirth that he can succeed in overcoming his culture, his "skin disease;" or as Deleuze says, "it is in his essence that man is called the skin disease of the earth,"[41] in his essence and not in his capacity for metamorphosis, his process of becoming. So it is that Nadège can redeem Anne's temptations to let herself be co-opted by "civilization," by "whiteness," because she accepts the process of becoming and its end result, death. She understands intuitively what Walter Kaufman says of Nietzsche, that "self-overcoming involves a measure of suffering and also of cruelty, not only in the individual's relation to others but also in his attitude toward himself."[42] Because Nadège surrenders herself to change and polysemy, Anne learns from her the value of ambivalence and ambiguity, rejects Apollonian clarity, "immaculate perception," as symbol of the Western will to power *over others*. Instead, she comes to an understanding of the value of difference, of the plurality of meaning in the person of Ariadne. As Deleuze says: "Dionysus teaches Ariadne his secret: the true labyrinth is Dionysus himself, the true thread is the thread of affirmation. . . . Affirmation is the enjoyment and play of its own difference."[43]

This power to affirm difference is the secret Anne(-Ariadne) learns from Nadège: the privileged difference of *métissage*. The power of affirmation is the Dionysian will to power over oneself, which allows Anne to accept the past and to let it recur, because, according to Deleuze "the lesson of the eternal return is that there is no return of the negative. . . . Only that which affirms or is affirmed returns."[44] To put it another way, for Nietzsche, "the idea of recurrence is intended to heal the disjunction between time and eternity and especially the resentment against the past which divides the consciousness of the alienated person."[45] Once we understand this

[40]Nietzsche, *On the Genealogy of Morals*, 2:16, p. 85.

[41]Gilles Deleuze, *Nietzsche et la philosophie* (Paris: Presses Universitaires de France, 1962), p. 192, *Nietzsche and Philosophy*, trans. Hugh Tomlinson (New York: Columbia University Press, 1983), p. 167.

[42]Kaufmann, p. 211.

[43]Deleuze, p. 188.

[44]Ibid., p. 189.

[45]Ofelia Schutte, *Beyond Nihilism: Nietzsche without Masks*, pp. 67–68 and 122–23. For Nietzsche, everything, good or bad, recurs, but it is up to the individual to refuse to be resentful in order to allow only the positive, the active (and not the reactive) to recur and thus prepare the world for our children.

affirmative side of eternal return, we can see Anne as reaching a point of self-integration and self-acceptance which allows her to put into perspective her maternal legacy of *ressentiment* and to surrender to her (forbidden) desire for the unknown ("l'Indien interdit," Aunauth, whose name phonetically conveys "zero," the excluded middle, the locus of a narcissistic illusion, the void: o-naught).[46]

Finally, the appropriate and conclusive image regarding this kind of "skin disease" is furnished by the island itself: in Mauritius, the *earth* literally suffers from a disease of color. In fact, there is a place, a "lieu-dit" in a mountainous region of the island called Chamarel where strata of volcanic lava, rich in minerals, were sedimented in layers of different colors, forming a curious area of rainbow-striped hills where no vegetation grows, where the earth is barren. This desolation has an awesome beauty that exerts a definite attraction on Anne's imagination: "But I will escape; for now, inert on the warm cement, I am a chrysalis; if my muscles are numb, that's because they are getting ready to take flight soon. . . . everywhere in the stifling air, armies of perfume are coming toward me, and instead of drowning me in their heaviness [pesanteur], they will carry me up, take me to the pinnacle of the great mountain chains over there, far away over there, beyond Chamarel with its earth sick with colors [ses terres malades de couleur], and where life begins" (164–65).[47]

Like a butterfly about to emerge from its chrysalis or a bird trying to outsoar tradition, Anne has the urge to shed the dead weight of convention, the "pesanteur," the spirit of gravity, which weighs her down like Zarathustra's camel.[48] That weight is her old self, the resentful one that she wishes to shake off, as Zarathustra's dwarf is

[46]Although this pun is more convincing in English than in French, I want to emphasize that it is nonetheless fairly obvious to a reader familiar with Mauritian society, since Mauritius, like Canada or Belgium, is a multilingual society. Indeed, English is the official political language of the island, even though Creole and French are more widely spoken. Furthermore, Aunauth is an Indian politician who was "graduated from the University of London" (432) and thus represents a *difference*, a linguistic and political interference in the French text of the novel.

[47]This passage could be compared to Nietzsche, *The Gay Science*, 2:60, p. 123: "Does my happiness itself sit in this quiet place—my happier ego, my second, departed self? Not to be dead and yet no longer alive? A spiritlike intermediate being: quietly observing, gliding, floating? As the boat that with its white sails moves like an immense butterfly over the dark sea. Yes! To move *over* existence! That's it! That would be something!"

[48]Nietzsche, Z, pt. 1, On the Three Metamorphoses, p. 138; pt. 3, On the Spirit of Gravity, p. 305.

shaken off the prophet's shoulder when they both reach the gateway where "two paths meet,"[49] the "moment" when the past and the future come together in the eternal recurrence of things. Mauritius—like Anne's text—is such a crossroads of spatial and temporal dimensions[50] and Anne's metamorphosis is a letting-go of bitterness and resentment in favor of a life-affirming vision of the future: she can finally be the face that says "yes" and can permit herself to walk through the gate. Like Nietzsche, whose *Ecce Homo* is subtitled "How One Becomes What One Is," she becomes what she is: the "âne," the donkey that says hee-haw, I-A, "Ja," and thus transcends traditional morality and dualism as the *Übermensch* would.[51]

In Chamarel, the earth is bare, but that is where "life begins," for Anne must be stripped of all her Western pretensions and beliefs before she can start living somewhat autonomously (like Sassita) and creatively (as a writer). This idea of desolation connotes another of Nietzsche's metaphors (at least in its French translation), a metaphor that relates directly to the author's choice of names for Nadège: "Partout de la neige, la vie est muette ici; les dernières corneilles dont on entend la voix croassent : A quoi bon? En vain ! Nada ! Rien ne pousse et ne croît plus ici." La neige, nada: Nadège. The phonetic similarity of these words implies a certain nihilism, a "value of nil" in Nadège.[52] But more important, it reveals that for the author, "Nadège" is nothing but a textual construct, a potentiality, a device that allows "Anne" to explore the "murdered visions" of her youth, "[her] happier ego, [her] second, departed self,"[53] as Zarathustra had on the "isle of tombs." In Nietzsche's ontology of self-healing, the will to power (over oneself) is a process of self-overcoming, a stripping from the ego of its masks, a creative rebirth, albeit a sometimes cruel and violent one.[54] Thus, Nadège's unconventional be-

[49]Ibid., pt. 3, On the Vision and the Riddle, 2, p. 269.

[50]Humbert's conception of the narrative as a crossroads of ideas and problems is not unlike André Gide's. He says in his *Journal*: "Le roman? . . . Un carrefour; un rendez-vous de problèmes."

[51]For discussion of the concepts of existential continuity and the *Übermensch* as used here, see Schutte, chaps. 3 and 5, pp. 57–75 and 105–32.

[52]Nietzsche, *On the Genealogy of Morals*, 3:26, as quoted by Deleuze, p. 170: "Here is snow; here life has grown silent; the last crows whose cries are audible here are called 'wherefore?,' 'in vain!,' 'nada!'—here nothing will grow or prosper any longer." See also p. 169 and the translation by W. Kaufmann and R. J. Hollingdale, p. 157.

[53]Nietzsche, *The Gay Science* 2: 60. See note 47.

[54]See Schutte, pp. 76–104 especially.

havior, her freedom from "pesanteur," casts her as the creative principle in Anne herself, a principle Anne can let be free (that is, free to
recur) by becoming "the child," "the god that can dance," "the wisdom that is woman."[55] This metamorphosis is only possible at the
cost of adopting and exploiting Nadège's impertinent dissimulating
strategies while rejecting the imitative ones of the "herd."

Herdlike behavior is synonymous with silence and death: such is
the mother's (and, at first, Anne's) predicament. In her effort to
conform to the image man and society impose upon her, she remains deaf and dumb, "often a silence directed at herself, too. She
closes her eyes to herself," as Nietzsche says in an aphorism that
exactly summarizes the self-denial of women in patriarchal culture.[56] Thus Nadège's self-denial, her act of uncalculated and un-
mitigated love for her sister is in fact a death sentence served ultimately because she allows herself to conform, on behalf of her
sister, to the prevailing social codes of the island. She denies the
"maternal" in herself, the maternal being understood here as the
creative, free-spirited "love of the artist for [her] work,"[57] as well as
her biological condition of pregnancy. This sacrifice amounts to a
kind of suicide brought about by the intransigence of Anne, who
cannot tolerate Nadège's radical otherness and attempts to steal her
face, appropriate her space within the economy of their specular
relationship as twins, because she fears disappearing into that unknown otherness. To be absorbed into, and eventually become,
what Nadège is means losing her very Western claim to a stable
subjectivity. Paradoxically though, for her as woman and as twin,
this "identity" is always already lost, since it is either conformity to
and imitation of the standards of the herd or a reluctant copying of
her double: "Fear would continually choke back my confession, the
same fear which made me copy her attitudes when we were youn-
ger, copy, like a faithful and recalcitrant reflection, whereas my
whole being craved emancipation" (314).

But Nadège's renunciation of the right to bear her *métis* child and

[55]Nietzsche, Z, pt. 1, On Reading and Writing, pp. 152–53.

[56]Nietzsche, *The Gay Science*, 2:71, p. 128.

[57]Ibid., 72. In *Spurs/Eperons: Nietzsche's Styles*, trans. Barbara Harlow (Chicago:
University of Chicago Press, 1979), Derrida comments on this fragment: "Nietzsche,
as is everywhere evident in his texts, is a thinker big with thought [le penseur de la
grossesse]. He is the thinker of pregnancy which, for him, is no less praiseworthy in a
man than it is in a woman" (p. 65).

her subsequent death in effect free Anne to become what Nadège had been all along, "woman" and "maternal," which, in the Nietzschean intertext of the narrative, means a creative artist, a writer, a spinner of webs, no longer Ariadne but Arachne (or perhaps "Ariachne," as Shakespeare's Troilus says of Cressida), as symbol of female creativity, as Anne-(Humbert)'s alter ego and textual persona: a symbol that links life and death together, since by giving life women also give death, for to be born is to be mortal.

Let us not forget then that Arachne committed suicide (by hanging) when Athena, jealous of her skill in weaving, destroyed her web: talent is not a blessing for the (female) writer whose work may end up ignored, if not destroyed, by Wisdom (the critics or the academy). Hence the strategies of textual and intertextual dissimulation I have tried to uncover in my analysis. *A l'autre bout de moi* is, first of all, an entertaining and spellbinding story. It became a best seller and received the "Grand prix littéraire des lectrices de *Elle*, 1980" reaching a wide readership. But it is also the creation of a writer who (self-)consciously reflects on the process of *écriture* and gestures toward a particular tradition of self-portraitists (Augustine and Nietzsche) while never allowing that reflexion to interfere in the *jouissance* of the process for either writer or reader. This, according to Derrida, is the recognizable trait of a Nietzschean style. He reminds us that "it is hardly necessary to know that this text is undecipherable for it to remain, at once and for all, open, tendered *and* undecipherable. . . . If the simulacrum is ever going to occur, its writing must be in the interval [l'écart] between several styles."[58]

Humbert's writing is a writing of the "écart," of the interval between subjectivities, races, cultures, styles, and languages—especially languages. Her mother tongue, Creole, is the key ("le fil") which allows me, as Creole-speaking reader of her French text, to enter into the language game hidden in the proper names of her heroines and to renounce any critical reduction of her work to a single system. It is in that interval that her utopian, and Nietzschean, vision of Mauritius as "a way, an episode, a bridge, a great promise," takes shape and becomes superimposed on the other mythical images to which the island has given rise.

[58]Derrida, *Spurs/Eperons*, p. 137–39.

Conclusion

> The social revolution . . . cannot draw its poetry from the
> past, but only from the future. It cannot begin with itself
> before it has stripped off all superstition in regard to the
> past.
>
> Karl Marx, *The Eighteenth Brumaire of Louis Bonaparte*

This investigation began with the image of a suicidal Francophone
male writer on his last bridge and ended on the utopian vision of a
female writer who uses her native island as a Nietzschean "bridge"
to a different future. To offer any kind of "conclusive" resolution to
this book would only trivialize issues and questions that are fundamentally political but can only be addressed within an aesthetic
framework, because, as Fredric Jameson has noted, aesthetics addresses individual experience and does not try to conceptualize the
real in an abstract way.[1]

My analysis has been primarily concerned with the politics of
racial, sexual, and national identity. But these questions are so complex that I can only hope to have set forth some of the boundaries
within which further explorations of *métissage* as a creative aesthetic
practice and an analytical tool might be continued. I am thus following in the steps of two Caribbean writers—Edouard Glissant and
Nancy Morejón—who advocate multiplicity and diversity as radical
critiques of totality. Glissant, in particular, has outlined the task of
the postcolonial intellectual: it is to give shape to a nonessentialist
aesthetics tied to the emergence of occluded oral cultures, to the
articulation of a reality that emphasizes relational patterns over autonomous ones, interconnectedness over independence, isomor-
phic analogies over unifying totalities, opacity over transparency; in
short, it is to elaborate the "aesthetics of a non-universalizing form
of Diversity [esthétique . . . du Divers non universalisant]."[2] Such
an aesthetics is potentially emancipatory because it creates a space
where the mimetic illusions of Western representational systems are

[1]See Fredric Jameson, "Cognitive Mapping," in *Marxism and the Interpretation of
Culture,* ed. Cary Nelson and Lawrence Grossberg (Urbana: University of Illinois
Press, 1988), pp. 347–57.
[2]Edouard Glissant, *Le Discours antillais* (Paris: Seuil, 1981), p. 465, my translation.

deconstructed. In that space, which is neither *ou-topia* nor *eu-topia*, differences are not sublimated and the ethnocentric self does not establish itself by selectively defining an "other" to be assimilated and subjugated. Rather, specificities are valorized and allowed to come into play, engendering a new mechanics of relational patterns, a new collective identity that does not invoke an "authentic" origin but forms the basis for a *project:* the transformation of polarities into multifarious units sharing a common goal. The creative tensions at work in the social body that accepts and values difference and diversity are analogous to the ones I have shown to exist in the narratives of the male and female writers studied in this book. *Métissage* and intertextuality are thus brought into implicit conjunction and constitute different ways of talking about the same thing on a personal, racial, cultural, or textual level.

If Humbert's novel seems to create images of utopia, it is because her insights are so at odds with the cultural realities of larger nation-states where the abstract myth of the melting pot did succeed in reducing cultural differences to the level of folkloric representations; today those differences are slowly being reencoded as the rich and valuable traditions they always were. (Such is the case in both the United States and in France, where regional minorities as well as new immigrants are struggling to voice their specificities.) Writers from Mauritius and the Caribbean islands who are engaged in creating new images of the future do stress the positive value of "utopian" inscriptions. Recently, two critics argue that "the Mauritian society of tomorrow will be able to give birth to human bridges [des hommes-ponts] who might very well become the real interpreters of the North-South dialogue. Being a microcosm of the world, Mauritius will no doubt be the living proof that understanding among the peoples of the world may not be just a utopian prospect."[3] I think that both Glissant and Morejón could subscribe to these statements, which might be applied to certain Caribbean realities as well. And Maryse Condé might concur that her vision of that "vast horizon which the Antilleans of tomorrow will have to discover" is convergent with Humbert's imaginary reality.[4]

[3]See Paul Turcotte and Claude Brabant, "Ile Maurice: Nuvo sime," *Peuples Noirs/Peuples Africains* 31 (Jan./Feb. 1983), 106, my translation.

[4]Maryse Condé, "Propos sur l'identité culturelle," in *Négritude: Traditions et développement,* ed. Guy Michaud (Paris: Editions Complexe/Presses Universitaires de France, 1978), p. 84, my translation.

How then is it possible to conclude? Indeed, what is the critic to do when caught between suicide and utopia? In a book titled *L'Utopie ou la mort* ("Utopia or death") thinker René Dumont argues that utopian thinking is perhaps the only way out of the impasse created by the neocolonialist strangulation of nations and peoples, whose slow but sure death has become nothing but a spectacle for a Western public opinion anesthetized by the visual medium of television. In *L'Afrique étranglée*, Dumont and Marie-France Motin say that the West must learn to "listen," "se mettre à l'écoute," in order to avoid the totalizing approaches of theoretical problem solving.[5] As for Frantz Fanon, he titles the last chapter of *Black Skin, White Masks*: "By Way of Conclusion." I would like to borrow his approach and offer, by way of conclusion, a few final remarks concerning the reading itinerary I adopted in this book.

Having focused on the languages writers use to translate the creative tensions of their plural realities, I have deployed a variety of reading strategies. Each chapter has attempted to analyze a particular work—or group of related works in the case of Angelou—and has scrutinized the organizing patterns that generate the polysemic meanings of the texts. Some contemporary critical theory has unfortunately been an appropriation, always arrogant, of literary texts through abstract theoretical concepts that did not always do justice to the contextually problematic nature of writing and reading, meaning and meaningfulness, dialogue and exchange. What I hope to have accomplished in this book is twofold: close attention to the language of the texts discussed but also concern for the ways in which this language embodies and reflects the social, historical, and political dynamics of the larger cultural realms that surround it and give it value and power.

My approach implies, in particular, a critique of early forms of negritude as well as a refusal of the "ghettoization" of women writers within a particular tradition of feminine styles, be it *écriture féminine* or any other essentialist approach to "Woman" as a category which might transcend historical or cultural differences. I adhere, however, to what I would call a "feminist practice of reading," understood as a resistance to reductionist theories or to the territorializing of texts by critics who remain deaf to the "confusion of

---

[5]René Dumont, *L'Utopie ou la mort* (Paris: Seuil, 1974); René Dumont and Marie-France Motin, *L'Afrique étranglée* (Paris: Seuil, 1980), p. 279.

tongues" by which these texts are inhabited. I have tried to show how a careful understanding of textual structures and verbal patterns can guide our interpretive strategies and enrich our experience of this diverse body of literature.

The works of Hurston, Angelou, Cardinal, and Humbert can help us imagine a future that integrates positive images of the past while encouraging critical and nonsectarian participation in the conflicts of the present. By contrast, Condé shows the impasses of unresolved historical conflicts. By reinterpreting Augustine's *Confessions* and Nietzsche's *Ecce Homo* in light of the autobiographical performance of these five contemporary women writers, who variously transform, adapt, or subvert their cultural and literary heritages, I hope to have shown that any reductive reading of the past *or* of women's writing needlessly limits our options and obscures the real links between past repressions and present morasses, links that must be recognized and articulated before they can be successfully severed.

Since it is not possible to escape from the voice of tradition (any more than one can hope ever to be "free" from one's upbringing), the Nietzschean question of transvaluation of values becomes an urgent one. Indeed, what we can learn from autobiographical writings is a new way of listening for the relational voice of the self, the self in us "of woman born," which becomes progressively alienated in language when culture, ethnicity, and historical contradictions inscribe their identifying codes on our bodies. Decoding these inscriptions could be called a form of "autoethnography," as Hurston's sophisticated approach proves. This amounts to a genuine way of perceiving difference while emphasizing similarities in the processes of cultural encoding from which none of us can escape.

There are many other writers whose works could be illuminated by this concept of textual *mé-tissage* of styles. The novels of Simone Schwarz-Bart, Assia Djebar, and Abdelwahab Medded might lend themselves to such an approach. Many Quebecois writers—belonging to the nation Pierre Vallières has called the "nègres blancs d'Amérique"—could also be included in such a study, as could South Africans Bessie Head and Nadine Gordimer. Once we understand the emancipatory value of *métissage* as concept and practice, the possibilities become endless.

Index

Library of Congress Cataloging-in-Publication Data

Lionnet, Françoise.
  Autobiographical voices.

  (Reading women writing)
  Includes index.
    1. Autobiography—Women authors—History and criticism.
2. Women—Biography—History and criticism.
3. Literature, Modern—History and criticism. I. Title.
II. Series.
PN471.L56   1989   809'.93592   88-43236
ISBN 0-8014-2091-1 (alk. paper)

DATE DUE